Dedicated to the day when Russ Columbo gets his overdue star on the Hollywood Walk of Fame.

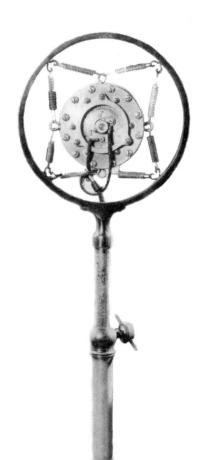

RUSS COLUMBO AND THE CROONER MYSTIQUE
©2002 JOSEPH LANZA AND DENNIS PENNA
ALL RIGHTS RESERVED

ISBN: 0-922915-80-6
FERAL HOUSE P.O. BOX 13067 LOS ANGELES, CA 90013

WWW.FERALHOUSE.COM
INFO@FERALHOUSE.COM
DESIGN BY HEDI EL KHOLTI
10 9 8 7 6 5 4 3 2 1

RUSS COLUMBO

══ AND THE ══
CROONER MYSTIQUE

JOSEPH LANZA AND DENNIS PENNA

CONTENTS

COLUMBOS ADORE BAMBİNO
Baby of Family Now Topnotch Crooner

Los Angeles Examiner, September 2, 1934.

THE
ALTAR BOY
AND THE
THUG

Russ Columbo resembled a lovelorn altar boy as he fell to his knees, folded his hands and gazed heavenward, fully unaware that Bing Crosby was aiming a gun in his direction.

There was Crosby, scowling in gangster drag beneath a cocked hat; his leering eyes and pursed lips revealing a man of no pity—a frosty hybrid of hoodlum and Martian.

In contrast, Columbo embodied the ever-huggable man-child. He was the "cream of the crooning crop," the "flashing Adonis of Hollywood" who, bedecked in clothes only a mother would select, predated Pat Boone in his preppy dinner jacket and immaculate white shoes. The caption beneath him read like a pitch from a sympathetic referee in a boxing ring:

> *IN THIS CORNER! Russ Columbo, crooning baritone, who once was in the same orchestra with Crosby and now is a screen and radio star in his own right.*

This was the scenario emblazoned across a two-page puff piece in the *Los Angeles Examiner* on Sunday, September 2, 1934—a symbolic assassination pitting two "Romantic Rivals" against each other. Little did the *Examiner* know how much its fictional battle of the baritones would rebound to haunt them as fact.

On that very day, sometime in the early afternoon, as thousands mulled over these *Examiner* pages after sundry church services, a real bullet tore through Columbo's left eye, penetrated his brain and fractured the back of his skull. In one hideously absurd instant, a radiant career was dashed, the history of popular song was altered, and scores of Columbo fans were left adrift in a romantically underachieving world.

The creepy coincidence between Russ Columbo's media-generated and actual assassinations put the finishing touch to a life that had all of the beauty, tragedy and fevered dreams of a surrealistic melodrama. Dead at the age of 26, with a modest 26 legitimate recordings, and a fame spanning roughly four years, Columbo entered and passed from the planet like a comet's flash, with relatively little tome fodder for biographers. He left behind, however, something much more important: the inspiration to write his life more as an impressionistic history than a conventional biography.

Dubbed the "Romeo of Song" the "Valentino of Radio," and, of course, "King of the Crooners," Columbo was a voice of authority in songs about romantic longing. Columbo not only sang and wrote about the aspirations of love-struck dreamers; he lived them out on a daily basis. This perfect meld of art and life illuminated his singing style. As perfunctory plot summary alone, the story of Russ Columbo offers an emotional helter-skelter—a violent contrast between the innocence of romantic balladry and the demons that lurk to subvert romantic ideals.

Resembling Valentino in both looks and temperament, Columbo represented a composite of new world men: the Latin movie idol, the sensitive aesthete, and the gifted eccentric. His mellifluous but melancholy tones spoke to many Americans still drifting in the malaise following the First World War. He paradoxically offered comfort yet affirmed the sense of emotional loss many faced as they entered the Great Depression.

With a respect for melodic traditions rooted much more in opera than anything resembling jazz or "the blues," Columbo could deliver the simplest of ballads in a smooth, sonorous and bedeviling style. He mastered the dual role of being easy on the ear while dramatizing romantic dejection on songs like his timeless "Prisoner Of Love." His was a special sound that surged from the heart but gazed into space, commanding what one critic called "a sly delivery of tone that weaves its way through a song hard to describe." Another put it more aptly: "Signor Columbo is three jumps ahead of the Vallees, the Crosbys and the Downeys, for he probably is the only other idol who looks the way he sounds."[1]

A couple of years before Columbo's death, a novelty song called "Crosby, Columbo And Vallee" joked about a crooner triumvirate. When Columbo passed on and Vallee resigned himself to a future as a comic more than a singer, Crosby claimed all of the crooner kudos. He would make many more hit records, shoot golf with the most hallowed of celebrities, accompany Bob Hope on numerous Hollywood *Road* trips, and essentially consign the crooner mystique to a lackadaisical everyman peeping behind a Father O'Malley façade.

Following Columbo's fatality, Crosby emerged in many minds as a virtual culprit. It was not that Columbo and Crosby were really enemies. There is ample reason to believe the two men got along fine and respected one

 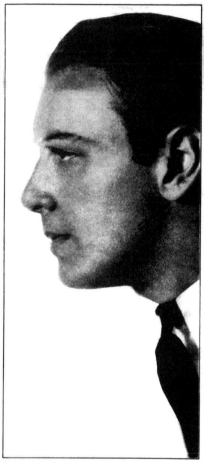

Rudy Valentino   Russ Columbo

Echo of Valentino?

Is Russ Columbo, the crooner, reminiscent of the beloved Rudy?

You'll see him in a prominent part in "Broadway Through a Keyhole," the Walter Winchell story which Darryl Zanuck is producing. Russ Columbo has been a radio Romeo for a long time, but it will remain for the movies to popularize his good looks. According to the two profile portraits, above, Columbo has some of the same Latin charm that made the late Rudolf Valentino the motion picture idol of his time. Will Columbo impress screen audiences also? See his film and let us know what you think!

3

another's talents. Crosby had even served as one of Columbo's pallbearers. But from 1934 on, Crosby had won the crooner duel, if only by default.

Depicting Crosby as the thug and Columbo the altar boy, the *Examiner* editors offered less a contrast between good and evil and more a clash of sensibilities. More than half a century later, some journalists still pit Columbo and Crosby as doppelgangers. Jazz proselytizer Gary Giddins, in *Bing Crosby: A Pocketful of Dreams*, asserts, "Columbo was the obverse of Crosby. He was a crooner merely, a ballad singer who initially favored a tenor range and could barely handle an up-tempo number, let alone swing."[2]

The premise behind Giddins' study in contrasts reflects many modern-day critics who pass off their jazz-happy prejudices as learned discourse. But such a world where swing is king can easily be turned on its head. This book shall, therefore, attempt to rectify decades of slanted scholarship with a counter-slant. Readers shall encounter a viewpoint in which the phrase "obverse of Crosby" is an inverted compliment and Columbo's disinclination to play it "hot" is a positive attribute. Here, sensitive and sentimental ballad singers are the heroes. Judging Russ Columbo on the basis of whether he could "swing" is akin to assessing Louis Armstrong's ability to yodel. So, if crooners were the modern-day equivalent to romantic troubadours, then Columbo was a master at his craft.

Decades later, Columbo's ghost returns from time to time to cast doubt on the legitimacy of *Der Bingle's* crown. To this day, many Columbo enthusiasts listen to all of the sweet and lovely tunes Crosby recorded through the years and pine over how much better they might have sounded had the Romeo of Song gotten a stay of execution. If only Columbo had been allowed to croon more of the great American songbook!

Tiny Tim, who was much more than just a zany media personality, had a vast knowledge of crooner lore. He outshines most "respected" critics with his splendid appraisal of Columbo's charms:

> [Columbo] did not sound at all like Bing Crosby. Crosby was strong, powerful, and magnetic, and Columbo was soft, smooth, and romantic. His voice was very beautiful, like a violin that he played... Columbo had a very smooth, ahead-of-his-time, modern, late Thirties-Forties voice, before Mr. Sinatra, Mr. Como, Bob Eberly, Ray Eberle, Vic Damone, Johnnie Johnston, Andy Russell— all Forties and late Thirties singers. He was ahead of his time.[3]

The discerning James Bedoian, founder and producer of the vintage reissue label Take Two Records, voices a similar view:

Columbo was what Crosby did later on in his career. Crosby's singing evolved from the rhythmic whiskey-voiced baritone to a smooth crooning style, similar to what Columbo had been doing all along. While Bing's singing did get smoother over the years, unlike Columbo, he never sang love songs as if he really felt them. There was always a rather casual, off-the-cuff quality in the way he performed his numbers, whether a love song, a Hawaiian tune, cowboy song or novelty number. I always felt that even his big hit 'White Christmas' was a bit dispassionate. Columbo sang lyrics with much greater feeling—perhaps even overdone by the standards of the late Thirties and Forties. It would have been most interesting to see how Columbo might have influenced popular music had he lived or, for that matter, how his style might have changed to fit the musical trends.

Without a doubt, Columbo's death—which journalists have much too often made the focus of his life—pervades his legend. As writer Peter Dempsey puts it in the notes to a British compilation of Columbo's work: "Columbo's life rests within a truncated span forever bounded by its duration within the space of eternity, his persona will therefore remain, as it were, frozen in aspic."[4]

Many other crooners sang the praises and dirges of love found and lost, but Columbo's songs are among the most purified hymns to the secular religion of romance. Like most religions, romance has its paths of illusion and temptation, along with its trials of devotion.

The following narrative speculates on Russ Columbo's days wandering through romance's desert. Here he shall try to keep the faith while enduring the indignities of Hollywood typecasting—the politics of radio celebrity; the slippery managers, press agents, lawyers, gangsters, and psychological grifters; the hyped-up "romances" with stars like Pola Negri; the somewhat motherly bond he established with Carole Lombard; his sometimes strained connection to his parents and siblings; and his ambiguous relationship with his greatest friend Lansing Brown.

Deriving much of its information from personal letters, diary entries, court records, newspaper articles, periodicals, biographical accounts, photographs, reviews, sheet music, songs, movies, and sometimes Columbo's own words, *Russ Columbo & The Crooner Mystique* portrays a man vexed— as well as inspired—by vibrant personalities, beautiful insecurities and confused emotional attachments. A marvelous paradox lurks within these fables and facts: a singer who beamed a soft light over troubled times while getting swept up in a whirlwind of joy, frustration, glamour, and ultimately horror. Like the visions that Lewis Carroll's Alice encountered in a parallel world, the history of crooners and love songs gets "curiouser and curiouser" through Russ Columbo's end of the looking glass.

Young Russ, a doe-eyed ragamuffin in schoolboy attire.

THE
THIRTEENTH CHILD

Oh! That old-fashioned mother of mine,
She's the dearest of mothers to me,
She is old-fashioned but mighty fine,
With her silvery hair,
I can see;
How I miss her sweet kiss of tenderness,
And her smile that I adore...

"That Old-Fashioned Mother Of Mine" (1925)
—Lyrics by Russ Columbo & Howard Coombs; Music by Russ Columbo

Russ Columbo had already achieved semi-mythical stature when he emerged from the womb with his head wrapped in a placental "caul"—a fetal membrane that antediluvian folklore regards as a sign of great health and success. Columbo's inventive family members, who claimed a blood link to Christopher Columbus, used this divine detail as a salvo in their last-born's evolving legend.

Among the olio of stories and fibs woven into his biography, Columbo's birthdate—January 14, 1908—and his birth name, Ruggiero Eugenio di Rodolpho Colombo—are among the precious few incontrovertible facts. His actual birthplace, however, has been open to controversy. Some, including Columbo himself, have cited San Francisco; others have designated Philadelphia. But an existing birth certificate originates from Camden, New Jersey, a place where the highly mobile Colombo family had apparently spent some time after residing in Pennsylvania.

Giulia and Nicola Colombo took pride in being not only Ruggiero's parents but also his de facto press agents. Their first efforts involved a manipulation of numbers. Paul Yawitz, Columbo's future press agent, would write of a document existing somewhere in the annals of Ripley's "Believe It Or Not" that revealed Ruggiero Eugenio being born the twelfth child of a twelfth child. To reinforce this numerological edge, father Nicola even claimed that he had to make twelve attempts to reach a doctor on the night of Ruggiero's birth, due to an electrical storm that had knocked out local telephone lines.

While the "official" number of Columbo's siblings remains debatable (even those brave enough to check census records are liable to come with up half a dozen names at best), the standard tally is twelve. The known names include Antonio (the first-born), Florence, Alfonso (later Albert), John, Carmela, Anna, and Fiore. Giulia and Nicola would have been loath to publicly acknowledge an alleged third birth in the family line— a stillborn boy. Such an ungainly detail would have branded the blessed Ruggiero as the thirteenth child.

Nurtured as he was on the lucky number "twelve," Columbo never discounted one story that allegedly took place on the 13th day of 1913. While visiting a friend's house, he spotted a violin on the piano, walked over to it, picked it up, and miraculously played it by ear. Years later, in one of his many well-prepared statements to the press, he gave his childhood talents a more earthly spin: "When I was first able to get around the house without falling on my face, I began tripping over musical instruments. The whole family loved music, a common devotion among Italians. At seven, I started taking violin lessons. I learned to play other instruments more or less haphazardly."[1]

Whether or not Ruggiero's future greatness was cosmically triggered remains an open question, but mother Giulia was an undoubted force behind his melodic pursuits and emotional makeup. She was among the very first to intuit how much music would help ease her boy's nerves and encouraged him to take up the guitar. Lazy stereotyping might evoke images of a squat Italian matriarch lording over her flock with Roman Catholic pieties and a wooden spoon, but Giulia Colombo was likely more complex.

While still in the Old Country, Giulia Pesari worked as a schoolteacher, a highly exalted profession in economically strapped Southern Italy. But around 1885, following the death of her parents, she took her chances on the New World. She arrived in New York but settled in Philadelphia, where she married Nicola, another recent immigrant who worked at the time as a stonemason.

The details of Giulia's life, though scant, suggest a woman who, despite physical and perhaps emotional ailments, endured more than the average American mom. Besides living to see at least half a dozen of her children die, she faced constant intimations of her own mortality with health problems that had manifested when Ruggiero was still a child. To compensate for the waning control over her own body, she nurtured her son with a silver cord and an invisible leash, showering him with genuine but desperate affection.

Nicola Colombo in one of his many occupations.

A proud prodigy.

In contrast to his mother, Columbo's father wielded a disciplinary hand and appears to have been less emotionally accessible. As a breadwinner whose trade varied from construction worker to grocer to real estate agent, he was more preoccupied with supporting a large family through what sometimes turned out to be wayward business ventures. Besides, he already had his share of roughhousing with several older sons and probably viewed the shy Ruggiero more as a delicate toy than a typical boy.

In the summer of 1913, the Colombos entered a talent show under the sunny skies of Atlantic City's Steel Pier, giving Ruggiero his first chance to sing and strum before an overheated but appreciative crowd. Though his guitar outsized him, the puckish five-year-old relished the kudos. Continual praise made him an applause addict.

When the time came for him to evolve from the guitar to his ideal instrument, Ruggiero took his first violin lessons from Antonio Laveri, a music teacher who had recently emigrated from Rome and lived in a neighborhood tenement. Accordingly, the boy showed a facility for the instrument within the first "twelve" months of instruction and started showing up the other family members whenever they commingled to play anything from Italian folk songs to operatic arias.

In 1916, by the time he was eight, and following the deaths of two of his brothers, Ruggiero departed with his family for the left coast, leaving behind Anthony (who preferred to stay rooted with his Pennsylvania Railroad job). Being that Alfonso and Florence had already made the milk and honey migration, family reunification was one reason for the Colombo family's wanderlust. But there was also the allure of Napa Valley's wine country, which was home to a Calistoga health resort perfect for Giulia's heart ailment.

By the time they moved to San Francisco in 1919, the Colombos incurred another tragedy when sister Florence died from influenza. Giulia placated her grief by seeing to it that Ruggiero became a violin virtuoso, even if it meant sitting beside him to make sure he finished his dreary finger exercises. His first attempts may have sounded like cats mating, but to her ears he was already nearing the greatness of Fritz Kreisler. Sensing her son would be distracted from his muse, she once refused to sign permission papers from this school that would have allowed him to play extracurricular baseball.

In between his classes at Everett Grammar School, Ruggiero got a spellbinding education from Dr. Joseph Czech, a German violinist who tolerated no nonsense. Bellicose and brusque, with a pudgy frame disproportionate to his towering disposition, Czech took merciless delight

Officers

Mr. Stanley Gray	-	-	President
Mr. Max Leon	-	-	Financial Secretary
Master John Heinzer	-	-	Librarian
Mr. Joseph Czech	-	-	Instructor

Members

Miss Marie Bovo	Master Arthur Domergue
Miss Aileen Blondell	Master Ferdinand Domergue
Miss Elsie Meier	Master Marius Figeac
Miss Dagmar Paulson	Master Louis Figeac
Miss Alice Ross	Master Joseph Gunter
Miss Viola Ross	Master John Filomeo
Miss Dagmar Thorsen	Master John Leiser
Miss Helen Sjogren	Master Fred Lackstrom
Miss Rachel Rondebush	Master Paul Laurens
Miss Iniz Zetterblad	Master Thomas McKenna
Miss Emilie Weisser	Master George Madrieres
Miss Josephine McCarthy	Master Allen Zetterblad
Mrs. Ivy Williamson	
Mrs. Annie Ohland	Mr. Stanley Gray
	Mr. John Heinzer
Master Willie Buschman	Mr. Max Leon
Master Russel Columbo	Mr. Hubert Redemeyer
Master Roy Carlson	Mr. H. Schreiber
Master Henry Dietz	Mr. Chas. Williamson

Czech's Violin Club

ASSISTED BY

MR. H. SCHREIBER, CELLIST

YOUNG MEN'S INSTITUTE BUILDING

SAN FRANCISCO

MAY 15, 1921

2:30 O'CLOCK

RHODES PRESS, OAKLAND

For the music student Mr. Czech offers considerable as a teacher. The pupil is given proficient individual attention in connection with ensemble players, under the personal direction of Mr. Czech. Two such ensemble groups are functioning—The Treble Clef Club in Oakland and Czech's Violin Club in San Francisco.

In past years of teaching, many who have studied under Mr. Czech's direction are now enjoying great success throughout the United States.

Among the talented pupils are Russel Columbo, N. B. C. Radio and Talking Picture Star; Miss Dagmar Thorsen, playing for the Goodwin Studios in Southern California; Marius Figeac, best known in the French Colonies in San Francisco, and many others.

The individual and class Czech system of teaching which has helped so many finished musicians and stars can be applied to others who have the desire and receptive music talent.

Additional information regarding the class system will be gladly given by our representatives.

Dr. Czech's program reveals that Russ used the "Columbo" spelling as early as 1921. A program from the previous year also lists a "Master Russel Columbo."

in giving orders from his stuffy parlor, subordinating his little protégé to the beat of the metronome. He would detain Ruggiero for what must have seemed interminable stretches of time, screeching "One-two-three-four!" over and again with the same relentless regimen of musical scales. If Ruggiero happened to make the slightest mistake or pause to rest his weary hand or chin, Czech would erupt into hang-wringing, expressionistic fits. Oliver Twist came face-to-face with Dr. Caligari!

Suckers for ethnic sentimentalism might glean an ideal scenario out of these browbeating sessions: the offspring of earthy Italians honing his skills at the crack of an icy Teutonic whip. Perhaps Czech was also keen to this interplay of ages and ancient bloodlines when he entertained grand designs of whisking Ruggiero off to Germany. There he could crow to his compatriots about how he had transformed a doe-eyed ragamuffin into an internationally renowned child star. But when Czech inquired about adopting him, a more frightened than flattered Giulia declined the offer.

By age twelve, Ruggiero was already shifting from mother's reach to face a ruffian world. One of his first initiations into peer cruelty occurred when playmates insisted on calling him just plain "Russ." This distressed his parents who, perhaps leery over some Old World superstition, believed the abbreviation to be a sign of bad luck and continued to address him as Ruggiero Eugenio.

Around this time, young Russ had demonstrated a facility for the "classics." As a regular contributor to Czech's Violin Club, he participated in a series of concerts given at the Young Men's Institute Building on San Francisco's Van Ness and Oak Streets. Those puzzled as to when "Colombo" became "Columbo" may refer to a Czech's Club program for the afternoon of May 9, 1920 that lists "Master Russel Columbo" as the violin soloist for Paganini's "Caprice." A year later, he was still performing solos for Czech with melodic bouquets like Schubert's "Ave Maria."

Columbo's specific reason for putting a "u" in his last name remains arcane. Perhaps it was the result of a serendipitous typo in Czech's program. Maybe he relented after too many people, associating his name with "Columbus," misspelled it too many times. The circumstances were somewhat illuminated thirteen years later, when his numerologist friend Trix MacKenzie detailed to him in a written correspondence how "Russ Columbo" adds up to the astrological "vibration" of 9—a number "governed by the great and beneficent planet Jupiter."

Restless to wander beyond Dr. Czech's cloak, Columbo responded to a newspaper notice calling for a violinist at San Francisco's Imperial Theater. There he made his theatrical debut as a soloist in the "Prologue" to a fantasy production entitled *The Land of Make-Believe*. On New Year's Eve of 1921, he skirted any existing child curfews with his "boy violinist" solo for a "kiddies' revue." The occasion was an all-night carnival-ball on behalf of the California Boys' Club, sponsored by the San Francisco Commercial Travelers' Association and the Native Sons of the Golden West. For this extravaganza, held at the Civic Auditorium, the city's Mayor (and future California Governor) James R. Rolph made a special appearance.

On the following January, Columbo encountered more gilded prospects while working at the Granada Theater. He performed in another "Prologue," this time to the screening of *My Boy*, in which Jackie Coogan played an immigrant orphan running from the authorities. Columbo was among the twelve "All-Star Juveniles" to join the "Cantonese Prima-Donna" Lady Lo Wah for a staged tribute entitled "Twenty Minutes at Ellis Island." "Russel Colombo" (another example of recurring vacillations with his name spelling) performed violin solos of "Meditation" and "Thais."

In February, the Garden Theater in Burlingame, California had booked "Russell Colombo" as "The wonder violinist of the 20th Century Kids." There, accompanied by Ray Lucas at the organ, he engaged in other prologues to movies like *The Foolish Age* and *The Lane That Had No Turning*. Supreme satisfaction arrived on Valentine's Day, when he played several "new selections" to honor the screening of the Metro Pictures production of *Camille*, a modernized version of Alexandre Dumas' story of love, obsession and physical consumption that starred Alla Nazimova and Rudolph Valentino. The film most likely left an indelible impression on Columbo's permeable mind.

In so many ways, Valentino's portrayal of the woebegone lover Armand Duval resembled the persona Columbo would later project. Facing off gaudy set designs and the over-emoting Nazimova as his consumptive lover Marguerite Gautier, Valentino was delectable as the hypersensitive romantic. This was evident in a key scene when Armand receives Marguerite's letter commanding him to "Go home and forget!" The circles under his eyes bespeak emotional hunger as he looks up from the note, crushes the flower she had left him, grows faint, and sobs hysterically. In another scene, he creeps to Marguerite on his knees, crying out: "I wish I were a relative—your servant—a dog—that I might care for you—nurse you—make you well!"

While still at the Granada, the fourteen-year-old Columbo experienced further feats of surrealism. This is where he supposedly entertained another of his early romantic obsessions. One day, while playing in the orchestra pit, he noticed a pretty blonde dancer rehearsing on the stage. Too intimidated to greet her or even learn her name, he found himself frittering away chunks of

WEEK OF FEBRUARY 12th

GARDEN THEATRE

M. F. LOWERY, Resident Manager

BURLINGAME, CALIF.   Phone Burlingame 8

Matinees Saturday, Sunday and Holidays at 2:30
Evenings 7:15 and 9:00.   Loge Seats Reserved

SUNDAY, FEBRUARY 12—Matinee and Night
You'll laugh till you cry—It'll tickle you pink.

DORIS MAY in "THE FOOLISH AGE"

Special added attraction—

RUSSELL COLOMBO

The wonder violinist of the 20th Century Kids,
Accompanied by RAY LUCAS at the organ.

COMEDY   PATHE REVIEW   SCENIC

NOTE—Chances on the $65 Bicycle will be given at matinee and evening performances. Send the kids to the matinee. No advance in prices.

MONDAY AND TUESDAY, FEB. 13-14.

Nazimova and Rudolph Valentino

—in—

"CAMILLE"

A modernized version of the Dumas masterpiece—and
RUSSELL COLOMBO, the kid violinist, in new selections.

TORCHY COMEDY   NEWS   PRIZMA COLORED SCENIC

Admission, 30c; Children, 15c; war tax included.

WEDNESDAY ONLY.

Agnes Ayres

In her first starring screen romance

"THE LANE THAT HAD NO TURNING"

By Sir Gilbert Parker.

Cast includes Mahlon Hamilton and Theodore Kosloff.
Final concert of RUSSELL COLOMBO.

COMEDY   Usual admission.   KINETO REVIEW

THURSDAY AND FRIDAY, FEB. 16-17.

It's joy time again for big kids and little kids.

JACKIE COOGAN furnishes the laughs in his latest— "MY BOY"

"SCHOOLDAY LOVE"—a special Campbell Kid Comedy.

FOX NEWS   TOPICS OF THE DAY   SPORT REVIEW

Special matinee Friday at 2:30 and 3:45. Send the kids—bring the kids—get the kids here somehow. Regular admission.

SATURDAY, FEB. 18—Matinee and Night.

"BIG" BILL RUSSELL

In the perfect punch play—

"SINGING RIVER"

Monte Banks in "SQUIRREL FOOD"

"WINNERS OF THE WEST"   MUTT AND JEFF

Coming Sun., Feb. 19—Eugene O'Brien in "Is Life Worth Living"
Flowers for the Garden Theatre from Peterson & Haywood.

Patrons Desiring Program Mailed, Kindly Leave Name at Box Office

Advance Print   Burlingame

As "Kid Violinist," Russ shares the same billing with his idol Valentino.

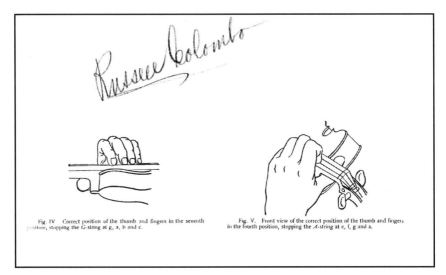

Fig. IV   Correct position of the thumb and fingers in the seventh position, stopping the G-string at g, a, b and c.

Fig. V.   Front view of the correct position of the thumb and fingers in the fourth position, stopping the A-string at e, f, g and a.

Russ' personal copy of his early finger exercises.

each succeeding day in hapless adoration. He would sit in the theater's front row, transfixed less on her flesh and more on the platinum tresses that glided with her body like gauze descending from the clouds. On the day of his final Granada assignment, he gazed for one last time on a presence so phantasmal and disorienting that he almost left without his violin.

Once he graduated from Calistoga Union elementary school in June of 1923, Columbo joined his sister Carmela in Los Angeles. The rest of the clan came down the following year. He continued his musical pursuits at the newly opened Belmont High School, conveniently located between downtown L.A. and Hollywood. Studying under a reputable instructor named Calmon Luboviski, he became first violinist in the school orchestra. He also joined the Belmont glee club just as his adolescent tenor edged into a high baritone. Making connections, he soon studied voice with Alexander Bevani, an opera performer who registered displeasure after learning about his pupil's dalliance with popular melodies and the "hot fiddle."

Columbo, like many growing up in musically inclined Italian families, thrived under opera's shadow. His older siblings eventually devised a way to share this gift with a paying public by opening a spaghetti joint on Western Avenue called *Gigi's*. Amid the sawdust floors and intoxicating scent of marinara sauce, Columbo sometimes wore a tasseled tango dancer's hat as he lulled customers with violin serenades. For him, as well as for his older brother Fiore (who managed the establishment), Gigi's had an additional resource: it was close to the Central Casting Office.

Still, the varying accounts of Columbo's early family life suggest a scenario more problematic than the boilerplate tableau of mandolins and red-checkered tablecloths. Destiny played a much more intriguing game by luring the Colombos westward from their quaint East Coast trappings to the feet of Movieland's Moloch. Fiore, who had also developed into a handsome specimen and was the first of the Colombos with movie star aspirations, had an understandable effect on his younger brother's shifting worldview.

Sharing Fiore's good looks, having precocious musical smarts, living near Hollywood, and reaching adolescence in the frenzied Twenties, Columbo was blessed and vexed with high expectations. Everyday, he confronted the glaring contrasts between the bucolic heritage of his European forbears and the deracinated environment into which his parents had transplanted him. This was an era when the science of public relations became an art, electronic sound transformed the human presence into ghostly echoes, and religious conventions buckled to cinema's cultic trappings. The matinee idol proved a much more tangible deity.

As Columbo played his first notes, he and his family were already enjoying the benefits of an advancing electronic age. As early as 1906, the Victor Talking Machine Company had put out a mechanically repro-duced performance of Enrico Caruso singing with an orchestra. By 1915, Victor also brought out its popular Victrola phonograph, a device designed to compete with the American home's once ubiquitous piano. By the early Twenties, phonographic and radio technology introduced new and eerie ways to morph singing into a kind of melodic ectoplasm. People were already bandying about the term "crooner" to denote the new singers of the airwaves.

The era was also rife with what a popular Twenties song called "Masculine Women, Feminine Men." Two major icons, Jack Dempsey and Rudolph Valentino, personified stark contrasts of the male ideal. Boxer Dempsey seduced America after winning the heavyweight championship in the summer of 1919. He was the Jazz Age hellion, the testosteroid who would never dream of compromising his legendary left hook by holding a Martini with pinky erect. But as Dempsey's fame grew so did his need to succumb to Hollywood's ballyhoo and its attendant manicures, facial appliqués and, according to some, the cosmetic surgeon's knife.

Columbo, like many boys of the time, also caught a bout of media-induced Dempsey fever. He even fancied becoming a professional fighter and practiced by sparring with Alfonso and Fiore in the summer evenings. Pugilistic prospects came to a halt, however, when his irate dad jumped into the fray, shouting: "You're not ruining your hands after your mother wasted all this money on your music lessons!" He then took off his coat, put up his own fists and hollered, "You're going to fight me, bambino." Even before he could position himself to meet dad's challenge, Columbo succumbed to a sucker punch that knocked him humbly earthward.

In public at least, Columbo took this profile in patriarchal terrorism like a good sport: "He gave me the worst beating I ever got in my life," he would later recollect. "I decided that if my own father could clean up the ground with me I'd better give up. And I did."[2] He was from then on more averse to aggression, dreading that even if he were brave enough to face off one adversary, another tougher oaf might lurk in the wings to polish him off. Worse, any further acts of hooliganism could worsen his mother's mounting heart problems. Besides, he was made of finer stuff. Later on, memories of Dempsey would trigger ghastly afterthoughts.

Happily, Columbo alighted toward the Valentino prototype: a much more attractive and rarefied role model who could be unmistakably male yet flaunt a rose-petal softness. With his dark, "Latin" features, Valentino was a novelty for movie audiences corn-fed on preppy heroes from the Midwest. He also exemplified how the entertainment media exoticized darker Caucasians from foreign lands. He may have been a bit swarthier than Wallace Reid but was still white enough to seduce the fair maidens without violating any production code strictures that forbade miscegenation themes.

As the rapacious Englishman masquerading as an Arab in *The Sheik*, Valentino elicited alternately glowing and scathing press. The female fans swooned and their dates seethed, while the more sensible and sensitive men either aped him or longed to date him. He was also brazen enough to mollify the gals and menace the jocks with an even more threatening image, that of the effete dandy.

Besides sharing the name Rodolpho, Columbo felt a deeper connection to the controversial Sheik. Perhaps it was Valentino's wistful frown, the impression he gave of someone too intelligent to surrender to the role of pasteboard Casanova without at least a pout. Valentino was, by many accounts, a moody guy who grew increasingly dissatisfied with fame's anti-climax. The astute H.L. Mencken wrote of a man who often appeared dejected, drained and alienated when forced to mingle with Tinseltown's crazy-makers. "Like Valentino, [Columbo] carried a mirror in his pocket, and had no inhibitions about gazing at himself in public," Warren G. Harris opines in his *Gable & Lombard* biography. "This led, as it also did in Valentino's case, to considerable speculation about his masculinity."[3]

Many crooners charmed their fans by playing hide and seek with the specter of effeminacy; in this sense, Columbo was all the more appealing

Years later, Russ, his brother and interceding father jokingly re-live a chidhood brawl.

Howard Coombs
Pianist

Howard Coombs, though young in years, is a wizard of the keyboard. He looks the virtuoso and plays like one. His audiences, impressed by his personality before he strikes a note, are spellbound by the force and poetic feeling with which he expresses himself through the medium of his chosen instrument. He produces effects of exquisite delicacy—draws forth singing tones of moving beauty—builds tremendous and dazzling climaxes—all with ease and surety.

His accompanying is of an artistry rarely heard—doubly rare in one who plays with such commanding brilliance as a soloist. Both as soloist and accompanist Mr. Coombs is favorably known to audiences of East and West. He has won the approbation and praise of distinguished artists and musical critics. In the Los Angeles Times and elsewhere his fineness of touch and feeling have been declared remarkable. At a special program in the world-famous Hollywood Bowl, celebrating the opening of Mulholland Highway, a vast audience acclaimed his playing a thrilling success.

Gifted with rare aptitude, Mr. Coombs began his piano studies at an early age, and continued them in both East and West, having been for some time with Burritt Lincoln Marlowe of New York and Los Angeles, who was a personal pupil of Leschetizky.

Mr. Coombs' interpretations show an exceptional mental grasp. More than that, they live in the memory by virtue of their wonderful emotional appeal. His extensive repertoire, great technical facility and several years of concert experience enable him to present programs by which his audiences are fascinated, and he is always enthusiastically applauded and recalled.

Howard Coombs is headed for the heights.

Howard Coombs—Russ' literary soul-mate and song collaborator.

because his elusive butterfly of a personality complemented a mannish appearance. One female reporter, professional on the outside but doting on the inside, would later describe him as "5 ft. 11—weighs 175 pounds—black hair—brown eyes... is chivalrous and well poised. Altho of Italian parentage, he is as handsome as a Greek God."[4] Another, this time a male, would marvel at how "his hair is so black that it shines; his eyes are equally black, and his shoulders are as broad as those of a football player."[5]

Columbo most likely had a difficult time reconciling the glaring disparity between the financial stresses of his family life and Valentino's screen glamour. Just as today, Hollywood in the early to mid-Twenties offered an extreme contrast between lords and serfs. Whether the neighborhood was squalid or just barely middle-class, its inhabitants had only to gaze upward toward the wealthy hillside hamlets for reminders of their lowly status. The long dead Roman ruins never threatened the Italians in the Old Country, but Los Angeles supported a very extant and greedy empire.

Sometime in the early 1920s, one special individual helped Columbo to cultivate a means of mental escape from penury and all else that reeked of the ordinary. Whatever happens to a young man in the interlude between childhood and adolescence marks him for life—so there is reason to suspect that his friendship with a bright and apparently sensitive pianist/poet named Howard W. Coombs forged an artistic and emotional link that became frozen in time.

Described in his promotional literature as a "wizard of the keyboard," Coombs had been recognized in the *Los Angeles Times* for his stage presence and musical flair. When the city celebrated the Mulholland Highway's grand opening, Coombs performed at the Hollywood Bowl for an audience that was "spellbound by the force and poetic feeling with which he expresses himself through the medium of his chosen instrument."

Columbo tended to forge ties with men he mildly resembled. Judging by an existing photograph, Coombs shared some of Columbo's fine features, along with the smartly slicked-back hair and intellectual high forehead. Coombs was quite young but commanded the presence of a mature virtuoso. He also possessed what dedicated English Literature students might instantly recognize as a poet's mug: the discerning eyebrows and the intense stare of a dreamer impatient with the "real" world's persistent let-downs.

Coombs articulated his feelings by channeling the lofty visions of Romantic poets like William Wordsworth, resorting to a language considered too anachronistic and precious for the hardened 20th century. Columbo was also inspired each time Coombs' pen begot ornamental couplets like "Winter's Wooing":

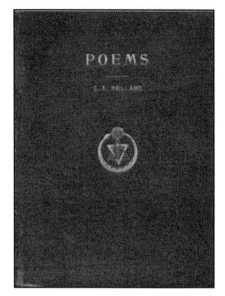
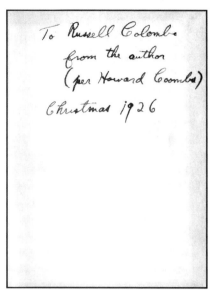

POEMS

C. F. HOLLAND

To Russell Colombo
from the author
(per Howard Coombs)
Christmas 1926

A book of poems by C.F. Holland given to Russ by Howard Coombs.

> *With sad winds wailing doleful dirges drear*
> *The earth forlornly mourns for summer's flight.*
> *With him fled all that made her beauty bright;*
> *Unadorned, woe-worn, she grieves in the fading year...*

Or such clashes between darkness and light as "The Sun-God":

> *More surely and fleetly as lives pass like days,*
> *With strength e'er renewed in the long, starry nights,*
> *Climb the steeds of the Spirit Divine in each soul,*
> *From passion's dim swamp-lands to heights beyond heights...*

As one of the very first kindred spirits to waft in and out of Columbo's path, Coombs probably helped him combine the roles of violinist, singer and songwriter. Of the many songs Columbo had registered with the Library of Congress, at least five were collaborations with Coombs in a span from 1925 to 1931. One fine example is "That Old-Fashioned Mother Of Mine." While Columbo composed the tune, Coombs collaborated with him on the lyrics. The first (barely legible) verse, which Columbo had curiously crossed out in his handwritten manuscript, shows how much he shared Coombs' themes of dreamy grieving, albeit in a simpler language:

I left behind my dearest pal,
When I chanced to roam,
I miss her most of all,
And I miss my 'Home Sweet Home';
I'm feeling so sad and lonesome too,
And I don't know what I'll do...

"That Old-Fashioned Mother Of Mine" had all the doleful trappings of older Tin Pan Alley themes about wayward sons and holy moms. (The title is even identical to a 1919 tune by Horatio Nicholls and Worton David.) Its lyrics suggest that Columbo was, in some respects, similar in temperament to the great American composer Stephen Foster, who has been described in various biographical accounts as melancholy, reflective, distracted, introverted, and mother-fixated. Foster was also more comfortable with the wistful parlor ballad, as opposed to the nerve-racking minstrel songs for which he cared less and has since been most unfairly associated.

Like Foster, Columbo wrote melodies and lyrics infused with beatific, nurturing and ultimately unattainable images. He was inclined to wrap his mother and himself in sugar-spun recollections of a gilded age, aided by lyricists like Coombs who sought refuge from the primitive present through the styles of a more genteel yesterday. With his "old-fashioned mother" as his paragon and Coombs his inspiration, Columbo proceeded to form attachments to motherly women and brotherly men for the rest of his life.

The second verse to "That Old-Fashioned Mother Of Mine" reveals how Columbo, even in his teen years, experienced the pangs of nostalgia expected from a much more weathered man:

I wish that I were back again,
I always wish I could have been,
With her so she'd be near,
I pray every night that she'll forgive,
And I hope it's not too late...

Maybe it was already "too late." Hollywood was too close to home sweet home. Paramount Pictures and other image factories were luring him away. With the safety of his protective family bubble in jeopardy, Columbo slipped through a rabbit hole to Wonderland.

Pola Negri once called herself "the high priestess of the Valentino cult."

MOOD MUSIC
FOR
POLA NEGRI

You are the girl from that English children's book, who walked through the glass into a world full of crazy people! And do you know who I am? I am the March Hare!!

—Pola Negri, from the 1964 film *The Moon-Spinners*

Lansing Brown was among those special individuals gifted and burdened with a gravitational face. While photographs of him reveal a propensity to droop and frown, his facial gravity was not the kind usually associated with sagging body tissue. His was a psychic gravity, a force so strong that a simple glance into his eyes could pull onlookers into a dense maw of artistic inspiration and emotional panic.

Specializing in Hollywood portrait photographs, Brown had a knack for absorbing souls by looking at or through them, especially those willing to pay handsomely for the privilege of preening in front of his camera. He was born Lansing Van Woert Brown, Jr. on August 24, 1900 in North Dakota, the product of a proper all-American family and the son of a railroad clerk. Around 1920, he pursued his undying interest in photography once his family moved to California. He had a knack for acquainting himself with influential people and eventually moved into exalted Hollywood circles.

Brown became an assistant to Melbourne Spurr, another Hollywood portrait photographer highly celebrated in the profession. Through Spurr, he got to sit alongside such luminaries as John Barrymore, Mary Pickford, and the doomed director William Desmond Taylor. This was a pioneering era for celebrity portraiture—a profession that started in women's periodicals but in due course sated the feminine appetites of both sexes in picture magazines like *Harper's Bazaar* and *Vogue*.

Brother Fiore, who had his own movie star aspirations, introduced Lansing Brown to the Columbo household.

In 1924, Russ Columbo's brother Fiore, scouting around town for bit parts, fell into the vortex of Brown's stare. Brown's affinity with filmland's bluebloods incited Fiore's actorly ambitions. Soon they became friends. In one particular photograph, Brown captured Fiore as a misty-eyed Mediterranean with dark, wavy hair brushed back to accentuate a slightly furrowed brow and eyes that drifted into the distance. Though he sported an immaculately white shirt, Fiore appeared a bit rougher around the edges than the younger brother he had always tried to protect.

On the day Fiore introduced Brown to the Colombo family, the sixteen-year-old Russ was especially charmed. Brown had an intrinsically elegant way about him, a taste for stylish finery and choice libations. He could carry on highly literate conversations and had a vast musical knowledge. To put it in the romantic language of the time: Brown's eloquence on all matters of art and life—especially his film star stories—reeled through the young Columbo's synapses like smooth Stradivarian bow strokes.

Impressed by Columbo's Valentino resemblance, Brown encouraged him to pursue work as an actor and even offered to take some headshots. Like Howard Coombs, he became a metaphysical confidante off whom Columbo could bounce ideas. Brown, eight years his senior, inversely saw in Columbo a vicarious escape to a lost boyhood, a second chance to engage in frolic and impish lunacy. For example, they delighted in a morbid little game. Whenever hearing the blast of a backfiring automobile, both would clutch at their chests, contort their faces, slump over, and cry, "Ach! They got me!"[1]

He may have found Brown's Valentino comparisons flattering, but Columbo initially entered the motion picture world more via his musical acumen than his looks. Gino Corrado, a friend with connections at Famous Players/Lasky studio, advised him that he could eke out a modest living as an on-location troubadour to the stars. In no time, the Junior Valentino who once brandished his sweet violin from table to table at Gigi's was weaving romantic tunes for some of the leading screen divas.

The notion of live musicians on silent movie sets may seem peculiar today, but background players were often essential in that era. The right musician with the right melody could conjure just the right atmosphere for actors to assume the required mood. The trend supposedly began as early as 1914, when D.W. Griffith hired an orchestra to motivate his star Blanche Sweet through the poignant moments in *Judith of Bethulia*. Even though the actual audience heard only music from the theater organ or piano, this on-site "emotion music" or "sob music" bolstered many subsequent screen narratives.

As a mood maestro for the silent screen, Columbo became Pola Negri's enabler when the cameras rolled.

From *Motion Picture Classic*, May 1925.

He played background music for the likes of Clara Bow, Evelyn Brent and Betty Compson, but Columbo had his most enriching and enervating experience devising counterpoints to the celluloid antics of that most tempestuous of starlets: Paramount's raven-haired "Queen of Tragedy"—Pola Negri.

Negri flaunted both the grandest and most abysmal qualities of a romantic. In her autobiography *Memoirs of a Star*, she admits to being troubled by what she called "a vast sense of melancholy yearning"[2] and regarded herself as a "child of destiny." Born Apolonia Chalupec in Lipno, Poland, she adopted her stage name in honor of one of her idols, the Italian poetess Ada Negri. Tubercular in her youth, Negri also described herself as "withdrawn, hypersensitive, given to poetic fantasy..."[3]

In relationships, Negri acquired a taste for lumpy cocktails of equal parts fame and frustration, throwing herself into the arms of millionaires, movie stars and statesmen. But when it came to cultivating lasting love, she had a black thumb. Her once happy affair with an English millionaire (who had a penchant for aviation and fast cars) crashed along with his plane. Her first husband, a Georgian prince, also underwent the death plummet in a polo accident.

Negri made her Hollywood debut as an evil vamp in the 1923 film *Bella Donna*, where she flashed an array of Egyptian turbans and gypsy accoutrements. Off the screen, she made a point of being chauffeured in a white velvet upholstered Rolls Royce and would occasionally traipse along Sunset Boulevard with a pet tiger pulling on her leash.

Like Valentino, Negri was an "exotic" European. With dark hair, olive skin, a round face, and robust demeanor, she had a bearing that could register as either Eastern European or Mediterranean. That is why she was best at portraying foreign females with attitude: hysterical courtesans, Ruritarian wenches, and tainted "half-castes." And like Columbo, she dreaded being romantically condemned, stating in her autobiography: "No matter how hard I attempted to find happiness with a man, something always intervened to destroy it, something beyond my control."[4]

Temperamentally, if not medically, Negri was not far from the fictional Marguerite Gautier in *Camille*—a character she would also eventually play—who was driven by a persistent fever in the blood. She saw in Columbo a fresh, new Armand when, taken in by the Valentino likeness, she hired him as her personal accompanist for a then generous sum of $100 per week. She soon goaded him into serving as her melodic enabler when the cameras rolled. His dreamy background airs placated her panic spells one moment, while his volatile tremolos sated her hunger for attention the next. His violin approximated each nuance, each affected spasm, and every glycerin tear that oozed from her batting eyelids.

Columbo's phantom chorus was the likely force behind Negri's portrayal of the Countess Elnora Natatorini in *A Woman of the World* as she brandished her whip to seduce a pious reformer. Columbo's heart-wrenching crescendos must have fueled her in *Hotel Imperial* as she played a meek Austrian chambermaid fighting off a Russian general's slobbering advances. And only Columbo could have fiddled while Negri burned with agitation in her role of the proud French farm girl in *Barbed Wire*, especially as she wept over the corpse of her father who keeled over after seeing her in the arms of an enemy German.

Negri's mating glances had all the benevolence of a black velvet noose once the cameras stopped and the klieg lights went dim. Her relationship with the masochistic Valentino was, by her own confession, a passion attack seasoned with moments of self-doubt, dark moods, and the Great Lover's "private inner war." "When things were going well," she explained,

A 1926 photo that Valentino had apparently written to Russ' brother Albert.

"he was often morose; when going badly, he would be gleeful as if he deserved misery rather than happiness."[5]

Columbo meanwhile experienced the anxiety and excitement of being caught in the crosswinds between two of filmdom's most irrepressible legends. He was present one day on the Lasky lot when Valentino arrived to pay Negri a visit and even got to shake his idol's hand. For Valentino it was another perfunctory greeting, but Columbo cooed inwardly.

Events soon spoiled his giddy infatuation. "I remember the day the news of Valentino's death was brought to the studio," Columbo would later recollect. "They were shooting scenes for the picture *Barbed Wire*. Pola fainted dead away, and I can vouch for the fact that it was no act."[6] The incident also made Columbo break out into a cold sweat. From that moment on, he got the creeps whenever the subject of Valentino entered conversations.

Valentino's untimely demise in August of 1926 led to a funeral in New York City that epitomized Roman Catholic camp. The occasion afforded Negri with not only a self-fulfilling prophecy of doom but a thespian's tour de force. According to Irving Shulman's hilarious Valentino biography, Negri passed out upon her ceremonious arrival at Grand Central Station and again when she checked into the Ambassador Hotel. When she approached the funeral bier and draped the casket with a curtain of roses spelling her name, she went into prayer, wept and, as the cameras and scribes stood on alert, lapsed into one more signature fainting spell.

Soon afterward, Negri immersed herself in the occult to propitiate the forces of a great spooky beyond that she would manage to avoid for three more decades. Years later, she would adopt a more sober approach to these events. "The void created by his death," she would write in her autobiography, "had to be filled by me as the living symbol, the high priestess of the Valentino cult."[7]

What a contrast Negri made to Lansing Brown. Instead of nourishing Columbo with philosophical succor, Negri burdened the seventeen-year-old neophyte with even more psychic baggage. A legend surfaced shortly after Valentino's burial. Negri supposedly anointed Columbo as her new Armand by presenting him with an opal ring that Valentino had supposedly regarded as a talisman. Hollywood mythmakers would later speculate that the ring was cursed and that Columbo triggered a chain of calamities by accepting this wearisome gift.

The true nature of Negri's "relationship" with her Valentino replacement remains an enigma. Were they paramours in the Biblical sense? Was Columbo little more than a platonic escort? Did she perhaps bait him into a nexus of evil?

Her capricious interests notwithstanding, Negri was gracious enough to introduce Columbo to the crème of her society. He hoped to achieve stardom by osmosis whenever chatting with Ramon Novarro, Gloria Swanson, Erich Von Stroheim, Cesar Romero and a still scandal-plagued Roscoe "Fatty" Arbuckle. Columbo also grew to enjoy the company of celebrities with whom he bore a vague physical likeness, such as the dashing Gilbert Roland, one of few actors to use his "Latin" countenance to great advantage in a post-Valentino climate.

This stellar circle of pals, while congenial and professionally resourceful, offered none of the comforts of Brown's new and exclusive photographic studio, located on posh Wilshire Boulevard. The smartly decorated enclosure offered a neural detour from the Paramount lot and all its disarray. While meting out his customary helpings of anecdotes, witticisms and fine wine, Brown also had a Victrola, an impressive stack of 78-rpm records, and a grand piano on which Columbo pounded away to his favorite sheet music.

Brown's camera eye would capture the likes of Stan Laurel and Loretta Young, but Columbo presented the ideal photographic venture. Standing a comely five feet, eleven inches in height, Russ had by now developed a frame that was tailored for impeccably pressed suits. He continued to be shy and somewhat awkward, with a shaky reserve and an ethereal neuroticism usually credited to obsessed artists.

In the hundreds of photographs Columbo accumulated of himself during his short career, Brown's portraits were the most fascinating and flattering. In one picture, Columbo would appear spruced up in a tuxedo, looking deeply engrossed against a spotlight while playing his violin. In another, he could be in full or semi-profile, looking downward as if concentrating on something profound and troubling. He could also look inscrutable and moody by adopting a slightly demonic grin.

Brown was essentially a crusader, armed with a photographic arsenal. Whenever Columbo grew despondent, Brown saved the day with a fresh fusillade of esteem-building snapshots. But Brown's camera was not all fluff and flattery. It was also a mental fencing tool: a sword, rapier, knife, dueling pistol, and sharpshooter's viewfinder all in one. Their photographic collaboration veered into more exotic and bizarre directions. In one set of shots, Columbo appears as a helmeted Prussian officer, grabbing at an amorous strumpet and waiting for a kiss with his eyes closed. He truly gets caught up in the drama when dressed as a gypsy, wielding a bloody knife and staring maniacally at the murdered woman in his arms.

There was a faraway look in Columbo's eyes during those evenings when he sat around with Brown and friends. He was boyish and vulnerable among these older sophisticates but rarely flinched when they affectionately teased him about his long Italian name. Journalist Walter Ramsey recalled those singular evenings when he (and sometimes his wife) would join Columbo and Brown at the studio. "For hours we'd sit around talking, recounting stories, airing our hopes and ambitions and discussing life in general. Of the entire group, Russ was the youngest and most retiring, had the least to say."[8] Columbo was also the first to leave and admitted only to Brown that he needed to keep his mom from waiting up for him.

In contrast to the publicity thin "romance" between Negri and Valentino, Russ Columbo and Lansing Brown shared a camaraderie more profound than any euphemisms at the time could describe and far deeper than shallow customs of "male bonding" usually encourage. A few years later, in an interview with *Motion Picture* magazine, Columbo invoked a Damon and Pythias scenario: "Lansa has been a great influence in my life... the best friend a man could have... one who asks nothing and gives everything... who would lay down his life for you if necessary."[9]

Columbo had taken this photo of Lansing Brown. Their relationship remains as obscure and suggestive as this dedication that Lansing had inscribed to Russ in Spanish.

Photo: Lansing Brown.

Photo: Lansing Brown.

Photo: Lansing Brown.

Photo: Lansing Brown.

Parade of fashion held at the Cocoanut Grove, Juanuary 27, 1938. Herald Examiner Collection / Los Angeles Public Library.

PRISONER
OF THE
COCOANUT GROVE

They opened their mouths on the screen and my voice came out. I was just a ghost.

—Russ Columbo, from a 1934 Universal Studios press release

Situated in the Ambassador Hotel on Wilshire Boulevard, the Cocoanut Grove was the most famous of Los Angeles nightclubs. The outside was stately, but the interior would have offered a visitor from another planet fantastic glimpses into humanity's conflicted self-image.

From the time it opened in the early Twenties, the Grove was a somewhat isolated enclosure where screen actors, producers and attendant sycophants could get intoxicated with a combination of contraband hooch and dizzying décor. The gents and ladies of Hollywood's elite intensified the glitz by donning their respective black ties and white gowns for a night of dinner, dance and suave conversation. Here, rising stars like Joan Crawford competed at Charleston dance contests with the likes of Carole Lombard (when both still had their original names).

By the late Twenties and early Thirties, the Grove took on a more exotic, pre-Disneyland jungle look—the kind of postcard hodgepodge favored by the Occidental tourist. Here, the eye candy of big-screen epics assumed three dimensions as the murals of a Polynesian paradise complemented Moorish archways, Oriental paper lanterns, ersatz palm trees (supposedly left over from Valentino's *The Sheik*), and plastic monkeys that dangled from the branches and rafters.

The nattily tailored bigwigs at these proceedings giggled at the simulated simians, but they often betrayed a queasy kinship with their arboreal ancestors. From time to time, when the plastic monkeys dangled prizes while suspended on strings, the plastered patrons were known to claw, punch and slap each other just to acquire trinkets that would be of little value to them outside this alternate reality. These Prohibition-era revelers also arranged ahead of time to stash their favorite spirits under their tables, ever ready to upstage the chorine cavalcade once the liquor kicked in and the egos swelled into flying fists.

This human zoo required a zookeeper, a job usually left to the dashing bandleader and his minions. Special honors, however, also went to the hotel orchestra's crooners who, dressed as manicured pixies in bright suits and bow ties, had to set an example by continuing, against all odds, to look human in the midst of Darwin's nightmare. These ultra-civilized song warblers, so soft and supple, took on a role similar to all those captive jungle goddesses who languish in the Western mind's Dark Continent fantasies. Unlike the half-ape in a Franz Kafka story, who had to choose between being degraded in a menagerie or performing in a variety show, a crooner at the Grove could manage both tasks with little noticeable strain.

As the Cocoanut Grove's resident orchestra leader, Gus Arnheim was a zookeeper extraordinaire. He had proven to be a formidable talent from his days as an accompanist for Sophie Tucker and for composing an occasional gem like "Sweet And Lovely." Knowing how well Columbo's voice matched his violin, Arnheim courted him to become a member of Gus Arnheim and His Ambassadors. But the often-pushy Arnheim alienated the singer, demanding that, upon joining the band, Russ would have to forsake other activities, including the quest for screen roles. Russ, now in a position to bargain, held out.

At the time, Columbo started to come into his own as a local media star. As a violinist, he flourished in various pockets of greater Los Angeles. By 1926, his stringsweeps wafted in the orchestra pit of Hollywood's Pantages Theater when he joined the Slim Martin band. Then on to downtown's Mayfair Hotel, where manager George Eckhardt Jr. hired him to play in the Mayfair Club Orchestra for $75 per week. When the Beverly Hills Hotel needed a second violinist for its society orchestra, Russ arrived just in time. There, amid the otherwise standoffish hordes of movie world nobility, he made friends with the musician and character actor Leon Belasco. Sporting similar suits and coifs, Russ and Leon soon made a fetching pair as The Hollywood Serenaders—an instrumental guitar duo that even strummed a few tunes over the L.A. airwaves.

Despite all of these opportunities to flaunt his musicianship, Columbo felt an inner calling that rumbled from his diaphragm, pressed against his thyroid and craved the open air. He finally got the chance to share his voice in 1927 during his engagement as a violinist for "Professor" Moore's Orchestra. The occasion was the grand opening of the Hollywood Roosevelt

FORMER
ENGAGEMENTS

RAINBOW ISLE
HOTEL MAYFAIR
LOS ANGELES

HOTEL DEL CORONADO
CORONADO, CALIF.

CAFE LAFAYETTE
LOS ANGELES

LATEST
RECORDINGS

BROADWAY
MELODY HITS

Wedding Of The
Painted Doll.

Broadway Melody.

You Were Meant
For Me.

Coquette.
(Mary Pickford's
Theme Song)

Walking Around
In A Dream.
(Ted Lewis' Theme Song)

My Sin.

GEORGE ECKHARDT, JR.
and his
RECORDING ORCHESTRA

INSTRUMENTATION

Piano
Violin
Three Saxophones
Two Trumpets
Trombone
Banjo
String Bass and Tuba
Drums

SPECIALTY COMBINATIONS

Three Violins, Cello, Viola, Flute,

Guitar, Piano, and String Bass.

Two Solo Voices.

Piano Soloist.

Vocal Trio.

Russ (third from left) joined George Eckhardt, Jr.'s Recording Orchestra in the mid-1920s.

Russ with Leon Belasco as "the Hollywood Serenaders." (Courtesy of Max Pierce.)

Hotel, a hotly anticipated event hooked up for a live CBS radio transmission from the grand ballroom. A crisis occurred, however, when the Orchestra's regular vocalist fell ill. When Professor Moore got his boys together to decide on the right replacement, Columbo instantly volunteered. That evening, the man who would later be dubbed the "Valentino of the Air" passed two milestones: his first public singing performance and his debut as a radio crooner.

The Valentino comparisons notwithstanding, Columbo got very embarrassed and flushed the first time admiring fans sent him love letters. "What am I supposed to do with these crazy things?" he once confided to Lansing Brown and Walter Ramsey. "Prof [Moore] says I ought to answer them. It's good business. But they make me feel like such a fool!" [1] He bristled less when Arnheim eventually sent him something on par with a love letter: an amiable contract. By April of 1928, Russ had signed the pact that awarded him a modest $150.00 per week. He would be a star violinist and singer while continuing to pursue his cinematic dreams on the side.

To their bandleader's specification, Columbo and his crooning cohorts harmonized in the style of the light-hearted, helium-hewn tenors that were

First from left: with George Eckhardt, Jr.'s Recording Orchestra.

so much in vogue. Reluctant to inflame the potentially riotous patrons with "hot" jazz, Arnheim, along with his arranger Jimmie Grier, preferred a fascinating hybrid of sentimental waltzes, ragtime, novelty forms of Dixieland jazz, and even skip-happy variations on the polka. The Ambassadors' regimen of bouncy ballads and foxtrots was typical of the sweet bands that dominated hotel ballrooms.

In 1928, OKeh released "Back In Your Own Backyard," a 78 single credited to Gus Arnheim and His Ambassador Hotel Cocoanut Grove Orchestra. Beneath the camouflage of humorous horns and a rollicking beat, Columbo performed the vocal solo sounding like many a hyper-caffeinated band singer paid to keep the patrons overjoyed.

Another OKeh release captured Columbo with his two co-singers, a performance preserved not only on record but also as part of a short film. Between 1928 and 1929, Arnheim and the band appeared in at least two such featurettes produced by Warner Brothers for the "Vitaphone Varieties." In the first, entitled *Gus Arnheim And His Cocoanut Grove Orchestra*, the trio begins with a quick intro to Irving Berlin's "Always" before proceeding with a quirky version of Berlin's "I Can't Do Without You." This

Russ with Hawaiian Slack-key guitarist Eddie Bush (right).

recording alone reveals how Arnheim made a point of retaining some nostalgic Americana in his shows, particularly in the way he fashioned his trio to evoke the olden days of barbershop quartets.

Though irked by his prized violinist's refusal to shun the cinema lights, Arnheim had no problem displaying Columbo at camera center. In the same Vitaphone short, there is a violinist to Columbo's left and a ukulele player to his right. The trio (like the rest of the band) sports black tuxedos and bow ties to resemble groom figurines on a wedding cake. Still, Columbo looks less composed than the rest as he rocks back and forth while trying to suppress a boyish smile. After playing music that goes from jaunty to spicy to romantically tempestuous, the orchestra gets silly again with "Stay Out Of The South," a raucous number that also gives Columbo an opportunity to fiddle to a hillbilly beat.

The second Vitaphone short, simply called *Gus Arnheim & His Ambassadors*, opens with the blithe dance tune "If I Can't Have You (I Want To Be Lonesome, I Want To Be Blue)." Immersed in a sensorium of clarinets, saxophones, Arnheim's piano, and a discreet vibraphone sprinkling mysticism into the mayhem, Columbo goes into another of his frenetic fiddle

Sally Blane: "I used to go to the Grove just to sit and stare at the boy whose soft voice made one dream...
And then I met him... Our introduction grew into a warm and understanding friendship."

interludes before re-joining the trio. The film's most fascinating moments occur, however, when Russ sits down to wait for his next violin cue. Here, he displays his idiosyncratic and meticulous nature by fidgeting, staring at his wrist, picking at the lint on his lap, straightening his pants, stroking his outer thigh, and casting wandering glances on the staged proceedings.

Both Vitaphone offerings came close to capturing the finesse and frolics of a Grove show. Guests from the most regaled walks of life continued to pour in and out of the club each night just to listen to and watch Arnheim's stylish curiosities. This was also a fertile social ground in which Columbo met one of his more significant friends, the actress Sally Blane. Blane, who was every bit as pretty as her sister Loretta Young, would co-star with Rudy Vallee in *The Vagabond Lover*, but Columbo was the budding crooner she found most mesmerizing. "I used to go to the Grove just to sit and stare at the boy whose soft voice made one dream," Blane recalled. "And then I met him... Our introduction grew into a warm and understanding friendship."[2]

By July of 1929, Lansing Brown was still there to offer respite when Columbo needed to escape from the demands of his Ambassadorship. Lansing's role as nurturer got augmented when Columbo's brother Fiore died in a car crash at the age of twenty-five. "Lansa was a wonderful friend to us during all that tragic time," Columbo would say in a 1934 interview. "It was then that Mother and Father took him right into the family. Our home was his home. We never thought of having a holiday celebration and dinner without having him there. MY mother cooked the things she knew he loved. We have spent every holiday together for years."[3]

To make up for Fiore's failed attempts at being a matinee idol, Columbo may have felt pressured to pound Hollywood's pavements even harder. On the days after the long Arnheim nights, he sought out more roles and sometimes had the good fortune to befriend someone with influence. Actor Monte Blue tried to help him along at Warner Brothers, but the brass there responded like all of the other Hollywood moguls who slapped him with the tired old canard about looking "too Latin." All of the sumptuous photos Lansing had taken of him were temporarily filed away when Russ settled for taking jobs as a musical ventriloquist.

Ben Hecht once wrote: "The more we let others sing, dance and perform for us, the more empty we become."

But as a ghost voice for stars in the still-evolving talking picture medium, Columbo occupied an even more frustrating vacuum. He began as a silent movie violinist the audience never heard; now he had to contend with being a singer the viewers never saw.

Lupe Velez. From *Hollywwod*, March 1932.

A ballad Columbo was originally slated to sing in his role as Ambrosia Gutierrez for the 1929 Paramount Famous Lasky film *Wolf Song*.

For the 1929 Paramount film *Wolf Song* (starring Gary Cooper and Lupe Velez), Columbo was billed as a character named Ambrosia Gutierrez. Many believe footage exists of Columbo singing off-camera while Cooper mouths the words. But according to sheet music found among his possessions, Russ was slated to serenade Velez' character Lola Salazar with "To Lola," a ballad that Leo Robin, Richard A. Whiting and Harvey Ferguson wrote "to be sung slowly and sweetly." But, as he later told the *Philadelphia Bulletin*: "After working six weeks (and thinking all the time I had a great break) along came the cutters, and when they got through with their scissors I found myself mostly on the cutting-room floor."[4]

That same year Clarence Brown, distinguished for directing several of Garbo's silent gems, tackled MGM's (now long lost) *Wonder of Women*. In this story glutted with the ambiance of European opera, Columbo supposedly dubbed over Lewis Stone on the German tune "Ich Liebe Dich." He soon was rumored to have ghosted for Gary Cooper in Paramount's 1930 film *The Texan*. For this project, Columbo was at least slated for a bit part as a "Singing Cowboy" at a campfire.

Columbo had his most haunting off-screen moments in the 1929 Radio Pictures production *Street Girl*, where he served in a ghost orchestra with the rest of Gus Arnheim's Ambassadors. Wesley Ruggles directed Betty Compson as a down-on-her-luck Viennese musician who ascends to stardom after the members of a traveling combo salvage her from poverty. Arnheim's band provides the genuine music while the screen musicians—led by stars John Harron, Jack Oakie and Ned Sparks—do a fine job of pretending.

Compson's character plays her violin so beautifully, especially on "My Dream Memory," an angelic melody that Oscar Levant and Sidney Clare wrote to lend some dreamy perplexity to an otherwise uninviting plot. Though once billed as "The Vagabond Violinist" during her vaudeville days, Compson merely assumes the motions, while Columbo likely played a pre-recorded track.

The sight of this wraithlike blonde pantomiming to Columbo's off-screen performance suggests the same female alter ego who left him captivated years before on the Granada Theater stage. Both figures merged in Columbo's mind as a single golden-haired sprite, whose strands formed a gossamer stairway leading out of surroundings that were banal, coarse and, like a night of revelry at the Cocoanut Grove, civilized only on the surface.

IN THE PUBLIC EAR

By FREDERICK L. COLLINS

*An ardent radio fan picks his favorites out of the
air—and asks you,"Who are yours?"*

Bing Crosby
is called the
Clark Gable
of the air

Russ Columbo has all
the glamour of Valentino

The three Boswell
sisters—Connie,
Vet, and Martha

Our Jessica
was one of the
first popular
radio singers

Vaughn de Leath is the
Sweetheart of the Radio

If you've missed Kate
Smith, you've missed
the biggest hit in radio

Rudy Vallee takes a lesson
from our old black-face
friends, Amos 'n' Andy

LANGUID LOVE STUFF

I'm always yearning, for your returning, dear...

—"(What Good Am I) Without You?" (1930) from the film *Hello, Sister*
Lyrics by Jack Gordean; music by Russ Columbo

When the movie *Dynamite* was released in December of 1929, the nation already had a few weeks to ponder over the Wall Street Crash. This story about a smug rich girl humbled by extraordinary circumstances arrived at theaters just in time to mirror a growing view of the world as an emotional and financial minefield. Life appeared so safe and normal one moment yet (as the film's title implies) was ready to explode at any time.

Silent epic master Cecil B. De Mille wanted to pack this, his first sound film, with an optimum audio and visual charge. Refusing to let the clunky technology of early talkies cramp his flair for spectacle, he embellished the MGM production with Mitchell Leisen's posh (Oscar-nominated) set designs and an elaborately staged mining disaster.

Dynamite's most shattering scene, however, takes place in a prison. Charles Bickford, playing a miner convicted of murder and waiting to hang, gets a visit from a high-living aristocrat (Kay Johnson) who entices him with a proposition. In return for having his indigent younger sister financially compensated and saved from the orphanage, Bickford will marry the socialite during his final hours. There is, of course, a darker motive to the woman's designs, for she must get hitched in order to gain her dearly departed grandfather's inheritance.

When the moment comes for the bride, groom and executioner to tie the knot, the clangor of scaffold construction drowns out the ceremony. And amid the bedlam, a gorgeous sequence of notes floats into the soundtrack, saturating the atmosphere like a beatific vapor in a man-made Hell. Russ Columbo appears as a mustachioed serenader in an adjacent cell, an unbilled

As the melodic "Mexican boy" in *Dynamite*. (From Lou Miano's *Russ Columbo*.)

role that the original dialogue continuity script described as a "Mexican boy." He is truly a prisoner of love, crooning and strumming all alone on his guitar while casting a wayward gaze at his lost amor's photograph:

> *Oh, how am I to know?*
> *Will it linger on*
> *And leave me then?*
> *I dare not guess*
> *At this strange happiness—*

As the minister tries speaking over the racket of hammers, the guilt-plagued bride summons just enough strength to mutter, "I do." Then, she lets out a scream and a rant: "Oh, why are they hammering like that? Can't you stop it?" "Believe me, lady," Bickford replies. "I'd like it stopped a lot more than you would." The marriage contract is finally forged and the crooning continues, even after a fellow inmate yells out: "Say buddy! Not so loud with that languid love stuff! The other prisoners are kicking!" Graceful but petulant, Columbo snaps back, "Let them kick!"

For oh, how am I to know?
Can it be that love has come to stay, dear? . . .

The banging at the gibbet gets louder, but Columbo's voice lingers on as the bride walks her solitary way and the scene fades to black.

These majestic screen moments allowed Columbo to flaunt his "languid love stuff" in his high baritone signature. Even though Dorothy Parker got livid when De Mille altered her original lyrics, the public reacted favorably to Columbo's mixture of Spanish *canción*, Italian operetta, and Tin Pan Alley ballad—all tied together in a slipknot of gallows humor. In his modest way, Russ Columbo helped to embellish the sound era's first phase.

Crooners, who were often as mildly manic as Columbo's "Mexican boy," emerged at the same time that jazz made its advent into popular venues. But the two forms were certainly not intrinsic to one another. If anything, crooners thrived *despite* jazz and its ultra-urbane, melody-mashing and anti-romantic nature. Tracing their origins in the Twenties, musician and historian Ian Whitcomb has keenly referred to crooners as "the new troubadours, offering up medieval romanticism in an age of flappers, vamps and machine gun gangsters. They were the civilized side of the jazz age."[1]

The term "croon" has a long and ambiguous history, purportedly of Scottish origin and usually used to denote a groan, a whimper or a low hum. The *Oxford English Dictionary* points out that in 1848, Charles Dickens mentioned, in his novel *Dombey and Son*, a character "crooning out a feeble accompaniment." George Eliot in *Adam Bede* wrote a decade later of "cocks and hens" that "made only crooning subdued noises." A recent edition of the *Merriam Webster Dictionary* designates "croon" as a verb meaning "to sing or hum in a gentle murmuring voice."

Through the years, "crooner" would metamorphose into a nebulous catchall term, applied to practically anyone with the inventive audacity to sing in tune. But roughly from the mid-1920s on through the Thirties, the most prominent crooners either delivered their songs in half-speaking, near whispers or evoked softer and more ethereal variations on the modes associated with Italian gondoliers or Celtic tenors. Their voices conveyed the woozy effect of clarinets when the dance bands got dreamy. They also reflected something unequivocally modern: the ghostly glow of early electronic sound transmission.

In the winter of 1919–20, radio pioneer Lee De Forest incorporated singing into his primitive microphone experiments. On a frosty December, he persuaded Miss Vaughn De Leath to join him at the top of New York

City's World Tower Building. There, De Leath was confined to a nine-by-nine room as she sang into a telephone attached to a large horn. She was so nervous about damaging the sensitive transmitter tubes that she piped her tune very softly. A fan letter followed, informing her that she had "inaugurated *a new form of song*."[2]

Soon after De Forest dubbed her "the original radio girl," De Leath set a standard for subsequent gentleman singers who—whether consciously or not—followed her demure example. Not until around 1925, when microphones were in common use, did the role of the ballad singer—like that of all musicians—change considerably. Approaching the microphone as if it were a serviette, crooners had garnered the reputation for being a bit diffident, mannerly and outright fey. Of course, crooners with integrity did not care what anyone called them, too enrapt in themes of courtship and romantic sorrow to anchor their feet, let alone their voices, in gangly notions about "proper" male behavior.

In contrast, blues and jazz singers gave the impression of being rugged and suffering. Al Jolson may have implored his "mammy" to "croon a tune from the heart of Dixie," but crooners earned their distinction precisely by refusing to be Sophie Tucker tomboys. They were more like lovable sissy boys enmeshed in the gooey girl concerns of dream dates and broken hearts. As troubadours of the upper air, crooners had every right to sound light-headed.

Some who dreaded the onslaught of commercial popular culture in general did not appreciate such crooner niceties. To them, crooning was another malformation of modern times. Henry Ford, in his frequent columns for *The Dearborn Independent*, was among the most rabid. He once lumped crooners with other "dredges of the slimy bottom of the underworld" that could only result with "the entry of Jews into control of the popular song…" He fulminated about how a "dreadful narcotizing of moral honesty and the application of powerful aphrodisiacs have been involved in the present craze for crooning songs."[3]

For many others, however, crooning was an exciting innovation—a vestige of true romance reborn, in Frankenstein fashion, out of electronic currents. Electricity also had its paradoxes. It may have enabled singers to convey more intimacy, but the lovable sentiments could sound eerie when processed through the ether waves. Just as vocalists were acclimating to the microphone's new world order, inventor Leon Theremin was promoting an instrument that required a simple wave of the hand in its surrounding space to emit a new kind of music. The theremin's oscillating frequencies produced a continuous siren wail, not all that different from the crooner's near-supernatural moan.

While the diaphragm has been the traditional source of oratory power, many crooners seemed to sing from the thyroid—that delicate, butterfly-shaped gland located just below the Adam's apple and attached to the windpipe. When over-active, the thyroid melodramatizes the effects of a broken heart. It speeds up the circulatory rate and plays havoc with mood and memory while pushing the body and mind to the edge of an inter-nalized Lovers' Leap. The more exemplary crooning, the kind that captured that sinking feeling of romantic rejection, echoed such feelings of metabolic distress.

Even before wired recording, Nick Lucas (born Domenico Antonio Nicola Lucanese) was a crooning champion. The Newark, New Jersey native earned the nickname "The Singing Troubadour" after he started performing his soft and high-range ditties on the Vaudeville circuit. Brunswick Records took him on as "The Crooning Troubadour," a moniker that played well with the public once his first vocal hit—a cover of Walter Donaldson's "My Best Girl"—made it to *Billboard*'s #4 by February of 1925. Between 1925 and 1931, Lucas continued with 26 Top 40 successes and introduced songs like "Sleepy Time Gal," "Bye Bye, Blackbird," and "I'm Looking Over A Four-Leaf Clover." He had his greatest coup when staying at *Billboard*'s #1 for ten weeks with "Tip Toe Thru The Tulips," the inspiration decades later for Tiny Tim.

By the winter of 1925, Victor Records had introduced its Orthophonic Victrola, a device that helped filter out the tinniness of the superannuated horn (an enduring feature of RCA's "Nipper" logo). Enabling crooners to apply their aspirates and sibilants with less distortion, the Victrola also galvanized record sales and nudged radio with a smidgen of competition. Earlier that year, Columbia Records—in a mad dash to out-race the other labels—hired Art Gillham to sing what would officially be America's first commercial electrical musical recording, a composition he wrote called "You May Be Lonesome (But You'll Be Lonesome Alone)"; the other was a cheeky novelty entitled, "Cecilia, Does Your Mother Know You're Out?"

In truth, Gillham sang with sympathies more rooted in ragtime. His was a tempered variation on the blues that did not have much faint-hearted, ballad-friendly appeal. He also tended to be quite self-mocking in his song interpretations, essentially owning up to his less than adequate pipes by practically talking the tunes. Gillham did get creative when capitalizing on the fine art of the sob song, having his listeners believe that he was a short, bald and chubby "broken-down piano player jest tryin' to get by." In reality, he was rather dashing with his thin frame, wavy hair and black rimmed-glasses.

Some crooners also affected the indolence characteristic of the 19th Century dandy, fooling audiences into believing that their craft required little effort. One of the most beloved of these minimalists was born Jacob Schmidt in New York City, just as the 19th century ended. Due to a World War I injury resulting from a gas shell explosion, he suffered a vocal impairment that left him barely able to purr a note. He converted his handicap into a pleasant-sounding gimmick, changed his name to "Whispering" Jack Smith and became a maven of radio and records. Also referred to as the "Whispering Baritone," he vacillated in his clipped diction between low groans and elevated pitches to complement his simple piano backing.

Smith, like several other early crooners, was also a song-plugger. Tin-Pan Alley composers were notorious for demanding that their songs be performed exactly to sheet music specifications. No apoplectic fits of improvisation were allowed! The radio industry adhered to a general rule that the optimum melodic range for a broadcast song should ideally stay within a few notes from the piano keyboard's center. This made Smith an ideal shill for the newest melodies coming out of Irving Berlin's music publishing company.

Specializing in whimsy, Smith escalated on the charts with his 1926 #1 hit "Gimme A Little Kiss, Will Ya, Huh?" followed by "Me And My Shadow" (his biggest) a year later. He appealed especially to the English during his performances at London's Hotel Metropole, no doubt due to elocutionary affectations similar to those of the ever-beloved Noel Coward. But by 1928, Irving Berlin's appropriately titled "The Song Is Ended (But The Melody Lingers On)" became Smith's swan song. His novelty approach fell out of fashion by the mid-Thirties, but he continued to perform around the world.

London-born but Iowa reared John Leonard was another soft and unassuming song-plugger. He had a dynamic stage presence but a minuscule stature for which he earned the title Little Jack Little. His elfish demeanor, wispy singing and awkward charms prompted historian Anthony Slide to describe his live act as a "a jaunty smile and a movement of his arms reminiscent of a locomotive getting up steam."[4] *Variety* would later characterize Little Jack Little as a vocalist who "belonged to a generation of microphone-hugging artists who set the scene for the relaxed brigade—Bing Crosby to Perry Como."[5]

Oddly enough, several early crooners hailed from the rough and rustling region of Texas. While Houston's Segar Ellis performed "Shine On Harvest Moon" as if holding back a schoolgirl's tears, Smith Ballew (from the Lone Star town of Palestine) tempered his falsetto with a few high baritone dips in the pre-Columbo/Crosby era. When Ballew trilled a tune like "He's My Secret Passion," listeners could interpret that he was either singing to another man or flattering a gal through imitation to win her favor. Song composers and publishers of the Twenties and Thirties, by the way, usually demanded that the lyrics stay exactly as written, including the pronouns, regardless of the gender singing them.

Gainesville's Gene Austin used his breathless technique to strong dramatic effect, sounding like a guy too choked up and elated for "down to earth" pretenses. He may have performed some uptempo selections here and there, but he was best suited, and apparently most comfortable, with relaxing love ditties. By 1925, Austin was intoning through Victor Records' newfangled "Orthophonic" process, his high tenor fully suited to facile rhymes like "June/moon" and "bloom/perfume." With Victor's Nathaniel Shilkret and Leonard Joy (both soon to be Columbo's leading arrangers), Austin evoked melodious waterfalls while drawling poetically over ballads like "Ramona," "A Garden In The Rain," "Love Letters In The Sand," and that dizzy equation of passion and physics, "I've Got A Feeling I'm Falling."

There were famous singers like Cliff "Ukulele Ike" Edwards who, despite an early penchant for piping out "scat," made his biggest impact as the voice of Jiminy Cricket in Walt Disney's *Pinocchio*. Some stellar crooners fell into a subsequent obscurity that is absolutely unjustified. An excellent example is Frank Sylvano. An itinerant vocalist, known mostly for his work with orchestras conducted by Ben Bernie, Abe Lyman and Isham Jones, Sylvano made crooning a creamy-on-the-melody delicacy. Sounding airy and somewhat shaky, he put mystery into otherwise chirpy songs like "Swingin' Down The Lane." In 1931, he joined with the Isham Jones Orchestra on the hit "Lonesome Lover"—a snappy but sweet-tempered ballad that cried out, "Let me hold your hand for only, Just a moment while I'm lonely..."

Fame's fickle finger was kinder to Hubert Prior Vallee, a New England native who specialized in the saxophone. Around 1923, while attending Yale, he would play at dances in the New Haven area and occasionally sing through a large megaphone. The voice that inspired him was not Enrico Caruso or even Billy Murray but that of Marion Harris, one of the most popular Twenties singers, adored for her relaxed style. In 1928, just after graduating beyond the Ivy Walls, he got his big break in New York City, performing with his own band—the Yale Collegians—at the newly christened Heigh-Ho Club. Thanks to subsequent broadcasts from New

York's radio station WABC, Rudy Vallee became one of the very first voices to resonate through the ether to a wide audience—the pre-eminent crooner superstar.

Fan mail poured in, praising Vallee for being able to put listeners into a benevolent trance, for giving lonely radio devotees a sense that they were listening to a friend. He inspired sweetness and pathos; inspiration and peaceful sleep. Just days after the Crash of 1929, he proved an airwave success, spreading his oleaginous allure for NBC's Fleischmann's Yeast program. Columbo's voice approximated smooth violin layers, but Vallee crooned with the alto saxophone's higher pitches and breathier effusions. With Marion Harris as the guiding force, Vallee's voice also projected a subtle yet unmistakable androgyny, a mystifying quality that prompted some members of the press to dub him the "'It' Boy."

Vallee adopted the nickname "Rudy" not from the matinee idol but in honor of a musician he admired named Rudy Wiedoeft, a saxophonist whose sweet tones Vallee often approximated vocally. He also bore little similarity to Valentino. He was an Ivy Leaguer of French-Irish stock, with a wavy head of light hair and a lackadaisical hauteur that could be alternately charming and off-putting. Known for his voracious ego, Vallee did show some modesty by claiming that he did not have a voice so much as a knack for allowing audiences to comprehend the words to songs. Prospering in the microphone era, he nonetheless remained famous for his trademark megaphone, a prop that had a limited lifespan in crooner history but somehow survived as an eternal icon of the times.

Far from being intrepid clods, the best crooners practiced seduction through stealth. They won hearts and minds by playing the consumptive dreamer, the diffident swain and the effete melancholic. The brusquer baritones as well had inspired moments whenever they scaled the girly ranges. When their voices cracked, they elicited additional listener sympathy. Even frat boy Crosby, in his autobiography *Call Me Lucky*, admitted to wriggling a bit under the lavender light: "Back in the 1920s, lads—or even grown men—who sang with bands did so at the risk of having their manhood suspected. It was a time when tennis players or men who wore wristwatches were given the hand-on-hip and the burlesque falsetto-voice routine."[6] He avoided a near-violent altercation in his early years with a group called the Musicaladers when, during a performance in Spokane, Washington, he launched into a rendition of "Peggy O'Neil" and encountered some hoodlum in the crowd who called him a "pansy."

By 1929, while Columbo was De Mille's romantic prisoner, other crooners mugged for the movie camera. Rudy Vallee warbled beneath the

Hollywood lights in *The Vagabond Lover*, while operetta enthusiast Ramon Novarro, remembered more as a hyper-magnetic love idol than a crooner, introduced the Arthur Freed–Nacio Herb Brown classic "Pagan Love Song" in the part-sound MGM production *The Pagan*. That same year, Columbo contributed some original compositions to the James Cruze production *Hello, Sister*.

Hello, Sister's story, much like *Dynamite*, centers on high-toned Prohibition-era partygoers and their moral dilemmas. Made at the Sono Art-Worldwide studios (and not to be confused with a similarly named film by Erich Von Stroheim), *Hello, Sister* casts Olive Borden as a hedonistic blueblood who, in order to inherit her grandfather's estate, must refrain from all vices for six months. Pretending to be sinless, she organizes a stage production for a church bazaar that evokes the shade of an old apple tree from a previous era. Lloyd Hughes, appearing in an Edwardian overcoat, top hat, and a blatantly fake handlebar moustache sings Columbo's "(What Good Am I) Without You?"

> *When night is falling,*
> *My heart is calling, sweetheart...*

Border, as the fair maiden receiving these sentiments, totes a parasol, strikes a demure pose, and replies with eyes agog:

> *Now that we've parted,*
> *I'm broken hearted, sweetheart...*

The swain and his paramour proceed into a duet about a "moon above" and "nights of love" before several other couples in the same attire join them for a Gay Nineties-style revue. Each pair engages in a simultaneous kiss, but when they emerge from their embraces, the women end up wearing the moustaches. More congenial to a gaggle of barbershop quartet enthusiasts than a "whoopee" party, Columbo's wistful melody reflected his own long-ago and far-away glance, his premature pangs of nostalgia.

Columbo started to thrive in this "languid love" era. He grew confident enough to try and launch a solo career once he quit The Ambassadors at the close of their nationwide tour. But he had to swallow his pride by the summer of 1930 and return to the safe haven under Arnheim's wing. This Prodigal Son rebound had a price. He now had to contend with Bing Crosby, as The Rhythm Boys—consisting of Crosby, Harry Barris and Al Rinker—became Arnheim's new vocal headliners.

Far from sounding like a barbershop trio, The Rhythm Boys were often under the "hotcha" spell. Crosby led while Barris and Rinker filled in with a jazzy counter-tempo. Spasmodic singing was sometimes not enough. During some of their previous performances under the auspices of Paul Whiteman, Barris would keep time by slamming the top of his piano while Crosby took to, in his own words, "frim-framming a cymbal with a wire fly swatter."[7]

There were times when The Rhythm Boys could deliver a softer ballad, tender moments when Columbo probably felt more comfortable joining them for impromptu singing sessions on the Grove stage. According to Crosby himself, Columbo even engaged the Groaner in occasional duets. Living up to his nickname "Binge," Crosby was notorious for his off-stage carousing and tippling, a regimen of excess that sometimes climaxed in crescendos of vomit strewn along the bandstand. Columbo was on hand during some of these bleary-eyed deviations to take Crosby's place and save the evening.

These were relatively carefree days. As Columbo and Crosby sang at one another among the plastic monkeys, radio listeners glued to the Grove's broadcast hookups were challenged to guess which crooner was which. Controversies continued as to who copied whom. "Russ was not a rhythm singer," Arnheim later chimed. "Where Crosby could sing hillbilly or sacred tunes, Russ was best with love ballads."[8]

Renowned arranger, composer and conductor Buddy Bregman, who orchestrated Crosby's 1956 album *Bing Sings Whilst Bregman Swings,* is even more steadfast in his appraisal: "I think a ballad singer is truly as important as any jazz singer. Ballad singers bring us the one thing we all want in life—and that is romance. Russ Columbo was a great singer, and I think that in many respects Bing copied him."[9]

With the Hollywood offers still thin and prospects of being a provisionary Rhythm Boy uninviting, Columbo soon left Arnheim's band for good. But he exited with panache on June 18th for his final studio effort with the bandleader, the hit record "A Peach Of A Pair." For this occasion, in which Arnheim let Russ record in his natural high baritone, Columbo made a sporting effort to jaunt along to this relentlessly upbeat tune (co-written by Richard A. Whiting) about a courtship downwind from "the breeze across the fairway." This may not have been the kind of languid love song that the prisoner of love preferred, but it propelled him as he breezed from one gilded cage into another.

Operetta enthusiast Ramon Novarro, remembered more as a hyper-magnetic movie idol than a crooner, introduced the Arthur Freed–Nacio Herb Brown classic "Pagan Love Song" in the part-sound MGM production *The Pagan*. He, like Columbo, would succumb to Hollywood's "Latin" typecasting. From *Motion Picture Classic*, October 1925.

Photo: Lansing Brown.

ROMANTIC
DEPRESSION

My life was empty till you came along,
Then in my heart there seemed to start a song,
But when you're mean to me the world seems wrong,
I've been wond'ring,
Is It Love?

—"Is It Love?" (1931)—from the film *Hell Bound*
Lyrics by Howard Coombs; Music by Russ Columbo

The year 1931 faced two great Depressions: the increasing economic downturn and Russ Columbo's mood slump once he awakened from his dreams of instant Hollywood stardom. His only other screen-related job at the time was composing the song "Is It Love?" for the low-budget Tiffany Studios production *Hell Bound*. "I remember the Russ Columbo to whom nothing had ever happened so well," journalist Ruth Biery later recalled in an article about the singer's leaner times. "He used to sit in my living room night after night, with his pal Lansing Brown, and yearn for a break 'like other fellows.'"[1]

Columbo had every reason to brood over those "other fellows" and the misguided public sympathies that could turn such oafs into heroes. All of those leaden lummoxes like Gary Cooper, with faces that registered zero introspection; simps like Charles Bickford who sent skin crawling yet secured the hand of a catch like Greta Garbo in *Anna Christie*. Then there were the William Powells and Clark Gables—glorified mountebanks in moustaches.

In this bestiary of stark screen types, Columbo occupied a shadow world. He continued to fume when Valentino-fatigued producers dismissed him as looking too "Latin." Hollywood moguls of these pre-Don Ameche days were too awash in affable buffoons like Henry Armetta or malevolent thugs like Jack La Rue to comprehend any salable commodity in assimilated Americans of Italian descent who spoke perfect English and did not grind organs or wave guns.

Secretly, however, Columbo must have realized that there were more complex angles to his casting woes than tiresome ethnic issues. The truth is that he was too elusive a screen type to make either a good gangster or a conventional leading man. Though he fit the tall, dark and handsome frame, he had a different kind of allure, something more edgy. The physically plain and outwardly unruffled Crosby could get away with playing bemused and devil-may-care roles, but Columbo appeared too callow and earnest, too tentative and unpolished with his retiring smile and slight stoop.

Columbo wanted to portray so-called "real people" at a time when Hollywood seemed more preoccupied with proto-human exaggerations. In 1931, while Universal Studios brought out Bela Lugosi in *Dracula* and Boris Karloff in *Frankenstein*, Warner Brothers unleashed what was perhaps the most creeping terror of all: John Barrymore's *Svengali*—the manipulator of souls who turned the fair-haired Trilby into an international songstress. Columbo was also in need of his own Svengali, some form of miracle man who would appear out of thin air to market him into, if not a matinee idol, at least Trilby's masculine counterpart.

Biding time, Columbo concentrated on his music, playing and singing occasionally on Los Angeles radio stations KFWB and KMTR. While entertaining at the family restaurant, he also assembled a group to perform at a club called the "Silver Slipper." His brother Alfonso, now Albert, then went into a partnership and converted a Hollywood Boulevard garage into the Pyramid Café (sometimes called the Club Pyramid). At this stylish nightspot, Columbo nursed his Hollywood rejection wounds, limbered up his voice, and flashed a winning smile when guests like Gloria Swanson and Erich Von Stroheim paid a visit. This was also the smartly lit splendor in which he crossed paths with Con Conrad.

Various accounts had surfaced through the years about the people and circumstances of that fateful evening. A composite rehash of events has Conrad, composer Sam Coslow, musician George Olsen, as well as actors June Collyer and Jack Oakie walking into the Pyramid Café and requesting a discreet corner table. Conrad, the calculating and clever songwriter turned talent agent, feigned an interest in the menu but made furtive glances to the comely performer wooing the patrons. Signaling the waiter, Conrad arranged an audience with his new meal ticket.

The irrepressible Con Conrad.

Conrad backed his blowhard badge with impressive credentials. Born Conrad K. Dober in 1891, he was a native New Yorker who loved the piano since childhood. He proved his showbiz acumen by the time he quit high school, hoping to be an actor while eking out a living as a theater pianist for silent movies. Still a teenager, he teamed up with violinist Jay Whidden to tour Keith's theater circuit and, by 1912, published his first song—the melody to a Ziegfeld Follies number called "Down In Dear New Orleans." In 1913, while traveling with Whidden to England for a performance at the Leicester Square Theater, he also produced a show called *The Honeymoon Express.*

Returning to America, Conrad forged a lucrative songwriting career and, by the Twenties, set up a music publishing business. He penned novelty gems like "Ma, He's Makin' Eyes At Me" and "Oh, Frenchy," a favorite among World War I soldiers stationed overseas. His collaborators included Benny Davis for "Margy" (which Eddie Cantor turned into a #1 hit), Bert Kalmar and Otto Motzan on "Mandy 'n' Me," and Billy Rose for "Barney Google" (named after the comic strip figure).

Physically, Conrad could have wedged himself inside a character actor cookie cutter. Rudy Vallee recalled him being "a tall, slim man with a moustache; he reminded me of Basil Rathbone."[2] In photographs, he had a more comical bearing, with an alternately silly and shady face hatched right out of vaudeville. The great Barrymore required layers of makeup, a witchy nose and synthetically glazed eyes to wield demonic clout, but Conrad needed only to display his sly but infectious grin, hold out his glad hand and act the smoothie. One could imagine him yelling out pithy quips to the crowd, with a voice every bit as acoustically grating as that of Pat O'Brien, an actor who would end up portraying a Conradish cad in *Twenty Million Sweethearts,* the 1934 film with a plot somewhat akin to Columbo's career rise.

As intimidating as he had to be in his reptilian profession, Conrad exuded an even more terrifying aspect on those clammy occasions when his humanity surfaced. Like Columbo, Conrad was a flustered romantic. He supposedly had a nervous breakdown after his wife Francine Larrimore sued him for divorce. But Conrad snapped right back into a mercenary mode once his emotional snit subsided. He subsequently marveled over the free publicity he got when Larrimore started dating the famous George Jean Nathan. Later, he helped to advance the career of a dancer named Beth Berri, flirting with an almost penniless existence by showering her with funds and gifts. When the time finally arrived to face the altar, Berri fell for Conrad's publicity agent. Not missing a beat, Conrad issued a tongue-biting public response: "I wish she had married a famous actor—what's the angle in marrying a press agent?"[3]

Jerry Wald, the ellipsis-happy journalist and forthcoming Hollywood producer, would become one of Columbo's champions. He commanded a voice of authority when summarizing Conrad's post-Berri blahs:

> *His dreams and hopes were now nothing but exploded bubbles... His music business meant nothing to him... Song scribbling had lost its charm for him... Women had lost their fascination for him... Conrad was spoiled for love by love itself... He then turned to religion and found solace there... But he needed something on which to expend his pent-up energy and vitality... It was at this time that he heard and saw Columbo... Suddenly he came to a decision... He would forget his hurt and torment in aiding this lad, this unknown quantity... What he might have done for himself or for the unappreciative women in his life.*[4]

Since Conrad's reputation as both a songsmith and shyster preceded him, Columbo knew what to expect but nonetheless succumbed to the fast talk and flattery. Conrad told Columbo how impressed he was after hearing him sing on KMTR radio and how thrilled he was by his performance in *Dynamite*. He also stressed the truth behind an eternal truism, a permutation of which Crosby would later utter in a 1933 Mack Sennett short: "Prosperity is just around the crooner!"[5]

As the Pyramid started closing up for the night, Conrad continued to bend Columbo's ear with scenarios involving instant fame, scads of wealth, and the name "Russ Columbo" emblazoned across theater marquees in metropolitan centers from coast to coast. Most important, he explained how Columbo's star would naturally rise in the east beneath New York City's lofty radio spires.

This mostly one-sided conversation went on until 4:00 in the morning. Conrad succeeded in making a believer out of the world-weary 23-year-old who had little to lose. Anything was better than the ongoing grind of pointless movie auditions, playing the same ditties for the same paying customers, and accumulating a weekly salary of approximately $75. Trilby was ready for a makeover.

While Lansing Brown was the sympathetic confidante, Conrad now acted as Columbo's emotional power broker. In the process, he manipulated his client's insecurities by projecting his own. This personality badinage was also constructive. Through Conrad, Columbo would grow to sharpen the skills necessary to convert the experience of amorous rejection into creative inspiration. Conrad initiated this alchemy when finding the right Columbo theme song. Judging from some of his other compositions, with titles like "Lonesome And Sorry" and a lover's lament that Columbo would later record called "Lonesome Me," Conrad instinctively latched onto a tune that enticed vulnerable listeners with calibrated doses of romantic agony.

In his autobiography *Cocktails for Two*, Sam Coslow claimed that Conrad had initially approached him to write Columbo's theme. But, due to a previous commitment with Paramount for an eventually unmade musical revue, he had to pass. Coslow writes: "But Con and Columbo kept up their search. A girl named Gladys Du Bois, who earned her livelihood as a movie extra, ran into Con at a party and showed him a lyric she had written. It was her first attempt, and she called it 'You Call It Madness (But I Call It Love).'"[6]

Columbo and Conrad had a murmuring masterpiece on their hands, an affecting and quaintly titillating air about a hopeless swain addled by love's cruel and persistent memories. They collaborated on a melody with a deliberately paced tempo and enough euphony to suit the singer's temperament, especially when Columbo drew out Du Bois' sequence of moaning vowels. Autobiography and commodity became one.

Drawing up a contract, Conrad rattled off a Jabberwocky jumble of figures and stipulations that likely left Columbo more bored than mystified. One potentially cumbersome detail involved the inclusion of a third party. Jack Gordean, who previously co-wrote some songs with Columbo, also happened to be a partner in the Conrad Music Corporation. The contract secured Conrad and Gordean 49% of Columbo's earnings, along with an agreement that Columbo would get a regular salary even in periods when work was scarce. Acknowledging Columbo's monetary problems, Conrad also agreed to come up with the funds for their cross-country trip.

The auspicious journey to Gotham began when Coslow, at least according to his book, expressed his plans to take a train to New York for a pow-wow with Paramount's attorneys: "When I told Con I had booked a compartment on the Superchief for New York, a sudden brainstorm hit him. 'We'll all go—you, Russ and I...'"[7]

Several accounts claim that Columbo and Conrad departed within twenty-four hours after their first meeting at the Pyramid. But they most likely stayed in Los Angeles for at least an extra day or two—enough time for Conrad to sell his piano, radio set, and all of the furniture in his bungalow to cover the train tickets. In another (likely apocryphal) story, Conrad needed more money to finance the trip and, learning that Crosby was in the market for a new car, sold him his Ford. The gist of the tale is that Columbo's eastbound dream was partly bankrolled with Crosby's cash.

Columbo still lived with his parents at 1322 Tamarind Avenue and now had to prevail upon Giulia and Nicola with news of his departure. A few years back, Giulia had to reject Dr. Czech's grand scheme to take her last-born on a European excursion. Now she could only surrender to this new interloper. It was close to the end of June when Columbo said his goodbyes. Sally Blane was disconsolate and Lansing Brown resigned himself to another of his young pal's whims. As Conrad tugged him away, Columbo tried to comfort his mom, promising (like the fame-bound sons of many movie scripts) to buy her a big house once his plans for stardom and fortune materialized.

The train rode out of California and across America's Depression-era landscape. On their three-and-a-half-day passage, Columbo and Conrad engaged in predictably awkward spells of ego jousting and soul groping. They discussed strategies for courting the major radio networks and theater impresarios. They also fine-tuned the melody for "You Call It Madness," which they agreed would be the highlight of Columbo's auditions. As these two anxious nomads talked up dreams of success, an uncanny contrast of dusty plains, rusty tractors, idle smokestacks, and other signs of a traumatized economy whizzed past their compartment window.

In contrast to Sam Coslow, a made-man for Paramount who arrived in New York to the swanky St. Moritz Hotel, Columbo and Conrad shared a small apartment in the Carnegie Plaza. Both braced themselves for an unproductive spate, even though Conrad made every effort to comfort Columbo with exaggerations of their financial security. To supplement his bluff, Conrad sold a quarter of his New York music concern to Harms publishing. Still, Columbo had to borrow here and there and later joked with the press about the benches in Central Park being softer than those in Bryant Park. He also related a particularly worrisome moment when his last nickel got wedged inside an Automat machine slot and he had to wire his parents for funds.

Another version has Conrad braving all of the financial havoc so that Columbo could thrive in a dreamer's paradise. Intent on wresting control over fiscal and other matters, Conrad scheduled Columbo's gigs, regulated his evenings, planned his meals, and even oversaw any semblance of a private life that the singer tried cultivating in between appointments.

Like an overindulgent father with his hypersensitive child, Conrad would order breakfast from a 10th Avenue restaurant and serve it to Columbo each morning. He would dole out money for him to go to the movies without ever letting on that it might be a last dollar. Others would also meet Columbo and instantly want to protect him. New big city chums like

Jerry Wald, Johnny Meyers and Paul Moss acted as emotional shock absorbers, always ready to salve Columbo with encouraging words as they strolled down Broadway together.

Keeping up his braggadocio while depleting his wallet, Conrad somehow mustered the wherewithal to hire a press agent. His name was Harry Sobol and his brother Louis just happened to be a prominent Broadway columnist. Conrad also excelled in the art of ruse-by-wire, sending off phony telegrams to entertainment moguls to puff up interest. Among his targets was Florenz Ziegfeld, who one day got a wire stating: "Sorry but Columbo is unavailable. Con Conrad."[8] The tactic got Ziegfeld's attention. But even when Columbo auditioned with "You Call It Madness" and another tune he recently co-wrote with Leo Robin and Clarence Gaskill called "Prisoner Of Love," neither Ziegfeld nor the radio and stage celebrity Harry Richman were impressed. Columbo later admitted to being so excited about meeting the Great Ziegfeld that he was "in a fog all afternoon."[9] The dejection slump hit twice as hard a few hours later once the fog cleared.

Subsequent auditions with ad agencies, Broadway producers, and executives at NBC proved equally fruitless. On July 2nd, Columbo and Conrad took an enchanted walk over to Victor Records' 25th Street studios to make an audition disc. Conrad tinkled away at a piano while Columbo intoned a version of "Out Of Nowhere"—a now lost recording that the studio had slothfully filed away. With the Victor folks less than elated about further sessions, Conrad looked elsewhere. He understood that in cash-craving times, radio was the favored medium. It was free.

Of the several network executives Conrad had to nag, Mort Millman, a representative from the National Broadcasting Company's Artist's Service Bureau, was decent enough to visit the Carnegie Plaza apartment and hear Columbo's informal audition. Millman radiated lukewarmth but asked both gentlemen to report to the NBC studios for a follow-up microphone test. A tenacious Conrad sidestepped any potential waffling by convincing NBC to assign Columbo a four-week trial run. Major radio shows had sponsors, but Columbo was yet to find one. They settled for a sponsor-free or "sustaining" program that paid a flat, modest salary and aired each evening for fifteen minutes at the ungodly midnight hour.

The radio and Victrola were not enough. Surrounded by Broadway bigwigs, Conrad envisioned Columbo as a stage personality. At the time, Earl Carroll was the wonderful wizard capable of granting such a wish. A producer, director, composer, lyricist and all-around urban demigod, Carroll had exuded his charisma over theater since 1916, when he produced his first musical score. After World War I, he took to being a theatrical manager and owner before premiering the first edition of his long-running *Earl Carroll's Vanities* series in 1923.

Conrad arranged for Columbo to audition right in the producer's office. Carroll liked him enough to consider him for a part in *Vanities of 1931*, but the previous commitment to NBC's radio shows conflicted with Carroll's rehearsal dates. "Earl liked my songs and I guess he liked me, too," Columbo recounted in the theatrical newspaper *Zit's*. "He took me over to the Pennsylvania Roof and there Rudy Vallee was good enough to listen to my songs and then graciously allowed me to use his mike."[10]

Vallee gives his version of events in the autobiography *Let The Chips Fall*. He claims Conrad had given him a call, inviting him to dinner and to meet a talented "young Italian boy." When the three hooked up at Schrafft's, Vallee was surprised to see Columbo as somewhat older than expected. He was distinctly impressed, however, that the young gentleman "wore Johnson and Murphy shoes (which were sported only by men of the world who could afford them), with a little gold pin underneath his tie to hold the points of the collar together—something affected mostly by the sophisticated young men of Wall Street who set the pace of fashion in those days."[11]

Vallee's attitude went from blasé courtesy to tepid fascination when he sat across from Columbo and suddenly remembered him as the balladeer behind bars in *Dynamite*. From the moment he caught Columbo's lingering look, the overgrown preppy felt empathy for this newly-arrived aspirant who seemed so down on his luck. They may have also shared a deeper personality connection. Vallee, like Columbo, was easily blindsided by the wrong pretty face. A while back, he got quite enamored with the drawing of a woman on the cover of *College Humor* magazine. Finally finding someone who resembled her, he proposed. In no time, she was the imminently unfaithful Mrs. Vallee.

In his other autobiography, *My Time Is Your Time*, Vallee describes his own Depression of 1931: "I was supposed to be the toast of New York. I was appearing in a Broadway musical, leading one of the most popular dance bands in the country at the Pennsylvania Grill and one of the nation's top radio stars—yet I was the most lonesome, unhappy person in gay Manhattan."[12] So, it was perhaps the subliminal regard of one faint-heart for another that prompted Vallee's magnanimous gesture. He agreed to let Columbo take the stage at 12:30 a.m., a half-hour before closing time.

On the momentous evening, Vallee announced the arrival of a handsome young crooner fresh from California. The patrons, who were in the rigor mortis of revelry, got re-animated as the band struck up a dance tempo. After looking around the room and into Conrad's badgering stare, Columbo started singing. Vallee, whose subsequent animosity toward Columbo's success no doubt tainted his recollection, told the following debatable account through clenched teeth:

> As I heard him sing 'Ah, But I Surrender Dear-ear-ear' with the familiar Crosby half-trill on the word 'dear,' I fully expected shouts from the crowd of 'imitator!' 'phony!' But at three minutes to one they were clamoring for more, and I believe we played ten or fifteen minutes overtime that night before they were satisfied.[13]

Columbo finished the set with a sigh of pleasure after enduring what must have felt like an eternity of pain. If Vallee's account is true, Columbo took a big chance by greeting New York with his rendition of a Crosby hit. He emerged from the gambit unscathed but, from that moment, Columbo started to temper Svengali's demands with a countervailing mission: to show that he was his own man with his own dream and (contrary to any cretins accusing him of being a "Crosby imitator") his own sound.

FOREPLAY
SERENADES

Unlike a great many of his type of entertainers, Russ can cut loose with a powerful voice of almost operatic strength if he wishes. And as a boy if he hadn't thought that the violin was more suited to him he might have joined the ranks of opera singers.[1]

—Robert Grannis, *New York Evening Graphic*, December 1931

In the summer of 1931, Russ Columbo had no compulsion to regard Bing Crosby with any malice. His "Romantic Rival" did not figure into the stockyard of creeps blocking life's footway. Crosby was just an affable contender in a new school of low droners. The image fresh in Columbo's mind was still that of the diminutive Rhythm Boy with the jug-ears who could probably drink him under the table but posed no serious threat.

This situation would, of course, change—and not necessarily through either singer's volition. Before anyone had a chance to question whether the legendary "Battle of the Baritones" really existed, Con Conrad and a host of others with vested interests had already invented it. Conrad, as a mover and shaker on his protégé's behalf, worked with such tireless vigor that anyone witnessing his maneuvers would suspect otherworldly forces at play.

Following Columbo's impressive appearance at the Hotel Pennsylvania, Conrad hired additional press agents to spread word about the novel sensation from the West Coast. But no matter how Conrad tried to boost morale, the bluenoses at NBC remained tentative about Columbo's likely success on their Blue Network. They hemmed and hawed, even up to the crucial July evening when Columbo made his fifteen-minute debut along the Eastern Time zone, live from NBC's WJZ studios. Author Lou Miano, in his pioneering book *Russ Columbo: The Amazing Life and Mysterious Death of a Hollywood Singing Legend*, points out that Columbo made this first NBC appearance at midnight on July 27th (contrary to the September 5th date that has shown up in so many Columbo-related articles).

On the following day, Columbo got a glowing review from the *Evening Graphic*. Piles of fan mail soon greeted him; sacks followed. Still, the arbiters at NBC stayed pathologically ambivalent. The sweet music eluded their brainwaves. To them, Columbo was just one more sustaining artist in search of a sponsor. So, at least for a little while, he had to regard each broadcast with weary gratitude.

Columbo soon faced an even more tenuous situation. While on a sea cruise, William S. Paley, president of the Columbia Broadcasting System, became so smitten with Crosby's recording of "I Surrender, Dear" that he arranged to have the singer transported from California to New York for a regular CBS show. NBC's listless minions were suddenly jolted. A fresh infusion of shark's blood propelled them to lure Crosby with a better offer.

In keeping with the spirit of a corporate bureaucracy, NBC's hasty zeal to "Get Crosby!" was based more on philistine reflexes than any intrinsic regard for his music. They assumed that he must be worth getting if CBS was willing to pay him $1,500 per week—a sum considered hefty for just another sustaining programmer. In the melee, Columbo got short shrift. NBC's headhunters were too drunk on delusions of conquest to renew his contract when his three weeks ended. On August 22nd, as he moaned "You Call It Madness" for the last of his trial broadcasts, Columbo could see only a black hole where the moon once glowed.

When CBS finally secured Crosby, Columbo and Conrad must have gloated, remembering how shabbily the losing bidders at NBC had treated them. Not being one to let rightful grudges interfere with good business, Conrad immediately embarked on a campaign to convert NBC's sour grapes into honeyed liqueur. His first step to easing Columbo back onto the ether waves involved contacting Rocco Vocco, a potentate at the prestigious Leo Feist Music Company who had enough muscle to admonish NBC for abusing a great talent. At Vocco's irresistible urging, the already embarrassed network caved and welcomed Columbo back.

Conrad's next step involved conspiring with NBC to activate a Columbo media blitz equal to if not greater than the publicity CBS was lavishing on Crosby. By the last week of August, Columbo had started a revamped show for 11:30 p.m.—all the better to vie with the Crosby spot slated to begin a few days later at 11:00. Columbo also enjoyed the privilege of singing with an orchestra conducted by Erno Rapee, a veteran film composer known mostly for the silent-era classics "Charmaine" (from *What Price Glory?*) and "Diane" (from *Seventh Heaven*).

As Columbo's flurry of fan letters resumed, Broadway producers, composers and fellow performers were taking him more seriously as a new

lord in the crooner manor. One older contender, feeling elbowed out of the spotlight, started looking a bit differently on the upstart in the Johnson and Murphy shoes. No longer in the snooty position to practice *noblesse oblige*, Rudy Vallee started bitching to the press about Columbo and Crosby as if they were a problem brood he had errantly spawned. Morton Downey, on the other hand, was beaming. Keen to haze out any distinction between a crooner and a traditional Irish tenor, he was secure enough in his singular talents to flatter Columbo through imitation when performing his own version of "You Call It Madness" on a CBS show.

Those glued to the CBS network for the August 31st Crosby debut were disappointed when he once again had trouble with his vocal cords—a malady that (according to his throat doctor) ultimately made his voice lower and huskier. By September 2nd, Crosby rebounded. He fixed both his voice and a musician's union ban that had dogged him since his Arnheim days when, as a chronic no-show, he made the mistake of alienating the Cocoanut Grove's powerful owners.

While the Crosby airs wafted through the magnetic spectrum, Conrad smelled war. He was intent on instigating a rivalry between the brown-eyed fiddler and the blue-eyed tippler. The Baritone Battle's confederates consisted of NBC shills, copy-mad journalists and a horde of sycophantic sharpies. Paramount Theater impresario Bob Weitman would soon join their ranks as he prepared to hire Columbo and Crosby as crowd-pleasers for his respective Brooklyn and Manhattan houses. "Russ Columbo and Bing Crosby," Jerry Wald soon wrote, "buddies on the Coast, haven't even said 'boo' to each other since they've been in the East. Such is fame!"[2] He wrote in another column: "No matter what you read or hear about the personal friendliness between Bing Crosby and Russ Columbo, you can take our word for it that each hates the other's respective 'guts.'"[3]

Meanwhile, the Radio Corporation of America—the parent company to both NBC and Victor Records—took a wider view. The once apathetic Victor brass was now overjoyed to get Columbo back into the studio, even in the face of a declining record industry. In contrast to the vast market in 1927, record sales competed somewhat miserably against the surfeit of gratis radio programs, falling about 39% in 1930 and dropping further the following year. Victor, among the few labels to survive, was confident that Columbo would make a heroic climb up the *Billboard* ladder.

Columbo was pleasantly surprised on September 3rd, when he walked into the Victor studios for his first session. Expecting a phalanx of functionary engineers concerned only with contract obligations, he instead discovered an ideal sonic laboratory manned by a musically sympathetic arranger and conductor. Unlike Gus Arnheim, Nathaniel Shilkret proved very congenial to Columbo's aesthetic temperament and would shortly oversee some of the singer's best work.

Born 1889 as Naftule Schuldkraut in Queens, New York, Shilkret would later describe himself as "another famous Jew born on Christmas Day."[4] His Austrian parents had impressed enough of a European musical heritage upon him when he was a pre-teen to inspire his seat as a pianist for the Russian Symphony Orchestra. Apart from being a conductor for John Philip Sousa, Shilkret made his biggest impact as Victor's Director of Light Music.

Shilkret, like Andre Kostelanetz, was committed to bridging the gap between the highbrow symphony and the low-to-middlebrow "sob song." In 1927, he wrote a third-person account of himself in the *Phonograph Monthly Review*, stating his "intention to treat popular music in the classic manner and bring to its rendition all the resources of the classic styles."[5] He already established his flair as a crooner's mood maestro in 1928, when he and the Victor Orchestra crafted a lush background for Gene Austin: the #1 hit "Jeannine (I Dream Of Lilac Time)," which Shilkret had originally composed for the Colleen Moore film *Lilac Time*.

Most of Shilkret's crooner arrangements conformed to the style of the popular "sweet" bands—those noble holdouts against the "hot" band incursion—with unabashedly sentimental waltz rhythms and light-hearted foxtrots. As he indulged Columbo with dreamy violins and weepy clarinets, Shilkret demonstrated the fine art of converting romantic frustration into an applied acoustical science. The key was to facilitate Columbo's darkly evocative drama through under-arrangement.

Shilkret already had a full plate that day. Thirty minutes before Columbo's session, he led the Victor Orchestra on three foxtrots for singer Chick Bullock and another for Victor's prized crooner Paul Small. But the tone in Studio #1 changed considerably when Columbo started with "Guilty," a lament about "taking the blame" for a love gone badly, that Richard A. Whiting, Gus Kahn and Harry Akst had collaborated on that same year. Massaging the song's otherwise strict tempo with strategic lulls, Columbo hangs onto the mood notes as Shilkret's brother Jack mists in and out of the background with his piano.

While respecting the composers' melodic intent, Columbo takes liberties with Fred Ahlert and Roy Turk's "I Don't Know Why (I Just Do)." He shifts from a lower to higher range with no evidence of strain and staggers ever so cautiously through lines like, "You never seem to want my romancing/ The only time you hold me is when we're dancing." The second verse starts out slightly more upbeat until Columbo re-wraps himself around the melody, his notes stretching out in slow motion. Suddenly, a renegade clarinet foams at the mouth, breaking the mood with a jittery instrumental interlude that passes quickly enough to be a less than welcomed bit of comic relief, especially once Columbo restores poise with a calm, classy finish.

On "You Call It Madness (But I Call It Love)" Columbo once again glides with the strings and the strumming guitar while blowing soft kisses at the melancholy piano. His heartsick quaver, unlike Crosby's beefy wail, evokes the weeping of a jilted and somewhat tipsy swain. Some have dubiously attributed the crooner language of "boo-boo-boo-boo" and "vah-vah-vah-voo" to "scat" singing, but in this instance above all, the nonsense syllables sound less like jazz blather and more like someone sobbing into his cups over the paramour who "made a plaything out of romance."

The difference between Columbo and Crosby is no more vivid than in their respective versions of "Sweet And Lovely," a breezy ballad that Gus Arnheim had co-written. Crosby's is much sprightlier and never lingers on the notes long enough to suggest emotional conviction. Bob-bob-bobbing along to the brief outbursts of improvised clarinet, he sings as a carefree roué to the cheerful beat. Even in moments of faux sensitivity, Crosby still plays to the knaves, tacitly assuring them he is being paid to act seriously.

The record Columbo made on September 9th is a much different "Sweet And Lovely." He sings it with sullen command and swerves more gracefully with the melodic curves. Ever the incurable dreamer, he crystallizes cliché phrases like "sweeter than the roses in May" with an internal logic resistant to cynicism. Unlike Crosby, who often gives the impression of scaling the high notes on stilts, Columbo seems much more relaxed in the upper register. He puts all of his subdued intensity into each distended vowel, manipulating the notes by bending them in time. There comes a point, shortly after the obligatory "voo-voo-voo-vah" and the silky violin interlude, when the rhythm slows downward. Listeners have only to hear him pipe a deceptively hopeful phrase like, "When she whispers in my arms so tenderly..." to imagine dark clouds forming. The song's three most poignant words—"melody, haunting me"—seem to be written for Columbo alone as he wallows in the ballad's message about romantic recollection and inevitable distress.

These first four entries were just the start of an ongoing songlist—a document of Columbo's personal odyssey during his initial rise. Listening to these recordings, one gets the sense that his romantic longing originates not so much from a recent sweetheart's rejection but from some deeper, earlier trauma that hit him when he was much too young to put the pain into rational perspective. His is the cry of a lost boy trying to focus on a fuzzy picture of the actual person or incident that hurt him.

At least in the beginning of his venture to stardom, Columbo tried to keep a pure, albeit wayward, heart, especially when dealing with show business politics. His attitude toward the less genteel forces behind his publicity machine was (in contemporary psychology argot) passive-aggressive. While eager to achieve celebrity, he was averse to confronting the huckster machinations needed to keep his name in print. It was therefore Conrad's job to whore for slogans like "Columbus discovered America— now America is discovering Columbo." Columbo's callow sense of humor came out when a written release from the NBC-WEAF Press Relations Department listed his 11:30 program as "Salade Moderne Columbo à la Russ." Columbo wrote in the margin: "Name salads after me—tee hee!"

By late September, as his recording of "You Call It Madness (But I Call It Love)" reached #5, the media at large devised monikers like "Radio's Revelation," "The Romeo Of Song," "The Vocal Valentino," "Valentino of the Air," the "Voice from the Golden West" and sometimes simply "Romeo Russ." Walter Winchell, vying to do one better, came up with a curious alternative: "Columbo—the Gem of the Ozone." As Columbo's first month of radio exposure unleashed at least 2,000 adoring missives, NBC gave him a new one-year contract and a weekly pay that matched Crosby's.

The radio industry was highly solvent by the fall of 1931. Airwave celebrities with abounding cache volunteered for an array of charity appearances. In late September, the *Daily Mirror* hosted a "Bellevue Radio Festival" to promote RCA's recently developed "radio-pillow," a portable device engineered to comfort troubled patients with doses of network reception wired to their hospital beds. Several such benefits strived to raise enough money to furnish every infirmary in the New York Metropolitan area but focused initially on Bellevue Hospital. Following formal introductions from Mayor Jimmy Walker and New York's Commissioner of City Hospitals, Columbo appeared before the mike with his customary opening theme song. (Today, irony prevails when one imagines "You Call It Madness" performed before patients confined to a hospital destined for acclaim as a leading psychiatric facility.)

Despite altruistic moments, radio stars were essentially commodities beholden to sponsors. Jack Benny would eventually turn America on to

Jell-O while Crosby helped sell Cremo Cigars (and later Miracle Whip). When it came time to endorse his first product, Columbo soon neared madness not out of love but because of petty legal squabbles. He signed an agreement to do three half-hour shows (on a trial basis) for Maxwell House coffee at $1,000 per week. They would air via NBC's WEAF studio, also known as the Red Network, and reach a larger audience than WJZ's Blue Network. The 9:30 p.m. broadcast slot was also more accessible.

On September 24th, the Maxwell House engagement commenced with the soothing backgrounds of the Don Vorhees Orchestra. Columbo would croon such relaxing fare as "You Call It Madness," "Guilty" and "I Don't Know Why (I Just Do)" while an announcer intermittently pitched praises for Maxwell's refreshing, aromatic and nerve-kindling brew. All the while, Maxwell House representatives sat in an adjacent booth, monitoring Columbo's every vocal nuance and body movement to determine whether or not a Radio Romeo was suitable for the contradictory ciphers needed to sell caffeine.

Following Columbo's third program, on which he included a song called "Was It A Dream?," Maxwell's monitors canceled the show. They decided that crooning was not their cup of tea and opted instead to continue only with the Vorhees instrumentals. This insult worsened after NBC failed to send the William Morris Talent Agency, Columbo's other business associates, an agreed-upon commission that was due whenever the singer found a sponsor. William Morris filed a breach of contract suit against NBC, Conrad and Columbo. Though the matter was at last settled out of court, Columbo looked with trepidation on future commercial entanglements.

Until now, Columbo regarded Conrad as his Gibraltar, but he could not ignore a crumbling sound. In October, Conrad drew up a fresh contract, setting out the rules and regulations for a brand new company called Rusco Enterprises, Inc. Legalese was the last language Columbo wanted to hear, but Conrad assured him that the emerging enterprise was entirely legitimate, with bigger profits and no snags. The Rusco agreement had one decisive feature: the specification that Conrad receives 33 1/3% of Russ earned and netted revenue. The name Jack Gordean, third party to the first contract, was conspicuously missing.

Amid this finagling, Columbo was still obliged to smile and chant like a romantic hero. Such pressures coincided with the foreboding mood behind his next three recordings on the ninth of October, starting with Vincent Youmans' languorous ballad "Time On My Hands." The slinking violin and ever so slightly off-kilter piano help Columbo's voice melt, like one of

Salvador Dali's soft watches, into a limbo where "the day fades away into twilight" and the lover in Harold Adamson and Mack Gordon's lyrics vaporizes.

In 1931, famed bandleader Ray Noble had penned "Good Night, Sweetheart" by adapting themes from Liszt and Schubert. It turned out to be one of the period's saddest airs—the one dance bands often used as their official closing theme—and also became part of *Earl Carroll's Vanities* that same year. In his doleful interpretation, Columbo clings to every word as he chaperones "a dreamy dreamland" where the dancers briefly forget they are on a warping ballroom floor.

Transfixed in this netherworld, Columbo continues with what would be his greatest paean to melancholy intoxication, "Prisoner Of Love." Structurally, the song bears an odd similarity to "Body And Soul." Unlike John W. Green's tune, however, "Prisoner" has a simple, crest-fallen melody that avoids the smug nihilism of a blues beat. Here, Columbo, who collaborated on the words and music, intimates how a tragic aria might sound if performed more softly. Judging from how he puts the song across, he probably specified that the lyrics, when sung, should mimic crying.

> *Alone from night to night you'll find me,*
> *Too weak to break the chains that bind me,*
> *I need no shackles to remind me...*

A constant violin mourns along as he dignifies masochistic lines like

> *She's in my dreams, awake or sleeping,*
> *Upon my knees to her I'm creeping,*
> *My very life is in her keeping...*

That same October, Columbo returned to the Top 20. "Sweet And Lovely" registered at a modest #19 and "Guilty" went to a higher but scary #13. He outdid himself a month later, ascending to #3 with "Good Night, Sweetheart," his highest charting record. The escalating success had its disturbing underside. Columbo's loved ones and friends were thousands of miles away; his new pals were too closely linked to his profession for comfort. In this state of anomie, he reached out to somebody in the third dimension, creeping upon his knees to the lovely Dorothy Dell.

Columbologist Jerry Wald bragged of being the matchmaker for the couple he described in his *Evening Graphic* column as: "A nice lad and a sweet, wholesome girl."[6] Dell was born Dorothy Goff in Hattiesburg, Mississippi and, while still a minor, boasted an innate talent for snagging titles like Miss American Legion, Miss Biloxi, Miss New Orleans, and The Girl with the Perfect Back. In 1930, at age fifteen, she was crowned both Miss America and Miss Universe. A year later, she appeared in the final edition of the Ziegfeld Follies, for which she sang the nasty "Was I Drunk? Was He Handsome? And Did My Ma Give Me Hell?" Shortly after Columbo entered her sphere, she switched her theme to "And Then Your Lips Met Mine."[7]

Whenever they availed themselves to the nosy press, the twenty-three-year old Columbo and this sixteen-year-old blonde were matching aesthetics. Gossip columnists salivated at talk of an imminent wedding. Conrad had allegedly leaked the matrimonial news to Walter Winchell, who in turn wreaked havoc in his daily column by printing: "Dorothy Dell, the Follies dolly, and Russ Columbo, NBC's Romeo of Song, plan to middle-aisle it shortly."

By late October, the chimera of a happy heart inspired Columbo to treat his adoring *paesans* to an "all-Italian" NBC broadcast. Victor already released his third single: "Good Night, Sweetheart" with "Time On My Hands" as the B-side. But soon he was again reminded that time was anything but generous when romance took on the trappings of an onerous movie plot. Playing the matchmaker turned avenger, Wald coyly spoke in his column of an unidentified "interloper"[8] who had hatched a Mephistophelean plot to break Columbo and Dell up. Wald went on to declare that this mystery person frightened NBC's executives with prospects of their lucrative bachelor crawling to the altar and spurning his hormonally-charged fan base.

When the time came to put love asunder, Conrad was appointed the logical party-pooper. He went directly to Dell and burdened her with bleak scenarios about the possible harm she posed to Columbo's career. In a supremely selfless gesture, Dell voluntarily withdrew from the crooner's life. When confronted, Conrad confessed to everything. A livid Columbo stormed out of their apartment and vowed never to return.

For the next three days, Columbo would see Conrad only during broadcasting hours. A pall of silence fell whenever Svengali and Trilby crossed paths. Then, Trilby took some time to ruminate. He may have snarled, rolled his eyes in exasperation, and pressed a handkerchief against his brow to stem an approaching headache but, as always, Columbo resorted to being practical once the mental torture subsided. He was back in Conrad's camp. Two years later, the plot, as previously mentioned, to the Warner Brothers film *Twenty Million Sweethearts* bore a curious resemblance to these events.

ROMANCE of Dorothy Dell (above), "Follies" eyeful and winner of "most beautiful girl in the world" contest, and Russ Columbo, who objects to being called a crooner, may draw frowns of broadcasting company bigwigs, but Youth—and Love—must be served. That trembly feeling, stilled by official order a few months ago, started in all over again as result of chance meeting last week.

Columbo, always reminding himself of the need to convert such affective assaults into art, was among the precious few crooners who could sing about these romantic travesties and be entirely believable. His voice was masculine, but he (like Vallee) retained the vulnerable charms of both a torch singer and a heart-swept adolescent girl—a quality that invited listeners to project their own heart-stricken histories onto his every sound. One *Radio Guide* critic tried to reduce this ambiguous appeal to mere technique: "Russ Columbo is really a tenor and not a baritone, but sings low and close to the mike to get that certain effect."[9]

Returning to the Victor studio on November 18th, Columbo mastered the blurred baritone/tenor range in his recording of "You Try Somebody Else." Playing his "lover's farewell" against a skip-happy beat, he reveals the song's more woeful underpinning by leaping with panic on the glib line: "Let's take our fun where we find it…" After a sad wordless chorus, he pleads for his sweetie's reassurance that "we'll be back together again."

Despite the more raucous rhythmic trends that crept into the pre-swing era, Columbo found solace in lyrics and melodies reminiscent of 19th Century parlor ballads. The waltz was a perfect fit: so "old-fashioned" yet compelling enough to influence much of the output from Tin Pan Alley and beyond. Waltzes, by their very nature, had always signified frustrated romance. As Jon W. Finson writes in *The Voices That Are Gone*: "Disappointment in courtship at the end of the [19th] century stemmed not from distance but from proximity: the waltz held the promise of an intimacy that sometimes went unfulfilled."[10] Columbo reflects this state of mind on his version of the quaint German tune "Call Me Darling," delivering—in distended 3/4 time—his sad soliloquy about a most unlikely "secret rendezvous."

Columbo's star status was by now unquestioned. In the grip of glee, Conrad prepared yet another volley in the baritone war. Crosby, scouting around for a theme song to promote his CBS program, settled on "Where The Blue Of The Night (Meets The Gold Of The Day)." Much like Columbo's theme, this Fred Ahlert–Roy Turk composition exuded the right balance of melancholia and storybook fantasy, embroidered as a waltz structured on "Tit-Willow" from Gilbert & Sullivan's *The Mikado*.

About a month before Crosby had a chance to record it, however, Conrad had already arranged for Columbo to go over to Victor and press his own version. As expected, Columbo took to the misty-eyed melody as second nature. He ignored the unremarkable opening verse, coasted right toward the ballad's postcard perfect sunset, and, like a golden-toned Icarus, winged his way back up *Billboard*, again at #13.

RADIO STARS

Russ Colombo
may be the next
Valentino

A SORT of Cinderella luck has moulded the course of Russ Colombo's amazing career. Oh, he has worked and slaved and turned himself into a fine musician—all of which has been done by many another lad just as ambitious as he without receiving any reward—but great things have come his way with all the glittering inevitability of fate.

No one knew, back in Calistoga, California, where he lived when a child, that he was born for the limelight. They thought him just one of the Colombos—and what a lot of Colombos there were—eleven other children beside Russ! It was an old Italian custom.

Almost all of them studied music at one time or another but it was Russ who outstripped all the rest. At fourteen, he was playing solos in the Imperial Theatre in San Francisco. Then came periods common to the lives of almost all orchestra conductors. He played and sang in Hollywood, did a little ghost-voicing for the talkies, and opened his own night club in Los Angeles. There was a steadily increasing regard for his voice among his patrons but even then, no one dreamed ahead to his conquest of the air.

Lady Luck wasn't especially kind during his first efforts in Hollywood. Why, no one can say. But remembering, too, how the godly Gable was buffetted through several years of refusal, we can understand Colombo's case.

Con Conrad was the man who lifted him from the ranks. Con Conrad is one of our great song writers. He was visiting the West when he heard Russ sing and knew immediately that here was a radio "find." It was he who persuaded Russ to come to New York. It was he who sold Russ to the National Broadcasting Company—and who wrote most of the songs Russ sang. And soon Russ Colombo was a sensation and a name to conjure with.

His fan mail came into the studio in carloads. And there didn't seem to be a knock in a carload, either. Colombo was a hit, the like of which hadn't been seen since that chap from Maine, Vallee, first crooned through his megaphone.

And then—Fate again—the movies became interested. They learned that Russ was called the best-dressed man in radio. They learned that he was young and handsome and virile. So they gave him a Hollywood contract—and soon you may be remembering that other great Italian favorite, and predicting that here is a second Valentino.

42

Like many of the others, this recording suggests that, for Columbo, true romance was more about a vague, motherly nostalgia than direct sensual contact. Some crooners belched romantic perfume but slyly alluded to a gamy climax, but Columbo celebrated the maddening energy of protracted foreplay. The man and the music were so deeply interwoven that even his least prudish listeners are likely to find the mere thought of Russ Columbo going beyond kissing and cuddling downright indecent.

As the lachrymose lover, Columbo harmonized well with the economic doldrums between 1931 and 1932. Tin Pan Alley at the time churned out such melancholy masterpieces as Gus Kahn and Harry M. Woods' "(Just A) Little Street Where Old Friends Meet" and Joe Burke and Al Dubin's "When The Rest Of The Crowd Goes Home (I Always Go Home Alone)." Though no existing files show that Columbo ever recorded the latter, its publishers M. Witmark & Sons did issue his photograph on the song's sheet music, an indication that he may have included a version on at least one of his radio shows.

Writing in a November 12th *World-Telegram* column entitled "Sing a Sob of Love," Gretta Palmer resented the "morbid" crop of torch songs that, in her words, "have been monopolizing the microphone for the last few seasons." Palmer likened the "funereal despair" of tunes like "You Call It Madness (But I Call It Love)" and "I Don't Know Why (I Just Do)" to "a mournful tattoo, upon the ear drums and consciousness of the young." She also blamed Depression-era "sob-singers" and "night club divas" for "making self-pity seem a reasonable and rather picturesque emotion."

For Palmer, the "sentimental tendency to wring the last drop of tragedy out of any emotional upset" was a baleful cultural omen. This dismissal of songs about "love gone awry" did not deter her from sobbing her own pessimistic prognosis: "Only the most sanguine young girl, after being brought up in this atmosphere of musical frustration, would give a second thought to a member of the glacial and unworthy male."

Poor Gretta Palmer. She failed to appreciate how those sad and often-tragic love songs accurately reflected an era that, while transpiring in relative peacetime, posed economic woes that triggered a collective sense of foreboding. The crooner, wedged inside a social malaise between two world wars, spoke directly to the many who coped with the Depression by taking it inward. He activated childlike thoughts about rejection and the need for warm coddling—feelings that even the most sneering ironists probably experienced, albeit secretly.

THE VOICE OF

THE VOICE OF
Broadway
—By Louis Sobol—

Dem Good Ol' Days!

In eighteen thirty-one, you know,
There was no blaring radio,
No crashing planes, no food in cans,
No subway trains, no parked sedans.

There wasn't any prohibish,
There was no Wickersham commish,
No telephones, no Follies girls,
No saxophones, no rhumba whirls.

There weren't any Broadway "snoops,"
The language had no "boop-a-doops,"
No movie queens, no 'genie fad,
No blabbing screens, no "Times are bad!"

But, best of all, ah, stainless age,
There was no Bing Columbo rage!
                    —Al A. Ostrow.

From the *New York Evening Journal* (December 1931).

(Courtesy of Max Pierce.)

LOVE
AND
LISTERINE

Gay songs of gladness
Love songs of madness
I sing them all in vain;
Nobody knows of the sadness
Back of each happy refrain...

— "Only A Voice On The Air" (1931)
Words by Al Dubin; Music by Russ Columbo

With the opening of *George White's Scandals* in the fall of 1931, Rudy Vallee sang "Life Is Just A Bowl Of Cherries" as 305 American banks collapsed and one in every four wage earners faced unemployment. New York City's movers and shakers still held their noses high, inspired no doubt by those recently erected towers of might, the Chrysler and Empire State Buildings. A comparable spirit of semi-oblivious optimism fueled Con Conrad's campaign to make Russ Columbo the supreme romantic ware.

Historian Thomas Waugh invoked academic spin to declare: "Glamorous daydreams compensate for social powerlessness and economic deprivation." But Conrad knew by instinct why a figure like Columbo offered proper emotional nutrition in times of breadlines and hoopla. Whatever their financial status, many still hungered for fantasies involving candlelight courtship and strolls down a quixotic Lover's Lane.

Several critics responded to Columbo's charm with genuine appreciation. "He came to the air unknown," Jerry Wald would scribe for the New York *Evening Graphic* in a continuous show of support, "and within a few weeks his youth, personal charm and real ability brought him to the top. His case is concrete evidence that the radio audience plays no favorites."[1]

One of Columbo's most illuminating songs was "Only A Voice On The Air." Al Dubin wrote the lyrics, but their simple and bracing message about being disembodied in the ether offered another peek into the mind of the man who composed the tune:

> Tho' many hear me,
> There's no one near me
> When I need sympathy;
> After the 'broadcast' is over
> Nobody thinks about me;
>
> I am only a voice on the air,
> To the millions who listen out there;
> I am only a voice on the air,
> When I'm lonely there's no one to care;
> If the song I sing could only bring,
> Just a message from someone, somewhere;
> But there's no one whose dreams I can share;
> For I'm only a voice on the air

On one November evening, the lonely Columbo found company among politicians and celebrities at the Hotel Commodore. The occasion was a benefit for the Free Milk Fund for Babies, for which he volunteered to entertain along with stars like Kate Smith, Cab Calloway and Ethel Merman. The Muldoon-Tunney Championship Committee sponsored the event—an all-stag affair, except for Mrs. William Randolph Hearst and her small gaggle of lady escorts. The honored guests included the esteemed Bernard F. Gimbel (who functioned as the dinner committee chairman), Mayor Jimmy Walker, Averell Harriman, and the controversial Hollywood censor Will H. Hays.[2]

The Committee's namesakes—prizefighters Gene Tunney and William Muldoon—were also on hand to oversee the testimonial dinner that commenced in the Commodore's grand ballroom. When the meal ended and the coffee arrived, the women withdrew while the men loosened a belt notch or two to assume postures of camaraderie.[3] Columbo, engulfed in the stench of cigars and conversation, tried his best to participate. But his jaw soon dropped as he looked toward the center of the banquet hall. Like an altar straight out of Hades, a boxing ring rose from an opening in the floor. The hale and hearty laughter permeating the enclosure swelled into

Brooklyn Paramount Theatre
NEWS FLASH

ROMANTIC SINGER CAPTURES HEART OF BROOKLYN!

THE CAMERA CATCHES
THE ROMEO OF SONG
IN A VARIETY
OF POSES

GIRLS! HERE HE IS!

Brooklyn's New Thrill!

RUSS COLUMBO

"THE ROMEO OF SONG"

Featured Every Week at the

BROOKLYN PARAMOUNT THEATRE

THERE'S A THRILL IN EVERY VALUE AT BOHACK'S!

demonic caterwauling as several amateur collegiate pugilists started to spar. The wandering voice of the air was now a misfit in a bullpen full of screaming rowdies. Quietly cringing, he must have watched the fighters with dreadful memories of that youthful encounter with his father's fist.

The events inside that makeshift arena foreshadowed the more symbolic bout that followed. A couple of weeks later, on the Thanksgiving evening of November 26th, Columbo had his own fight—a Battle of the Baritones waged not in a boxing ring but in two of Paramount's prestigious New York theaters. While Bing Crosby and Kate Smith headlined at the Paramount Theater in Times Square, "The Romeo of Song" made his stage debut as master of ceremonies at the Brooklyn Paramount, his name spread out in lights and his face adorning a mammoth sign. Jack Partington (who once hosted a program in which a twelve-year-old Columbo appeared as a violinist) now returned to help organize this first engagement.

The show opened to a pitch-black stage as the Paramount Orchestra faded into "You Call It Madness." Like a little boy lost, Columbo called out from the darkness with the lines, "I can't forget the night I met you, you're all I'm thinking of..." Then, the lights, like artificial rays of requited love, beamed on the serenader as he stood at center stage. He was demure, polite and astounded at the thunderous ovation.

In between acts like the Candreva Brothers and the Whirlwind Dancers, Columbo continued to elicit applause each time he resumed the spotlight, crooning numbers like "Sweet And Lovely" and "Sleepy Time Down South." But when he proceeded with "Goodnight Sweetheart," the crowd resounded in fits of mad love, insisting that Columbo remain on stage. Each time he tried to announce the next act, the clapping and shouting for an encore grew louder. When he repeated the song, the cheers were almost deafening. Columbo waited several minutes for a semblance of calm before he reprised his opening theme, motioning for the lights to go dark again as the projector grinded out the premiere of the new George Bancroft picture *Rich Man's Folly*.

The following day, Richard Murray of the *Standard Union* complimented Columbo's "natty blue suit" and appreciated how much the singer truly resembled Valentino:

> *Columbo is not, as the Broadway historians would say, a wisey. He has infinitely more to recommend him... In the first place, he acts as master of ceremonies without resorting to the smiling quackeries of that profession. Tossing off an occasional joke but not underlining wisecracks, standing in the background without attempting to attract the spotlight, he emerges as a thoroughly agreeable and good-*

looking young man, introducing the various entertainers in amiable fashion. His ability to warble songs of rueful love is, of course, the selling point. An ovation somewhat akin to a riot indicates that his voice registers as well in the theater as it does over the air.[4]

Jerry Wald soon followed in the *Evening Graphic* but apparently derived warped pleasure out of sharing some awkward inside information:

When Columbo debuted at the B'klyn Paramount last Thursday, he kept the audience waiting a full fifteen minutes because he mistook the cue buzzer in his dressing room for a telephone signal and turned over and went back to sleep...[5]

More plaudits followed. On the evening after the Paramount premiere, an announcer for Columbo's WJZ program read aloud a letter from former San Francisco Mayor turned California Governor James R. Rolph, who praised the singer as a proud offspring of the Golden State. The November edition of *Radio Log and Lore* hailed him "King of Crooners." Crosby may have had the advantage of playing in the swankier borough of Manhattan with stellar co-stars, but the Paramount-Publix officials, perhaps skittish about Crosby's recurring throat maladies, had at one point wagered in Columbo's favor when estimating box office grosses. Sweetening matters, the *Sunday Brooklyn Times* announced on December 6th the results of a contest that Brooklyn's Warner Strand Theater held to promote the opening of the Walter Huston-Loretta Young film *The Ruling Voice*. The majority of contestants, vying to describe "in fifty words or less" their favorite crooner, chose the Vocal Valentino.

Preceding a different movie each week, Columbo lulled his Brooklyn audience into the Christmas season. On week three, Tallulah Bankhead's *The Cheat* was the new feature, while The Mills Brothers joined the roster. The Paramount also got a little more experimental with stage design. According to an account in the *Brooklyn Eagle*, the show—set around a highlight performance of "Prisoner Of Love"—was "divided into four episodes, in one of which Columbo sings two songs in Spanish."[6]

As anticipated, the language of love exacted a price tag. Starting on December 7th, Columbo earned an additional weekly sum of $2,500— just by lending his velvety voice to promote the throat-cleansing properties of Listerine mouthwash. In the past, perfume merchants sold elixirs that merely masked life's pungent recesses, but thanks to the efforts of antiseptic trailblazers like Joseph Lister, the religion of romance could flourish in a relatively germ-free environment. Being that Russ, like his crooner cohorts, sang the praises of the utopian kiss, the Listerine spot, reported to be among radio's "most expensive"[7] broadcasts, was a cross-marketing treat.

One reviewer, perhaps keen to this antibacterial link between crooning and chemistry, gushed: "Russ Columbo, the boy from the golden West, has a voice of gold, the fine melody of which has enthralled all who have come underneath its spell. There is poetry, romance and charm in his every tone and the Listerine people are fortunate in having secured him to help popularize their product."[8]

Listerine's coast-to-coast broadcast appeared in fifteen-minute blocks on Mondays, Thursdays and Fridays at 5:45 p.m. over WEAF-NBC's Red Network and Tuesdays, Wednesdays and Saturdays on WJZ-NBC's Blue Network at 10 p.m. Committing such an exacting schedule to memory was dizzying enough, but Columbo came close to tether's end when he had to balance these time slots with his four daily Brooklyn Paramount shows. Over the airwaves, he brilliantly camouflaged the strain. "Never an ardent crooner fan," critic and skeptic Ben Gross admitted after taking in Columbo's Red Network program, "this listener must admit his drowsy tunes have a soothing effect."[9]

Columbo would report for these Listerine assignments in his customary dark jackets, blue shirts and trusty white—sometimes two-toned—shoes. His hair shining and meticulously combed, he would smile and mingle with the studio personnel until airtime, when announcer Ford Bond eased the transition. Russ would step before the mike, summon his composure and stare intently on the rack of music before him. Raising his left hand to signal the orchestra, he would begin with a soft melody, tilting slightly on his right foot, swaying to the tempo and occasionally tugging at his tie. His wrinkling brow betrayed the only sign of his emotional attachment to the songs (and possibly his annoyance at legal folderol required to perform them).

David Bratton, writing for the *Brooklyn Times*, elaborated on the singer's demeanor:

> *Columbo is a slim little chap, or perhaps we should say of medium tallness, with a pleasant smile. He smiles when singing and is seldom still. His hands hold closely to his coat pockets and he prefers the military heel shoe to increase his size. His waist is slim, so slim that one would almost imagine that he holds it in, but believe us it is natural. With another couple of weeks on the stage, he will have a personality that will please all who see him as well as listen.*[10]

From the *New York Evening Journal*, December 15, 1931.

Early in December, the New York *American* announced that a "major victory in the rivalry between the baritone crooners of the two networks will be won by Russ Columbo, Dec. 14, when he will go into the Waldorf-Astoria as a dance band leader." The occasion for this leap into the laps of New York royalty was the unveiling of the Waldorf's Empire Room. Replacing an orchestra previously led by Joseph Moss, Columbo was now appointed to front a ten-piece band for "supper dancing" every night of the week except Sunday. The show was also scheduled for live broadcasts for three nights per week via NBC hookup.

Café-society bluebloods, who previously snarled at the mere thought of sharing their scented oxygen with radio artistes, were now reserving their tables well in advance. This changing attitude among the metropolitan elite surfaced in a satirical cartoon depicting a supercilious couple all decked out for an elegant evening. The only object in their penthouse not reeking of posh is the bawling brat in its bassinet. The matron, cross-legged in her plush chair and fumbling at her pearls, deigns to look in the direction of her maid who enters the room to announce: "Moddom, Masters Vallee, Crosby and Columbo have come to croon baby's lullaby this evening as you ordered. Shall I show them in?"

Under the glaze of klieg lights, the Waldorf honored Columbo's opening night by unraveling a red carpet for stellar guests like musical legend Paul Whiteman and silent screen idol Buddy Rogers. Columbo was disappointed, however, when the major columnists failed to appear. One radio journalist who did show up, Jack Foster of the *World-Telegram*, meowed: "Russ Columbo forgot his baton and used instead a rung from a coat hanger after he had been introduced to his orchestra."[11]

On December 29th, Columbo returned to the Victor studios to layer on more of what one critic would soon describe as his "slow, weaving, binding style."[12] Nat Shilkret assembled a piano, three violins, a cello, guitar, string bass, trombone, and a pair of saxophones for two more songs. The first was "Save The Last Dance For Me," a heavy-hearted waltz that composers

Walter Hirsch and Frank Magine probably intended for a particular sweetheart. Judging from his customary dream-weave, Columbo probably dedicated it to the many engaging but aloof faces that passed him in the daily haze. He followed with "All Of Me," a freshly published ode to romantic self-abuse that just panted for his interpretation. Beginning with a soft melodic massage but easing toward a dramatic buildup, he closed this ballad about "a one-sided love affair" with semi-operatic fortitude.

"Guilty," "Good Night, Sweetheart" and "You Call It Madness" made *Variety*'s Top 10 in sheet music sales. And as for records: "They sell so fast, these Columbo discs," the December 15th issue of *Variety* reported, "that the music stores are lulled into a beautiful day-dream that it's still old times. 'I Don't Know Why' sighs the moonstruck baritone, and he echoes himself with a tremulous 'Guilty.'"[13]

Toward the end of December, *Evening Journal* columnist Louis Sobol visited Columbo in his Brooklyn Paramount dressing room to capture Radio Russ in a fragile moment of glory. According to Sobol, Columbo was near naked as he reclined on a couch while "Gordon"—his elegant, "sepian" valet—coaxed the crooner to relax, close his eyes and not think about having to face the cooing crowd. Columbo took a few deep breaths and reflected:

> *Gee Louie... Can you imagine this? Remember when I came into town five or six months ago, broke? I can't believe it and now my mother and father are coming Sunday from the Coast and wait'll they see the house I've leased for them. And I wanted to be a prize fighter once.*[14]

NEW YORK
2¢ EVENING GRAPHIC

IN CITY LIMITS
3e ELSEWHERE

Vol. 8. No. 2245. NEW YORK, MONDAY, JANUARY 4, 1932 Fair Today

SEVEN STAR
**NIGHT
FINAL**

JAP ATTACK ANGERS U. S., PUNISHMENT IS DEMANDED

TREASURY REPORT ON PAGE 2 ——————————————————————————— STORY ON PAGE 2

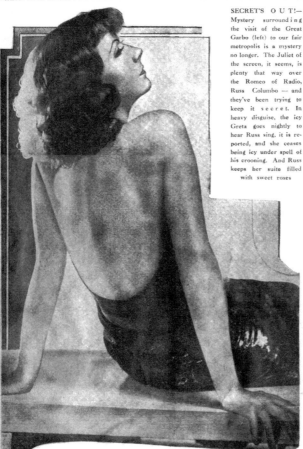

SECRET'S O U T!— Mystery surrounding the visit of the Great Garbo (left) to our fair metropolis is a mystery no longer. The Juliet of the screen, it seems, is plenty that way over the Romeo of Radio, Russ Columbo — and they've been trying to keep it secret. In heavy disguise, the icy Greta goes nightly to hear Russ sing, it is reported, and she ceases being icy under spell of his crooning. And Russ keeps her suite filled with sweet roses

"DEVIL-DOG'S" BRIDE-TO-BE, Ethel Peters Butler, daughter of the fire-eating former marine chief, Gen. Smedley D. Butler, is to marry Lieut. John Wehle, also a marine. Romance at Quantico, Va., brought about engagement announced today

GRAND HOTELS

Greta Garbo, Greta Garbo!
Have you fallen, too,
Just like other silly girls,
For Russ's gentle moo?

Russ Columbo, Russ Columbo!
'Neath your swarthy skin
Do you blush while on the air
'Cause Greta's tuning in?

Romeo of Radio, and
Juliet of Screen!
What a perfect match, me
   lads—
A Crooner and a Queen!

—Nick Kenny, New York *Daily Mirror*, January 4th, 1932

The New Year held promise for Russ Columbo as Victor Records proclaimed him its "Disc Leader" of 1931. For the duration of his Empire Room engagements, he moved from his Beresford residence at Central Park West to a luxurious Waldorf-Astoria suite. He had his scheduled recordings, his daily Paramount shows, and his Listerine programs, but still aspired to write the Great American Operetta. Yet every wave of solace had undercurrents of doubt. Ed Sullivan alluded to this in his *Evening Graphic* column when describing a circulating holiday greeting card that depicted Columbo "gazing sorrowfully at the roofs of the city." [1]

Ideally, Columbo should have felt unadulterated joy on his upward spiral, but his sense of alienation grew in direct proportion to his success. He looked forward to his parents visiting him soon and longed to go to the movies again with Sally Blane. He would even call up hysterical memories of Pola Negri. Most of all, Columbo yearned to see the man with the photo-probing eyes. "You know, Lansing Brown is a great lover of music," he would later tell an interviewer:

> When I first met him, I was all wrapped up in my violin. He would listen to me, praise me, and encourage me. And after I took up singing, I could not have gone on during some of the difficult times without his encouragement. We telephoned every day. When I was in New York sometimes, the telephone bills would reach a hundred dollars. Whenever I was worried about anything back there, I would wish that Lansa was with me to set things right. [2]

In Lansing's stead, Conrad tried being the void filler and mood leveler. Columbo called him "Pontoon"—a pet name Conrad probably earned by buoying his client out of troubled waters. "If you have faith," Conrad once offered as unsolicited advice to a reporter, "nothing reasonable in this world is denied you. You can have almost anything. You've gotta have faith, that's all." [3] Though his publicity stunts were an almost weekly affair, Conrad pushed his faith-testing limits after getting word that a major motion picture star was in town under the alias: "Miss Gustafsen."

Greta Garbo craved a rest cure when booking herself into the luxurious St. Moritz Hotel. With MGM casting her in movie after movie, she found the exotic scripts, splendid costumes and stately co-stars an insufficient fix for her emotional binges. Soon the world would see her whimper her famous "I want to be alone" in *Grand Hotel*—an inspiration for misanthropic fans otherwise reconciled to being drones in the swarm. These ticket-buying vassals accepted her aloofness and did not even mind collectively footing the bill as she took refuge in the ever-fresh faces and linens of grand hotels around the world.

Garbo's respite was short lived when it came time to promote her new film *Mata Hari*. Oddly enough, Pola Negri had anticipated taking this role as her RKO talkie premiere, but MGM wrested away the rights to this prized story about the real life spy of World War I. While Garbo portrayed the treacherous temptress, an insufficiently animated Ramon Novarro played Russian Lieutenant Alexis Rosanoff, her duped lover. MGM's publicity department, intuiting the public's desire to blur film with fact, spread news of a star-crossed romance between the two leads. "Greta

Garbo is my ideal woman," the exceedingly polite Novarro stated publicly, "but I shall never marry." [4]

By the time *Mata Hari* opened at New York's Capitol Theater, critical reaction was very mixed. The film came across as flat. The elaborate scenery seemed to drain passion from the players. Garbo went through her campy motions as Novarro made perfunctory gestures of reciprocity. With two of MGM's biggest headliners, an immortal story, elaborate wardrobe, chewable scenery, and chiaroscuro lighting, *Mata Hari's* absence of screen chemistry became a great fluke of early talkie history that nonetheless pulled in a box office windfall.

An equally contrived romance would soon eclipse the Garbo-Novarro charade. According to various, sometimes conflicting, accounts from Sam Coslow, Jerry Wald, Walter Winchell, and Columbo himself, Conrad threw an evening press party at the Waldorf's assembly suite on Monday, December 28th. The bash was supposed to be atonement for the Waldorf's lackluster media reception on Columbo's opening night two weeks previous. Conrad's real motive, however, was to plant a thought virus into the heads of the Gotham scribes, wheedling them into believing that the Swedish Sphinx really came to New York to be near her Italian troubadour.

The gaggle included folks like Coslow, Rocco Vocco, Agnes Ayres, Fifi D'Orsay, bandleader Abe Lyman, stage actor William Boyd, and, of course, Columbo's publicity honchos Harry Sobol and Paul Yawitz. As everyone consumed dishes of gossip and hors d'oeuvres, the telephone blared through the chatter. Conrad waited for three rings so that everyone could focus on him lifting the receiver and muttering pregnant replies: "Miss Gustafsen?" "The St. Moritz?" "Suite 2231?" "Mr. Columbo?" "Yes, he's here." "Oh?" "Well, I'll pass it along to him..."

The savvy schmoozers in the room knew that Garbo's birth name was Gustafsen. And in case there was any doubt, Coslow (still a St. Moritz resident) chimed in on cue to inform everyone that he lived just a few doors down from the screen diva's suite. Instead of suspecting subterfuge, most of those present entertained the more outlandish assumption that Conrad was on the up and up.

Winchell, supposedly in on the joke, acted as the pied piper of press hawks in his "On Broadway" column: "Ramon Navarro [sic], who Wasn't Acting in Their Newest Moom-Pitcher, at all!—now has Russ Columbo in his hair—GG sending Russ a mess of pashograms... 'Dun't misonderstend, cuss we unly goot frands'—Oh sure!" [5]

On Monday, January 4th, the *Evening Graphic's* front-page headline read: "Greta Garbo, Columbo Cooing." Beside her picture, a caption claimed:

"In heavy disguise, the icy Greta goes nightly to hear Russ sing, it is reported, and she ceases being icy under spell of his crooning. And Russ keeps her suite filled with sweet roses." Celebrity eclipsing world politics, the large photo of a reclining Garbo upstaged news of the recent Japanese military incursion into Manchuria.

Reporters, when not clawing into the St. Moritz lobby for a Garbo glimpse, were cramming into Columbo's Paramount dressing room, taking photos and demanding answers. Dazed, he stepped away to phone one of his press agents, returned with a twinkle in his eye and proclaimed: "Gentlemen, have a glass of wine, I have nothing to say! I refuse to comment on the entire matter. Best for myself and Miss Garbo, I think it wise to refer you to her." [6] Columbo's knowledge of (or complicity in) the Garbo hoax ultimately remains a mystery. He could have, as he claimed, been innocent of the scheme or, as others suspected, endorsed the ruse with one eye closed.

According to Coslow, Columbo got so inundated with phone calls that he finally snapped at one reporter: "'What the hell kind of a cad do you think I am? If the lady told you she has nothing to say, what makes you think you'll get anything out of me? Did it ever occur to you that people have a right to privacy?' Then he hung up quickly." [7]

Columbo was defensive, Garbo was silent, and the story mutated into curlicues. One version had Conrad hiring an anonymous blonde to impersonate Garbo and send phony telegrams to Columbo signed "G.G." Jerry Wald claimed that Conrad journeyed to a Park Avenue florist to send Garbo a hefty basket of roses with the note: "To Greta—I'm sorry they are bothering you. Hope this makes up for it. Russ." In another account, Conrad maximized the theatrics by taking measurements of the St. Moritz lobby elevator beforehand to assure that the basket was too wide to fit through the door.

Ed Sullivan typed out the rejoinder: "Chalk up another for burlesque humor… they're advertising Bing Lipschitz from *Columbo*, Ohio." [8] Dorothy Kilgallen surmised in her column that "Garbo must have liked the nationwide publicity—she never denied it." [9] Garbo continued to stave off interviewers, donning goggles and black hats while sometimes going by the name of "Gussie Berger." But Sam Coslow, a fly on the wall through much of this episode, recalled that even a seasoned recluse like Garbo could not escape the connivances of an *Evening Graphic* reporter who held a vigil outside her hotel entrance. One night, when she emerged from a taxi, he finally got the chance to pelt her with questions. She retorted: "I have *absolutely nothing* to say! Please go away!" [10]

On January 6th, Winchell came clean in the *Daily Mirror*:

> *Now poor Russ Columbo is the bait... His pals promoted a gal with a Swedish dialect to keep phoning him... She told Russ: 'I luff you so motch, I Garbo. Don't told nobody—I vuss by you place vare you sink and vuss so trilled!'...And spurious pash notes were sent to Russ signed 'Greta'... He spent a young fortune on posies for her... And some papers went for it, too; so Columbo lost nothing but his dignity.* [11]

Jerry Wald gave the *Evening Graphic* an even more jaundiced perspective:

> *Little Russy and Greta Garbo. I wonder how that all came about? You see, Russ always told me that he couldn't fall for a girl with big feet. And did you ever get a peek at La Garbo's pedal extremities? Puh-leeze... Now then, putting two and two together and making five, Mr. Columbo's press agents, the Messrs. Yawitz and Sobol, for a total expenditure of less than $250, got the said Columbo about $10,000 worth of grand publicity.* [12]

One night, Nick Kenny was strolling down Broadway when he ran into Jean Malin, an entertainer he described in his column as a "female impersonator." "DID YOU fall for the Garbo–Columbo stuff, Nickie?" Malin blurted. "Shame on you! Greta can't see Columbo. She was out with ME Sunday night! Russ must have sent himself those passionate telegrams signed G.G." [13]

As poetasters and songwriters celebrated the tabloid tryst with cute commemorations, other rumormongers still insisted that Garbo was traveling incognito to the Waldorf to watch her adorable crooner at work. But her only other reported encounter with Columbo occurred years before at the Pyramid Café. There, she returned his friendly glance with a chilly Nordic glare.

On January 14th, Columbo celebrated his twenty-fourth birthday with publicity poses at the Brooklyn Paramount. He stood in the lobby to greet the twenty lucky girls who wrote the best letters explaining in fifty words why Radio's Romeo was such a favorite with Brooklyn audiences. The frosting tasted bittersweet as the brooding baritone cut into his humongous cake, chatted with the breathy contest winners, and escorted them to their theater seats. After his romance with the MGM queen proved too perfect to be factual, this new round of adolescent adulation must have triggered an empty feeling. Only in Hollywood's most monstrously heightened reality would the woman notorious for wanting "to be alone" fall in love with the man bedeviled by loneliness.

Radio Guide

An ILLUSTRATED WEEKLY *of* PROGRAMS *and* PERSONALITIES

Vol. 1. No. 6   New York, December 5th, 1931   5 Cents

RADIO'S VALENTINO
RUSS COLUMBO NOW FIRST IN HEARTS OF WOMEN FANS

A success story from the pen of an Horatio Alger or a fanciful tale from the brilliant mind of a Hans Christian Andersen could well use as the hero the glamorous figure of Russ Columbo, the youth whose melodious baritone voice has catapulted him to the very top of the radio heap.

Russ
Columbo

* An eager brown-eyed lad of twenty-three, Columbo rides in the circle of success with the sheer joy and bewilderment of an urchin who has snatched the elusive brass ring on a merry-go-round ride.

But lo! The brass ring is not of brass. It is solid gold, encrusted with priceless diamonds. Russ Columbo, three short months ago an obscure singer and musician on the west coast, is today traveling up a path at whose end is the end of the Rainbow.

The reason? Genius and a splendid voice are undoubtedly his; a handsome physique and a winning personality are also undeniably his; and coupled with all this he has a native shrewd intelligence and real ambition.

But all this, strange as it may seem, was not nearly enough to bring him to the top. Something more was needed.

something most important. Good management! This meant the right presentation, the right approach to the right people, and ballyhoo! That latter, proper ballyhoo, is so very, very important. And Con Conrad, the famous song writer, was the answer to that problem.

But now we're a bit ahead of our story. Let us travel down the "memory lane" of Russ's start and growth and get really acquainted with him.

Russ was the twelfth son of a twelfth son. He maintains he is free of superstition, but we know he wouldn't trade that twelfth-son-of-a-twelfth-son birthright for all the glory in the world.

The name he was given sounds like a beautiful sequence of musical notes Ruggiero Eugenio Di Rudolpho Columbo. But he wasn't yet three years

Pola
Negri

Pola Negri's favor helped to shape Columbo's Destiny.

old when his playmates on the streets of San Francisco shortened that imposing symphony to plain "Russ". Innately, Columbo resents the coldness of the "Russ" diminutive and cherishes the memory of his full name as one might a lost bit of lyrical beauty.

Russ wasn't yet seven when a German violinist, John Czech, was hired to give him lessons. He proved an excellent pupil and (*Turn to page 9*)

ROMEO ROULETTE

The rise of Russ Columbo to radio fame reads like a fairy tale; a product of dreams which the most imaginative of dreamers would find hard to eclipse. [1]

—*Jersey Journal*, April 22, 1932

"Radio Romeo" was not a label Russ Columbo accepted with ease. Though a compliment, the tag implied self-defeat. When the time came for age to follow beauty, Rudy Vallee could always fall back on being the gangly life of the party; Bing Crosby always had his affable plainness; and Dick Powell, when no longer convincing as the boy next door, eventually traded his pixie smile for a middle-aged *film noir* scowl. But Columbo was already planning ahead for the day he too became another of Father Time's withered orphans. He knew that he had to survive more as a voice than an image.

The mantle of "crooner" posed an even bigger problem since it threatened to relegate his craft to a perishable fad. "No, I am not a crooner," he would say, "but instead a singer of soft music." He would sometimes resort to musicology's stodgy lingo: "I have a lot of trouble defining it. I'm not a crooner, or a blues singer or a straight baritone. I've tried to make my phrasing different, and I take a lot of liberty with the music. One of the things they seem to like best is the voice obbligato on repeat choruses—very much as I used to do them on the violin." [2]

Columbo was ever elusive about self-definition, but a 1932 Eveready Raytheon pamphlet entitled *The Eveready Book of Radio Stars* came to his aid. It described him as "tall, dark and handsome, 24 and single. His hobby is opera. In his private collection has every operatic work ever recorded." This bio-line was almost cryptically terse, but it underscored Columbo's important musical merit, particularly the affiliation with opera he had nurtured from the classical lessons of his boyhood.

One of Columbo's possessions, uncovered years later, may illuminate his earnest vocal pursuits—a book entitled *Caruso's Method of Voice Production: The Scientific Culture of the Voice*. The author, Professor Mario Marafioti, was an opera scholar and physician who would later become one of Columbo's voice instructors. Columbo could only mystify interviewers when stating that he simply "takes a song and reads it musically into the hearts of listeners," but Marafioti was better at articulating one of the Vocal Valentino's important features.

Marafioti impressed upon his readers "the belief that, from the physiological and phonological standpoint in voice production ... Italian is the most melodious and adaptable language for singing..." [3] Columbo likewise had a knack for combining wholesome American English with the deep, resonant and warm vowel inflections more congenial to what music historians loosely call "bel canto" singing.

Enrico Caruso would have belted it out over and beyond the rafters, but Columbo sings "You're My Everything," the second of two Victor sides recorded on January 12th, with the smooth and sad delicacy of an ultra-soft aria. The melody, typical of many Harry Warren compositions, was written to be infectiously light-hearted. Columbo ignored such sheet music specifications by pondering more slowly over its theme of love and self-effacement.

With a style that is simultaneously listless and passionate, Columbo makes a believable pitch to his honeyed ideal on lines like, "You're my only dream, my only real reality/ You're my ideal of a perfect personality." Other less dedicated singers might make Mort Dixon and Joe Young's lyrics sound like a Hallmark card, but with Columbo the lines are utterly believable, especially when he pushes his diaphragm a little harder for the closing phrase, "You're my winter, summer, spring—my everything." As usual, fans expressed sympathetic pains by buying enough copies of "You're My Everything" to send it to *Billboard*'s blessed #12 spot.

Columbo began the Victor session that same day with another imminent hit—the more directly autobiographical "Just Friends." Only gauzy violins could heal the hurt revealed in phrases like:

> Two friends,
> Drifting apart;
> Two friends,
> With one broken heart...

On "Just Friends," Columbo laments over a man's demotion from romantic to platonic, but in real life—at least in public—he sometimes took on an astonishingly blasé tone regarding the blurry distinction between being a pal and a paramour:

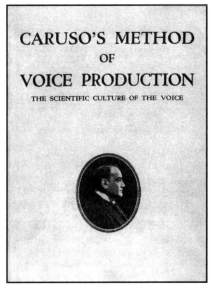

The billowy blonde alter-ego.

Columbo's personal copy.

Two friends,
Drifting apart;
Two friends,
With one broken heart. . .

As for Sally Blane, he once replied: "Sally and I have known each other for years, and I like her very much, but we weren't serious." Even Dorothy Dell, whose departure from the singer's life the press had treated as such tragedy, registered as little more than a pleasant memory blip when he declared: "Dorothy is a very sweet girl and I saw her a number of times in New York, but we weren't engaged."

As the song states, an actual romance outside of dreamtime "seems like pretending." Columbo's romantic obsessions, though instigated by real people, ultimately had no discernible face or name attached to them. He was blessed with an intelligent defense mechanism, an innate talent for casting a milky cloud over his perspective once the maw of rejection threatened to swallow his art:

We loved, we laughed, and we cried,
Then, suddenly love died—
The story ends, and we're just friends. . .

Meanwhile, Columbo's trip down the showbiz rabbit hole darkened as politics poked against his shrink-wrapped visions of art and romance. New trouble brewed on January 23, 1932, when New York's theatrical review *Zit's* blared the headline, "Russ Columbo Quits In Huff." Ever since his opening night at the Empire Room, Columbo's illusions about being the new Lord of the Waldorf ended. The Waldorf officials had already engendered bad public relations by turning away many reporters from Columbo's debut. Now, Listerine's executives decided that he was giving the Waldorf too much publicity at their expense.

Listerine accused Columbo of violating a contract that demanded he promote the mouthwash exclusively. Unless Columbo, Conrad and NBC rectified the problem, the gargantuans of gargle threatened to cancel the entire deal. As a result, whenever he made his live-at-the-Waldorf broadcasts, Radio's Romeo could only transmit the sound of his orchestra and violin, with neither a buzz from his throat nor mention of his name allowed. He once complained in song about being "only a voice on the air"; now he was the voice of love that dare not speak until the broadcast ended. Columbo had no other choice but to serve the Waldorf his letter of resignation.

Columbo's next air-castle collapsed when Paramount-Publix failed to renew his ten-week contract. So, on the day before he quit the Waldorf, he also gave his final Brooklyn Paramount show. That same month, Jerry Wald, in his "Not On The Air" column, initially claimed that "Columbo and the Paramount people are squabbling over money, with the Roxy, Palace, Earl Carroll and the rest of the producers trying to dotted-line the baritone..." [4] Then, in early February, Wald was much more forthcoming:

> *A radio outrage in its most vicious form is exemplified by the deal which landed Russ Columbo out of the Brooklyn Paramount, where for the last ten weeks he has been attracting patrons. Despite the fact that NBC's boy Russ' run at the Paramount had brought quite a huge box office return, he's not to be resigned for an additional ten weeks! And why? Here, you lucky radio audience, you, is the real reason:*

> *Columbia, rival chain of NBC, demanded his expulsion and held a whip over the Brooklyn Paramount in the form of a boycott. "Unless you refuse to resign Columbo," they were told, "we will never again permit you to use any Columbia stars on your bills." That's why Paramount wilted and the business-drawing Russ is out. Proof of the underhandedness in this deal is the fact that Columbo was willing to take a cut in his weekly pay compensation. You might call it madness, but I call it a big gyp!...* [5]

Impervious to this act of sabotage, NBC reacted to Columbo's sequence of mishaps by blaming Conrad, who now struck the network executives as a petulant boor with too many demands and an exasperating flair for contract dereliction. Conrad, in turn, saw NBC as a cadre of mental midgets concerned only with the bottom line. He was especially irate when the network knuckled under Listerine's ultimatum. Firing Columbo would have been too merciful. NBC instead reassigned him to a loathsome afternoon spot.

Conrad was indeed proving to be a capricious businessman and slippery ally. He made a significant gaffe in early February by signing Columbo for a two-week engagement at New York's downtown Academy and uptown Audubon theaters. Overconfident about the estimated audience turnout, Conrad took his chances by forfeiting any advance payment, asking only for a straight percentage based on actual ticket sales. The crowds, though decent, failed to amass enough profit. When his two weeks were over, Columbo depended on the theater owners' good graces when they gave him $2,000 out of appreciation and sympathy.

He may have been sliding as a shyster, but Conrad was useful as a stage sidekick, accompanying Columbo on piano for a new schedule of limited tours. In February, he and Columbo also participated in WOR's new "Radio Guide Hour" broadcasts. On a show that included Sophie Tucker and Barbara Stanwyck, Columbo opened as the first guest artist, backed by Merle Johnston's dance band and Conrad's trusty ivories. The show also included Radio Guide's "word-building contest." Whichever contestant assembled the most words out of the letters in the sentence "Listen to Russ Columbo" won a free round-trip winter vacation to Bermuda.

In the past, Columbo and Conrad could at least assume the roles of good and bad cop. While Columbo reacted to the stilted argot of contract law with a dreamer's distraction, Conrad made a good show of taking the brunt whenever the business end of beautiful music got ugly. He lost steam in this capacity, however, when the sorry politics behind Rusco Enterprises, Inc. finally came to light. Behind the lofty façade of its company name embossed in gold over frosted glass, Rusco proved to be a litigant's dream and a nightmare for just about everyone else.

When drawing up the contract for this merger in October of 1931, Conrad assured Columbo there was nothing underhanded about leaving Jack Gordean out. But this time, "Pontoon" carried Columbo into a typhoon. In this unfair universe, where the music of romance invariably yields to the tintinnabulation of commerce, Jack Gordean—the lovelorn lyricist who once collaborated with Columbo on songs like "(What Good

Am I) Without You?" and "Yesterday's Dreams (Of You)"—was now at a loss for poeticisms. He relied instead on the written injunction that his lawyer Jerome Wilzin filed in United States District Court against the singer and his Svengali.

Claiming it was he who originally convinced Conrad of Columbo's talents, Gordean accused both men of violating the original agreement signed in June of 1931, which stipulated that he and Conrad would get 49% of Columbo's stock, Columbo would get the other 49%, and the remaining 2% would be allotted to Gordean's father. Along with Rusco, the suit's co-defendants included NBC, the Lambert Pharmaceutical Company that sponsored the Listerine program, the Paramount-Publix Corporation, and the Skouras Theaters Corporation—all of which were involved in brokering apparently illegal Columbo performances that never earned Gordean a penny. [6] Gordean demanded an audit of the singer's earnings and threatened to prevent any future performances if Columbo did not cough up remunerations.

Even in the face of a Federal Court, Columbo and Conrad availed themselves to journalism's ink. *Daily Mirror* columnist Lee Mortimer summarized the controversy: "Russ' personal press department made capital out of the prospect of packing the musty courtroom with female admirers of the romantic singer..." Mortimer also detailed a subsequent interview with Columbo, who was "clad in silk robe and pajamas, received reporters and explained to them that Gordean had been an employee of Conrad and that when Conrad decided to branch out into a new business he had used Gordean's name as a dummy." [7]

Conrad in the interim contrived his own explanation for the *Evening Graphic*: "Gordean had been working for me in Hollywood. While I was here in New York, I got very unfavorable reports on his conduct in Hollywood so I discharged him. I never heard any more about him till this suit was started." [8]

Up to this point, Conrad, despite all of his clumsy chicanery, had a loyal friend in Columbo. "Pontoon" returned that loyalty in curious ways, at least in one case with a back-handed accolade. "He's just a slob ballad singer," Conrad blurted out to the *World-Telegram* when asked to explain his Trilby's appeal. "But dames write poems about him." [9]

Along with Gordean, another specter from Columbo's past soon materialized. Pola Negri, now embroiled in a court settlement of her own with former husband Prince Serge Mdivani, had already arrived in New York toward the end of January for the opening of her new RKO picture *A Woman Commands*. Facing the newspaper cameras with an ashy face and half-hearted smile, she was obviously recovering from an illness. One reporter described her as "a shadow of her former self."[10] But there she was—a raven impersonating a phoenix—re-emerging from the ashes and ready to bellow out: "Nevermore!"

Destiny played tricks two weeks from the time the "Queen of Tragedy" arrived. Word was out by mid-February that Russ Columbo and Pola Negri would soon appear together on the same stage for a vaudeville-style revue at Newark's Shubert Theater. The event was scheduled for a premiere on February 22nd. Comic and showbiz *mensch* George Jessel would be Master of Ceremonies to a roster that included Burns and Allen, Follies singer Marion Eddy, and the Albertina Rasch Dancing Stars. Advertisements for this "George Jessel Variety Revue" dubbed it "The Most Brilliant Stage Show Ever Given in Newark at These Bargain Prices."

The February 18th edition of the *Newark Evening News* announced Columbo's anticipated appearance, stating: "If those among radio audiences who find his work as delectable as that of Rudy Vallee and some of the other favorites specializing in crooning are as curious about his personality as they were about Rudy... there is likely to be a scramble for seats at the Shubert." [11]

As February 22nd neared, the Newark ads inexplicably replaced Columbo's name with that of actor-singer Dennis King. Fans soon confronted the harrowing fact that Columbo was a no-show. Was it simply the result of a schedule conflict? A sudden attack of the flu or a tension headache? A phobia of Newark? Or did he realize the conniption he might have during a public reunion with that Polish tiger tamer—that matriarchal vixen who left a cursed ring on his finger?

Negri, eager to make her stage debut on the east coast, remained on the bill. Even though she crowed to one reporter of her plans to cultivate a third husband (a Chicago millionaire who would be, in her words, "someone on whom I can lean"), [12] there was something about her opening night performance at the Shubert that cried out for help. "Miss Pola Negri exhibits herself as a tragedienne in a brief sketch that is remarkably done," wrote a critic for the *Newark Star-Eagle*. "Miss Negri speaks and sings of love and its inevitable bitter aftermath with all her vivid personality and feeling." [13]

Columbo soon had little time to brood over misguided reunions. As March approached, he was about to end his thirteen-week obligation to Listerine. This time, he did not need Conrad to goad him into rebellion. When Listerine mulishly adhered to a contract clause forbidding him to appear on any other radio shows, Columbo dared them by going into

song during an appearance originally planned as just a radio interview. Listerine was history. Besides, he never liked being crammed into NBC's afternoon slot.

On March 8th, *Variety* reported on Columbo's change of fortune: "From nothing to over $5,000 a week and back to almost nothing in six months is the rise and drop of Russ Columbo, whom the NBC and other radio authorities hold up as an example of what management can do to make and break down a radio personality."[14] He tried to change course on March 12th when starting an engagement at the RKO Palace Theater—a regimen that, like the Paramount, required four shows per day. Columbo joined emcees Jack Haley and Benny Rubin, along with musical acts by Tess "Aunt Jemima" Gardella and crooner Will Osborne.

After the Palace held him over for an extra week, Columbo earned enough new clout to arouse NBC's interest once again for another regular program. But he already made travel plans to head down to Baltimore for an engagement at Keith's Theater, where he would share the spotlight with crooner trailblazer Vaughn De Leath. Accompanied by Bob Iula's "twenty-piece orchestra" and a hookup via Baltimore's favorite station WFBR, Columbo coasted through a week of afternoon shows that NBC agreed to broadcast through its nationwide system. After offering signed photos of himself to the first 1,000 "ladies" attending the performance, he treated the crowds to standards like "Dancing On The Ceiling" as well as a medley of the songs that made him famous. One critic for the *Baltimore Post* observed: "Columbo, different from the usual run of 'mike' personalities, is as pleasing to the eye as to the ear."[15]

When he returned to New York for another Victor session on April 6th, Columbo reported to Leonard Joy, another prominent RCA Musical Director replacing Nat Shilkret for that day. The sound remained virtually the same, with three violins and a cello lording over two mood-altering melodies. The strings, saxophones, trumpets, string bass, guitar and piano glided ever so gingerly to Columbo's charismatic time-stretches. In a mere two hours and fifteen minutes, he made two of his best recordings.

By hooligan standards, Columbo's version of "Auf Weiderseh'n, My Dear" is brazenly fey. For those keen to the Columbo mystique, however, it stands out as his most exemplary tune: sweet and boldly sentimental, saturated with a love obsession bordering on the macabre as it invites listeners to "stroll down Lovers' Lane" and through "the lonely daytime." "Auf Weiderseh'n, My Dear" perfects the long, lyrical goodbye. It suggests in strong musical metaphors the images of lovers waving to one another in a perpetual train station departure. The people come and go, leaving only tenuous connections and ghostly mementoes.

Columbo's recording of "Paradise" is another correspondence of art and life. Hollywood composer Nacio Herb Brown wrote (with Gordon Clifford) this permutation on the woebegone waltz for Pola Negri to perform in *A Woman Commands*. A rumor circulated through the years that Columbo performed it on the stage for the film's premiere, but the spirit of his heavy heart was probably all that was present that night. That same spirit hovered through the Victor studio as Columbo opened with a verse about the incubus who "comes to me as she used to do." With his listless "va-va-va-voh" trailing each opening line, he revealed once again how captivating a man can sound on a torch tune intended for a woman to sing.

On the afternoon on April 15th, Columbo throbbed soft and low as he sang "Paradise" in person at the Mastbaum Theater, located at his childhood home of Philadelphia. Following a kid hoofer, a comic acrobat

Mobbed in Philadelphia (*Philadelphia Daily News*, April 14, 1932).

duo and a singing organist impersonating Walter Winchell, Columbo started his show with the quirky misgivings he often displayed toward his surroundings, struggling with what one reviewer identified as "a recalcitrant microphone."[16] Promptly taking a solitary place in the spotlight, he crooned a velvety rendition of "I'm Sorry, Dear" before retreating from center-stage to step behind the curtain. After some fumbling and "gentle confusion," he re-emerged, looking somewhat incarcerated inside of a heart-shaped frame—a perfect lead into "Guilty."

The local press, though kind overall, was slightly critical of Columbo's clashes with audio furniture. "If you want to know what Russ is like," a reviewer for the *Philadelphia Record* observed, "all I can tell you is that he is extremely good looking, handsomely groomed, and more timid of a visible audience than of one he can't see."[17] The *Philadelphia Public Ledger* described him as "the attractive, temperamental young man, whose voice was heard in the early talkies, who always has the 'mike' at his side, who croons and makes women sigh."[18]

Columbo appeared at the Mastbaum to inaugurate the premiere of the film *Misleading Lady*, in which Claudette Colbert played a wealthy but bored socialite who aspires to be a stage star until a swashbuckling hero (Edmund Lowe) sweeps her away. This Tarzan-and-Jane tryst was a sharp contrast to

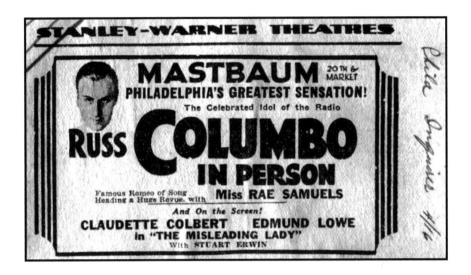

Columbo's non-encounter with Dorothy Dell. The *Philadelphia Daily News* reported that he steered clear of her after discovering she was also in town for a scheduled radio broadcast on the Fleischmann's Yeast program.[19]

For better or worse, the Philadelphia trip was a sensation. From the time Columbo disembarked from his train at Broad Street, the fanfare was splendid. A writer for the *Philadelphia Daily News* described him as: "Shy, retiring and just a little bit bewildered," especially when a "wildly gesticulating press agent, on the verge of apoplexy, grabbed him by the arm and insisted that he return to greet the station full of very insistent fluttering feminine fans and a bevy of newspaper photographers."[20]

For the first time in seventeen years, Columbo saw his brother Anthony, the one who stayed behind while the rest of the family journeyed west. Some of his best hours were also spent in a makeshift childhood during a photo-op on behalf of the Macfadden free clinic at an osteopathic hospital. He seemed a bit ill at ease holding a baby in his arms but was much more comfortable when posing with a group of slightly older youngsters whom he treated to a round of ice cream.

On the evening of April 20th, Columbo strayed from the safety of babies, brotherly reunions and ice cream junkets for some perilous fun. The festivities started at The Plantation, a Philadelphia nightclub on South Broad Street that, according to a newspaper advertisement, included Columbo for a "Celebrity Night." The Plantation had gained some notoriety since its purported operators were the Lanzetti brothers, major players in South Philadelphia's mobster ring. After an hour or two of

Ad for Columbo engagement at the Plantation Club, allegedly owned by South Philadelphia's notorious Lanzetti Brothers who bailed the crooner out of a gambling debt later that evening.

sundry salutations, Columbo left the Plantation. He and Paul Cranston (a feature writer for a local evening newspaper) slipped past the city limits to the borough of Millbourne.

They drove up Market Street, along a rather staid neighborhood highlighted by the elevated tracks for the city's "L" train, a Sears, Roebuck & Co. and an automobile showroom. Within this incessantly ordinary neighborhood stood a large but otherwise ordinary red brick house. Leaving their car, they ascended ordinary steps, knocked on an ordinary door, and received an ordinary doorman's greeting. Once inside, however, Columbo and Cranston entered a den of visually scintillating vice—a miniature Monte Carlo replete with paneled walls, Oriental rugs, festoons of champagne, spinning dice, and multi-colored chips flying like confetti from hand to hand. As society ladies in flowing gowns ogled high rollers in dapper evening jackets, an almost hallucinatory trail of platinum-topped chorines belted out the latest Tin Pan Alley ditties.

Euphemistically called the Quaker Outing Club, this exclusive gambling resort (said to be run by another cadre of thugs called the Duffy Gang) was infamous for luring prominent Philadelphians, fattening them up with drinks and slimming down their wallets with games of chance. Columbo and Cranston were not immune to such a seduction. They went to the second floor, where the gaming took place, walked past a velvet curtain and traversed a parallel world where a rock-faced croupier directed Columbo's gaze into the hypnotic gyrations of a roulette wheel.

Russ Columbo Has Bodyguard As Gamblers Nick Him for Alleged $11,000 Dice Loss

Russ Columbo dropped $11,000 to a local gambling syndicate during the last several days, with the  result that his stay in Philadelphia was marked by the presence of a heavily armed bodyguard.

That was revealed today as detectives took in several suspects for questioning, among whom

Russ Columbo were reputed to be the Lanzetti boys, Tio and Ignatius.

Tio Lanzetti   I. Lanzetti

From *Philadelphia Daily News,* April 22, 1932.

As in love, Columbo proved an equal glutton for punishment when playing the numbers. The wheel spit his every unlucky bid back at him. This non-reciprocal courtship with centrifugal forces continued until approximately 3 a.m. after he squandered $11,000—cash he did not have in hand. The club's on-site proprietors, more generous with libations than with credit, forbade both him and Cranston to leave the premises without making concrete payment plans.

Columbo managed to contact Ignatius and Tio Lanzetti, two of the crime family's five brothers, with whom he had likely chatted at the Plantation a few hours beforehand. They came to the club, fronted the money and vouched for Russ. Everyone should have been out of harm's way, but Cranston, the quiet bystander, was now thinking about the story he had planned all along about Philadelphia's gangsters. The Quaker Outing Club mishap would now be its centerpiece.

On the night after the crooner met the crooks, Cranston received an invitation to visit Columbo's Mastbaum Theater dressing room. He got there to find Ignatius and Tio waiting instead. The Lanzettis threatened to take him for the proverbial "ride" if he wrote his story. They then drove him over to a room in the downtown district where they questioned him until approximately 2 a.m. Meanwhile, some of Cranston's friends, already wary that the Lanzettis might be planning sabotage, notified the police. When Ignatius and Tio chauffeured Cranston back to his office intact, several detectives were already there to arrest them for making threats with intent to do bodily harm.

The Lanzettis, adept at outsmarting authorities, had a short custody. With all charges against them ruled insufficient, they signed their own $500 bail bond. Columbo nevertheless felt compelled to spend the remaining hours of his Philadelphia visit with armed bodyguards. Oddly enough, the casino erased its own existence before the state police could investigate any further. With all traces of the high-rolling revels gone, the Millbourne authorities denied there had ever been any prior complaints about any alleged player's paradise.

By the time the Millbourne affair became a front-page story in the April 22nd edition of the *Philadelphia Daily News*,[21] Columbo had already escaped to the relative calm of Jersey City. Upon arriving in Journal Square, he was greeted by the dulcet tones of the Potterton Choristers, an organization of child singers assembled to celebrate the crooner's one-week engagement at the local Stanley Theater. While there, Columbo confessed to a reporter his preoccupation with numerology, particularly the number "twelve." He claimed that, besides being the twelfth child of a twelfth child, he had met Conrad on June 12th (an arguably willful act of dyslexia since it was really on the 21st), was signed to NBC twelve weeks later, and was earning $1,200 a day for twelve weeks while piling up 1,200 daily fan letters.[22] Cold numbers, however, were not the focus when another infatuated critic saw the Stanley show's opening night and wrote in the *Jersey Journal*: "Russ Columbo is the cynosure of eyes."[23]

VERRA' IN PERSONA
L'Idolo di Ogni Italo-Americano

RUGGERIO EUGENIO di RODOLPHO COLUMBO
Da Millioni Conosciuto In Arte Come

RUSS COLUMBO

Il Romeo Della Canzone Alla Radio Per La Prima Ed Ultima Volta,
Apparira' Sul Palco Scenico Dei Warner Bros.

STANLEY THEATRE Journal Square Jersey City

SARA' IL PRIMO AD APPARIRE SUL PALCO

PER UNA SOLA SETTIMANA a cominciare da

VENERDI' 22 APRILE

Martedi 26 Aprile - - Serata Italiano

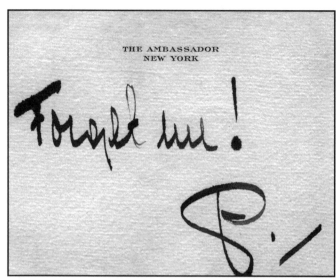

THE AMBASSADOR
NEW YORK

Forgive me!

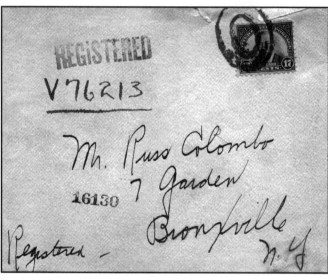

REGISTERED

V 76213

16130

M. Russ Colombo
7 Garden
Bronxville
N. Y

Registered —

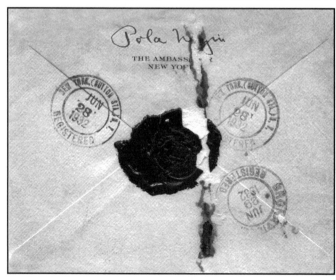

Pola Negri

THE AMBASSADOR
NEW YORK

TEARS
WITHOUT
MEASURE

Remember me as half lover and half mother.[1]

—Pola Negri, from *A Woman of the World*

"Forget Me!"—Russ Columbo recoiled as he read this verbal wallop smeared in blood-red sealing wax. These were the only words Pola Negri bothered to scribble as she luxuriated in her suite at The Ambassador in New York City.

The erstwhile silent star's missive arrived as a registered letter on June 28th, 1932, just in time for the sweltering summer to feed the romantic fevers of Columbo and many others. Here, Negri demonstrated her continual flair for melodrama, even as she faced a waning career in a new era when movies needed more than faces.

"Forget Me!" The fact that she felt compelled to write it at all suggests that Columbo, though busy fending off legal demons and straddling a rough ride of a career, still found the time to pursue (some might say hound) the thought goblins from his past.

"Forget Me!" The sinister sequence of letters had supernatural contours, forming a potent, cloud-casting hex when Columbo uttered them to himself. As he imagined Negri pronouncing these crass consonants, his thought-vapors thickened into bile. He took umbrage at this harridan and her guttural command. When the untouchable Garbo talked, her vowels produced enthralling moans. In contrast, Negri's handwritten goodbye called to mind the tempo of a brassy death march.

The events leading up to Negri's rejection started back on May 5th, when Columbo embarked on an entirely new project. A talent manager named Lew Erwin had booked him for ten weeks at the Woodmansten Inn, a club in the nearby town of Pelham. This engagement would be appreciably different from all the rest since it coincided with the formation of the Russ Columbo Orchestra.

Columbo and Conrad assumed that club audiences would respond more to a band that played dance numbers as well as ballads. In the past, Columbo had to adjust to various house orchestras that rotated different arrangers and players, but this patchwork approach backfired when members of the Happy Rose Orchestra (which had backed many of his NBC shows) would not commit to the Woodmansten schedule. He needed a permanent, reliable group that could travel from booking to booking.

With its *who's-who* of future big band and jazz figures, the Russ Columbo Orchestra reflected a fertile time in the pre-Swing days. Benny Goodman was at the hub—the band's contractor, organizer and overseer. Planning out the orchestra's personnel one morning at breakfast, Goodman decided on two trumpets: Bob "Bo" Ashford and Eddie Petrovicz; a cornet: Jimmy McPartland; Leo Arnaud on trombone; a lead and second tenor saxophone: Jess Carneol and Irving "Babe" Russin, respectively; Mac Ceppos on violin; guitarist Perry Botkin; twin pianos: Joe Sullivan and Roland Wilson; Gene Krupa on drums; Goodman's brother Harry on bass; and Goodman himself on alto sax and clarinet. Besides singing, Columbo also joined in on violin and an occasional accordion.

Stylistically, the music was more rhythmic and playful, but most of the songs retained a vital melancholic core. As a live show, the Russ Columbo Orchestra may have been a crowd-pleaser, but musically the results were mixed. Here was Goodman, the eager beaver of the jumpy beat who now had to submit to Columbo's tightly structured song preferences and ballad-friendly phrasing. For Goodman, this stint as Musical Director was, of course, only a job. But sometimes when Columbo stepped off the stage to mingle with guests, the band donned imaginary antlers and wolf pelts to revel in that musical equivalent to fraternal flatulence commonly known as "hot improvisation." If sour testosterone had a sound, it filled the Woodmansten hall the moment Columbo turned his back and left the boys in the band to their own designs. Conrad, for one, rightly objected to Goodman's sabotage, especially when the audiences got too restless to concentrate on the ballads. The band could never get loose enough, however, for the fidgety drummer. Krupa reportedly scoffed at Goodman for forcing him to play only the brushes.

John Hammond, the future mogul of Columbia Records, attended one of the Woodmansten shows and shared his views in his autobiography: "Columbo's band was a commercial group, the kind which plays the latest tunes for dancing in a corny, unimaginative style."[2] Being that what is "corny" to one can be "gratifying" to another, Hammond, like any dedicated music critic, aired his biases out in the open. A distant relative

Russ in his bandleader best.

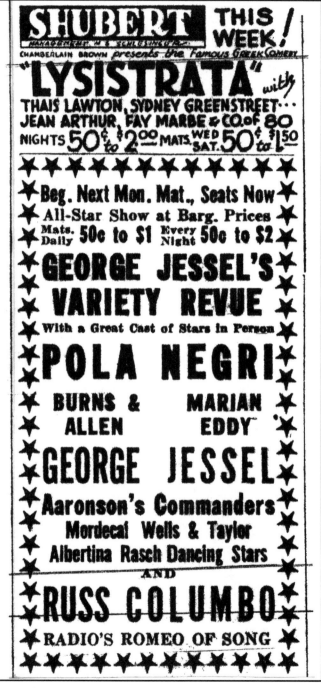

On February 17, 1932, this ad appeared in the *Newark Star-Eagle*. Columbo had mysteriously cancelled his appearance just days before the show's premiere.

of Cornelius Vanderbilt, Hammond was the pampered offspring of northeastern wealth who eventually flouted his social register status, dropped out of Yale, and atoned for his privilege by embracing the jazz rebellion and all of the wild-man weekends he fancied it represented.

Hammond became a jazz correspondent and champion, tooting his horn in favor of swing and against the sweet, "commercial" music that, through the decades and despite all the browbeating by the Hammonds of the world, continued to inform mainstream tastes. Failing to swing to a footloose goosestep, many a dance band risked being branded—in Hammond's words—"smooth and soporific."[3] Any romantic balladeer committed to his craft, on the other hand, would wisely invert Hammond's dismissal as a badge of honor. Not inclined to take urban jazz or rural bluegrass all that seriously, Columbo maintained a starry-eyed edge even when his band sounded choppy and grating. If anything, the problem with Columbo's Goodman-led group was that it often did not sound "smooth and soporific" enough!

Despite bits of political strife among its players, the Russ Columbo Orchestra drew comely Woodmansten crowds. Second-hand observer Jerry Wald assumed a dreamlike tone when writing about one particular celebrity gala. Columbo and his band enjoyed the limelight amid a human backdrop that included banjo-eyed Eddie Cantor; beloved torch singer Ruth Etting; comedian Bert Lahr; and the irreplaceable Royal Canadians, Guy and Carmen Lombardo.

What a shame that, in the midst of such revels, Columbo had to contend with the dreary shades of yesterday. He just happened to be singing "Prisoner Of Love" when he eyed Dorothy Dell in the arms of none other than heavyweight-turned-partygoer Jack Dempsey. Suddenly, the loving fans, fine clothes and other ego-boosters did not suffice. "Friends who were there have told me that Russ' face turned white when he saw Dorothy," Wald recalled. "Nor will they soon forget his voice as he sang that night. Dorothy and Jack danced by his place as he led the band."[4]

Dell soon vanished into the murky background, only for Pola Negri to loom in her place days later. While visiting some friends in the town of Larchmont, she felt galvanized by the sound of a familiar crooner being transmitted live through the radio from the Pelham club. Once getting word of the show's origins, she insisted on taking a little excursion to track down the same "Roosie" who failed to join her on the Newark stage a few months before. Once there, Negri initially reacted like an explorer baffled by her find. Columbo, who recognized her immediately, jogged her memory by holding up the hand that bore the opal Valentino ring. He still may have thought it a good luck charm, but the ring was more like a symbolic black force drawing bad energy.

They may have impressed passersby and reporters with star-crossed couple poses, but Negri—for reasons likely to remain a mystery—turned out to be Columbo's negative inspiration. Her written rebuff would be one more warning that Columbo was destined to be an emotional nomad lost in a crowd on a street of dreams. He had already anticipated Negri's "Forget Me" note twelve days before it arrived, enlightened by a Western Union preamble dated June 13th:

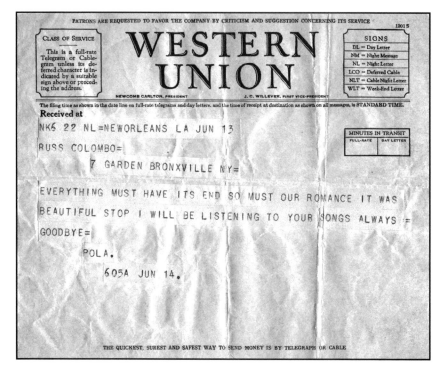

The message still reeled in his synapses three days later when he started recording his Victor 24000 series. These songs illustrated a hypnotically lonely voice trying to peacefully co-exist with restless players. Like the Woodmansten orchestra, this studio incarnation offered what was essentially pre-swing swing. In many ways, the arrangements lacked the subtlety, understatement and melancholy conviction of the Shilkret and Joy sessions, but Columbo's vocalese showed more muscle as he held his notes longer and put more force into some of his closing lines.

Since Victor's surviving session logs fail to list actual musical personnel, the likelihood that they included Benny Goodman, Jimmy McPartland, Gene Krupa and other members of the official Russ

Columbo Orchestra from the Woodmansten shows remains pure speculation. But there is little doubt that all eleven songs capture the dance band's sound and spirit—with two violins, two pianos, three saxophones, two trumpets, a trombone, a string bass, occasional chimes, and a "trapman" on percussion.

The first entry, "Just Another Dream Of You," is among the best of the lot. With a strict but tender waltz tempo suggesting a picturesque carousel ride, the music comes very close to Guy Lombardo and His Royal Canadians. Cushioned by sweet trumpets, violins and chimes, Columbo pays tribute to the older crooner style, gliding from high baritone to a higher Nick Lucas-style lilt. He also indulges this lovelorn lullaby with perfect pitch as he pines over "lovers in the moonlight" and "teardrops when we parted, leaving me alone and blue."

After his "Fox Trot" version of "I Wanna Be Loved" (rejected and apparently lost forever), Columbo caps the session with John W. Green's "Living In Dreams." Even though much of the recording has a blithe and brassy background, Columbo survives the impish rhythm and wiry piano solo. His wistful mood comes through with the brief but ornate appearance of twin pianos, along with verbal flourishes like:

> For all these years
> I cried out my heart
> In tears without measure,
> But with you to treasure,
> I'm living in dreams. . .

The Victor 24000 recordings started coming out just as the Woodmansten Inn's owners cuffed Columbo with a salary reduction and warned him of diminishing patrons. To compound this, disc sales for recording artists in general plummeted along with vaudeville bookings. Even Atlantic City's famed Steel Pier—one of Columbo's childhood haunts—was having financial woes. There was at least one stimulus to offset the drab horizons: the *Daily Mirror's* Annual Radio Popularity Contest listed Columbo as #1 in the "New Crooners" category.

The Russ Columbo Orchestra ended its Woodmansten Inn engagement by the second week of July but soon began a two-month tour starting at the Atlantic seaboard and spreading into parts of the Midwest. Road life was rough with predictable personality skirmishes and musicians grumbling over money. But the public enjoyed an ensemble that stayed well-kempt and always professional.

An evening at the RKO Palace Theater in Cleveland typified their concert itinerary. Broadcast from NBC's affiliate station WTAM to a nationwide hookup, the Palace show was a sell-out success, full of what Glen C. Pullen of the *Cleveland Plain Dealer* called "unusually smooth, sweet music with muted trumpet effects." Pullen also basked in the crooner afterglow: "When Russ Columbo steps up to the Palace's amplifying microphone and starts crooning oh-so-softly about such things as love and paradise, his palpitating feminine fans in the audience seem to fall into a blissful, dreamy state of unconsciousness..."[5] This gravy boat of admiration was well earned, considering that Columbo had to share the bill with such "guess you had to be there" sensations as the trained dog act "Hector & Pals," the singing Sinclair Twins, and a movie feature called *American Madness*.

Returning to Victor on August 3rd, Columbo began with the blissful and dreamy "My Love," for which he wrote the music and words. Musically, the song fulfills its romantic duties. The chimes come in at just the right moments during a misty instrumental interlude, the violins and clarinet swirling into an "adorable" and "kissable" serenade. Columbo's voice is soft and sweet yet commands the fawning enthusiasm that Nelson Eddy would later exhibit during his screen duets with Jeanette MacDonald. Though sounding at times as if he is a bit full of himself, Russ never comes across as oily. And though the lyrics at times suggest the niceties of a romance writer's phrase book, Columbo also luxuriates in a bit of warm-hearted self-parody on lines like: "Some call it madness and blame the moon above, but she is my love."

On "As You Desire Me," he placates the frantic and giddy beat with breathless submission, crying out: "Come take me, my very soul is yours/ As you desire me, I come to you..." The song itself was one of the year's big finds since several other highly regarded singers, including Morton Downey, recorded their versions all at about the same time. Composer Allie Wrubel named "As You Desire Me" after the title of a recently released Greta Garbo movie. Though it praised the elevated themes of passion and surrender, the tune also raised the eyebrows of censors with its licentious overtones. Judging by its success, this particular version—the Russ Columbo Orchestra's highest charting song at *Billboard*'s #6—pleased a vast, romantically inclined audience.

"Lonesome Me" was another melody about misbegotten affections was co-written by Con Conrad with Andy Rasaf and the famed Thomas "Fats" Waller. In his version, Columbo overcomes the cloying beat and ingratiating horns, bonding with the song's narrator: a man hoping somehow to overcome a life of empty arms and wasted charms.

Negri's "Forget Me!" note continued to linger as a negative after-thought as Columbo closed the session with "The Lady I Love," another story of a man compelled to place poetic wreaths before the idol who abuses him. Again, the insistent but uninspired dance beat compromises the song's melodramatic impact, but in some ways Columbo's elegant and (in this case) slightly higher pitch foreshadows his future emulator Jerry Vale.

Once the first Russ Columbo Orchestra tour ended on the Labor Day weekend, Columbo appeared in his trademark white shoes and white pants for a full-page ad on the back cover of *Variety* that touted the band's success. The engagement at the RKO Palace Theater in Chicago had "heavy patronage" while the RKO Palace Theater in Cleveland had to "stop selling tickets" when the band started a "new house record." The show did "capacity business" at Boston's RKO Keith's Theater and Atlantic City's overbooked Gateway Casino had to turn away "2,000 people." On the home front at New York's Loew's Paradise Theater, the act brought in the "largest house attendance since the inauguration of Vaudeville."[6]

Columbo recorded his last four Victor sides on November 23rd, roughly a year after his Brooklyn Paramount debut. The session began in a bit of a rhythmic rut. Even Columbo's sweet "moonbeam" invocation on Victor Young's "Street Of Dreams" had little impact against the oppressively playful "one-two" arrangement. "Make Love The King" suffered from a similar brainless backbeat but had the added handicap of one-dimensional lyrics that facilitated none of Columbo's innate tension. But on "I Called To Say Goodnight" (out of which Conrad wrangled another songwriting credit), Columbo and the band were in top form. For this thoughtful ballad, adapted from the German "Gut'nacht Mein Lieb Gut'nacht" ("Goodnight My Love Goodnight"), the musicians employ the sweetening effects of kind-hearted clarinets and muted horns while Columbo implores, in a soft but subtly dark manner: "Oh, cling to me sweetheart of mine, tomorrow the sun may not shine."

Columbo ended with another Conrad co-write, an accolade to solitary brooding called "Lost In A Crowd":

> *Wandering here, wandering there,*
> *Searching for love, heaven knows where...*
> *Sweethearts pass me by,*
> *Make me wonder why,*
> *Mine has never come along...*

This time the deliberative dance rhythm is an effectively sardonic contrast to Columbo's portrayal of a gentle and sad fantasist looking in all the wrong places for a phantom lover (and possibly a mother). Clutching the microphone's electrical umbilicus, he sang this just about the time his family was busy on the other coast, transferring the remains of his brother Fiore from Hollywood's Rosedale Cemetery to the Great Mausoleum and Sanctuary of Vespers at Forest Lawn. Respecting their last-born's new stardom, the Colombos saw fit to embellish Fiore's nameplate with the "Columbo" spelling.

NOW YOU CAN PICK A HUSBAND!
FEBRUARY IS WANING! HAVE YOU CAUGHT YOUR BACHELOR?

From *Radio Guide*, February 1933.

Hannah—And New 'Heart'

Russ Columbo, popular orchestra leader and radio crooner, with Mrs. Roger Wolfe Kahn, daughter-in-law of Otto Kahn, millionaire banker, who, it is said, will be married next week when Mrs. Kahn has obtained her divorce. Mrs. Kahn is the former Hannah Williams, musical comedy actress. Pitcure from International News Photograph Service.

MY
CRUMMY
VALENTINE

I wonder... WHY Russ Columbo doesn't draw the line on those phony publicity romances and try to win out on his talent, which is plenty good!

—Nick Kenny, *Daily Mirror*, April 1933

One day, when Russ Columbo was exiting a theater with pal Sally Blane at his side, a reporter asked him if the two had planned to marry. "I guess I should have been a poker player," Columbo responded. "I must be lucky at cards, I'm so unlucky in love."[1] Sally demurred, but Hannah Williams soon held the winning hand.

Dancer, singer, socialite, aspiring dramatic actress and soon to be Columbo's warden of love, Hannah Williams may not have been a blonde, but she still had the photogenic qualifications to be the Vocal Valentino's dream date. When they met, Williams was at the height of a show business career that started when she was a youngster singing at nightclubs with her sister Dorothy.

With an evident appetite for bandleaders, Hannah was just nineteen when she married Charles Kaley, a union she had annulled by 1927. In January of 1931, she married Roger Wolfe Kahn, an on-air orchestra conductor and the son of international banker Otto Kahn. When this matrimonial magic also withered, Mrs. Hannah Williams Kahn grew desperate to trim that dangling syllable from her last name. She anticipated a speedy divorce and was soon ecstatic to find in Columbo a willing ear for her tales of spousal stress.

The circumstances leading up to Columbo's meeting with Hannah began in the last weeks of 1932. Con Conrad had finally arranged to release Columbo from his NBC contract and market him as a freelancer. He booked Russ Columbo and His Orchestra into the prestigious Park

Central Hotel, an oasis of escape in the late Twenties and home to dance orchestras led by the venerable likes of Ben Pollack. By the early Thirties, this place "Where Hollywood and Broadway Meet" adopted a tropical look and became the new "Cocoanut Grove Room." For Columbo, this may have been an unsettling reminder of leaner times, when he served as a tuxedoed lackey at L.A.'s plastic monkey prototype.

In an interview years later, Madeline Graw, who (with co-President Genevieve Fitzpatrick) started the Russ Columbo Co-Ed Club in 1931, had hinted at the Park Central's disconcerting interior while relating the breathtaking encounter with her idol: "Russ was appearing at the Park Central Hotel in Manhattan. I wrote his manager, Jack McCoy, and asked if it would be possible to meet Russ. My sister and I attended his show at the [New York] Cocoanut Grove. During a break, he came over to our table. I was so nervous! He asked how we were enjoying the show, and my sister commented that all the Cocoanut Grove needed now was some monkeys, which Russ must have misunderstood, as he gave her a funny look!"[2]

On December 9th, Columbo made his Park Central debut. Welcoming a "20 Piece Orchestra" to augment his band, he joined the stage with both Williams and the erstwhile silent star Roscoe "Fatty" Arbuckle in a cavalcade of song that ended with another rendition of "Good Night, Sweetheart." Columbo and the band followed a similar routine each evening.

While waving farewell to 1932 in style during the Park Central's New Year's Eve show, Columbo focused his attention more on Hannah. She soon reawakened all of the tell-tale symptoms of love: fluctuations in body temperature, racing heart, muscle aches, periods of elation followed by self-doubt, and a mania for writing and receiving letters. His fondest hope was that his "Sweetch" (a Jabberwocky jumble of "Sweet Witch"?), as he liked to call her, would send him adoring missives in the event that he would have to leave her side.

According to columnist Harriet Parsons, Columbo even had his nose altered to conform more to what he at least thought were Hannah's specifications. The picture-perfect couple was soon an item among New York celebrity oglers. Russ and Hannah looked so optimistic together, staring into the Pools of Narcissus sparkling in each other's eyes. Jack McCoy, another of the singer's press agents, was eager to change Columbo's confirmed bachelor status by publicly stating that a bride and groom were in the making—that is, once Hannah's divorce from Kahn got finalized in Reno.

With Hannah and her sister Dorothy Mc Partland (left), who allegedly did not approve of Russ.

Columbo was by now accustomed to having his heartstrings tug on his fraying purse strings. Tallied profits for the Park Central holiday revue showed Conrad owing Columbo over $7,500. He reluctantly accepted Conrad's promissory note but quietly ruminated over the right time to sever ties with his now flaccid Svengali. He tried to cut loose in January of 1933 with merely a verbal agreement to dissolve Rusco Enterprises, Inc. Conrad also abdicated his position as Columbo's manager.

Jerry Wald offered a fond eulogy: "Always, Con Conrad had been his brains, a leader and patron to be obeyed unswervingly. Now, groping like an inexpert child, Russ sought to get his life back to its old level. Many things interfered, among them a childish resentment at being Fate's plaything, and a false notion that he had to present the same front he had shown in his $7,000-a-week days."[3]

At this point, Columbo was back in the good graces of NBC's Artists' Service Bureau, which had re-booked him into the Brooklyn Paramount for a one-week engagement. Opening for the all-star movie *If I Had A Million*, he was reunited with his old Hollywood chum Monte Blue, who acted as emcee to acrobats, jugglers, organist Jesse Crawford and "24 Freethy Aerial Beauties." NBC then arranged for the Russ Columbo Orchestra to go on a Midwest tour.

Hannah looked forward to joining the band on its journey but ended up having to stay behind and face messy marital matters. At a time when states across the country prepared to salvage their failing financial institutions with "bank holidays," Hannah suffered her own fiscal crisis. An embittered Roger Kahn devised a brilliant way to avenge his alienated affections, clamping her spending habits by posting a newspaper notice that absolved him of any future debts she might incur.

On February 4th, Columbo and the band departed for Detroit without her, but Hannah, with pen in hand, vented her conjugal frustrations (with enhanced punctuation provided by the authors):

> February 4, 1933
> c/o Book Cadillac Hotel, Detroit, Michigan
>
> "My Darling"
> Your wire was simply grand. It made me very happy. I have been thinking of you every second since you left, have been perfectly miserable, and shall continue being so until you return.
> Dearest, what in the world am I going to do without you? I feel lost, completely lost. Nothing exciting has happened since you left. It has been raining, just the kind of weather we like honey, which only adds to my misery.
> I really cannot bear the thought of not being with you for six long weeks. Oh my darling—come on, hold me, kiss me, tell me you love me more than anything in the world. Our love is so beautiful, dearest. We can't possibly be separated for any length of time.
> It was wonderful listening to your sweet voice this evening. I was so thrilled honey. I didn't know what to say. I feel so badly about your being ill, you must take care of yourself for me. If only I were there to take care of you. Oh my darling, we could make love, heavenly love.
> Sweetheart I must close. If I write any more, I shall cry my eyes out. I miss you so it's unbearable. I'm going to bed now. I know I shall have beautiful dreams of you. Goodnight my angel. Think of me and love me—
> I shall love you XX always XX
> Hannah

Judging from the letters found among his effects, Columbo got Special Delivery dispatches of Hannah mail almost daily. He apparently responded to her written entreaties. One can only imagine his replies—worry-lines in longhand, engorged with all of the lyrical desperation he expressed in his songs. Hannah's missives—executed in a scrawl resembling bat wings—illustrated romantic rapture's light-headed yet terrified state, a mutation of body and mind that, when left unchecked, thwarts the goals of workaday adulthood and impels people into outbursts of madcap swooning. In some ways, Hannah was essentially echoing the sounds of Columbo twisting under Cupid's heel. Twenty-four hours after marinating in thoughts about her marital plight, she shared her terror of impending lunacy:

February 5, 1933
C/o Book Cadillac Hotel, Detroit, Michigan

"My Angel"
I was so thrilled to receive your beautiful letter. Words cannot express how happy it made me. Oh my darling, I do love you so, and miss you terribly. I have read your letter over and over again and love it more each time. What a grand day this has been for me. I awakened this morning to find a beautiful letter from my love, a wonderful wire, and then looking forward to speaking to you dearest. It was simply heavenly hearing your grand voice again tonight. Oh honey, when I hear you say, I love you darling, I miss you so. I want you near me every second—it just breaks my heart. I can't stand, dearest, just cannot stand it, that's all. I must be near you always. I must feel your lips. You must hold me in your arms, you must love me, love me until I can't breathe.

Sweetheart I have never felt like this in my whole life—I'm speechless, I can't think, I don't want to do anything without you darling. We must be together always, never to be separated. Darling—Darling, you must come back. The thought of your being away for six long weeks is driving me mad. What are we going to do honey? I can hardly wait to talk to you again tomorrow night. I hope and pray I receive your letter in the morning. Dearest, I can't stop raving about your beautiful letter. It really is a masterpiece. I'm going to keep it forever. Honey, it's so sweet of you to buy a frame for my photograph. I hope you won't have trouble packing it.

I'm so happy to know you are almost well. I was terribly worried about you, honey. Please be careful. Oh my darling, I do hope you like my letters. I realize they cannot compare with yours. I'm not going to worry about it dearest, being as I write what I feel and you write what you feel. We both shall be happy. I'm going to say Bye Bye for now, my angel. Think of nothing except our beautiful love.

I love you more than anything on earth.
Goodnight Dearest—
XXXXX—A million of them, love you, love you, love you, madly.
Your Sweetch

Despite these verbal hugs and kisses, Columbo endured the rigors of a Michigan winter while Hannah fueled his imagination with much darker themes. Anticipating the trauma of her upcoming divorce, she edged into another of her favorite topics, mortality:

February 6, 1933
C/o Book Cadillac Hotel, Detroit, Michigan
"Sweetheart"—

Another beautiful letter from you this morning. Oh what a glorious feeling to know you think of me every second, and a still more glorious feeling to know you love me. I know I should want to die if you didn't. I love you so madly, dearest, and I'm praying we can be together very soon. That's all I want darling. Oh honey. Your letters are so beautiful. I love every word you say. You express your thoughts so beautifully. I haven't stopped thinking of you for one second since you left. I don't want to think of anything else except our beautiful love.

I have had several offers for nightclubs in Chicago. I haven't answered any of them. I'm only interested in cleaning this mess up first. Dearest, I'm terribly sorry I haven't any news for you. Nothing exciting has happened so therefore I have nothing to tell. My Darling, I must close now as I am sleepy and must get up terribly early.

Goodnight my angel. I love you, love you, love you.
"Always"
Your Sweetch
XXXXXXXX

The Russ Columbo Orchestra basked in swank during an engagement at downtown Detroit's exclusive Two-Two Club. While grateful that fans made the effort to show up in the freezing temperatures, Columbo could not help but obsess about uniting with his lost Lenore. But Hanna, like the Raven of Poe's poem, offered scarce comfort in her letter the following day. As her insomnia mounted, her prose got more delirious:

February 7, 1933 4:30 PM
C/o Book Cadillac Hotel, Detroit, Michigan
"My Beloved"

I'm so depressed. I doubt very much whether I shall be able to write a letter. Why oh why do we have to suffer like this? I promise you darling I'm going to do something desperate if it isn't settled one way or the other. I'm a nervous wreck. Everything I eat makes me ill. I go to bed early but cannot sleep. What am I to do, dearest? If only you were here, honey. I would be a different person. I love you so, darling. I can't possibly go on another minute without you.

You mustn't be angry with me angel. I'll admit I have been stupid, but those days are over forever. I'm thinking of only myself and of course my only love. You know I adore you sweet, don't you? Remember that always and never stop loving me dearest. Oh! How I've longed to be in your arms darling. That's all I think about. I want you so, sweetheart. It's driving me insane. Darling, darling, kiss me, hold me, hurry, come on, don't be bashful. Are you my Itta-Ca-Pwetch or not? (Hurray, I can spell it.)

It's bitter cold outside. I'd love it if you were here, if we were in a little house in the country, seated by a big fireplace, oh darling, and making such grand love. Excuse me dearest; I must relax for one second. How I'd love it, more than anything in the world sweetheart. I could cry my eyes out.

Goodnight my love. I feel so miserable. I must get into bed and cry.

Maybe it will make me feel a little better. Please excuse this short letter. I can't help it honey. I just can't write another line.

All my Love and Kisses to you dearest,

Always,

Your Sweetch

XXXXXXXX

Though a mere four hours elapsed since this last dispatch, Hannah was compelled to write another. This time she tempered her anxiety by contemplating psychiatric care. With dexterity, she oozed under Columbo's skin, enticing him by expressing the same kind of amorous genuflection he moaned about in his songs. At this juncture, the Russ and Hannah correspondences seemed to get more oblique. Columbo apparently scribbled back to her about some unpleasant mishap. And in a perverse form of sympathetic magic, Hannah's emotional tailspin seemed to exacerbate the nation's bank panic:

February 7, 1933 8:00 PM
To: Book Cadillac Hotel, Detroit Michigan

Hello My Love:
You are getting entirely too smart, writing such beautiful letters. Gee honey, they make my letters seem terribly dull and uninteresting.

You stop now or I'm afraid I'll have to hit you.

Before I say another word, I want to remind you to send my music. Oh yes honey, please tell your press agent Mr. McCoy to send my trapeze. It's very important. Tell him I can't do my standing sitting standing jack knife dive without it.

Dearest, I'm afraid the next time you hear from me I shall be in a sanitarium with a nervous breakdown. Slowly but surely I am losing my mind. I'm so worried and upset. I've gotten to the point now; I don't care what happens to me. If only we were together, sweetheart, nothing else would matter. I love you, and need you so my angel, what shall I do?

Now that you have told me why I am your little Sweetch, I'm going to tell you why you are mine. You are the finest and dearest person in the world. Secondly, I couldn't possibly go on without you. Thirdly, I worship the ground you walk on and love you with all my heart. Can I possibly say more, honey?

I'm so happy you are feeling a little bit better. But darling, you must get out and get some fresh air into your lungs. You are going to need strength, because when I see you I am going to kill you with love ooh and such love darling. I can hardly wait to speak to you tonight. Your voice sounds so grand, dearest. I just want to get on a train and come to you. Here's a big kiss for you. XXXXXXXX

My Dearest, darling, honey, sweetheart, angel, ooh my love—I had a beautiful dream last night, it was heavenly—I am going to close for now—

Loads of Love and Kisses to you My Darling.

Always

Your Sweetch

XXXXXXXXXX

Burdened by the lurid image of Hannah in a straitjacket, Columbo still had to assemble the other band members for the next leg of his tour. This time, they visited the somewhat more clement climate of Kansas City for a one-week show at the Main Street Theater. Hannah kept trailing him by post, inking out self-references so veiled they probably escaped her own detection. Case in point: her lavish praise for Lionel Barrymore's performance as a mad and manipulative Russian monk—a role that, given her hypnotic way with words, she may have been able to play herself, under a fake beard:

February 10, 1933
Mr. Russ Columbo
C/o Meulbach Hotel
Kansas City, MO

My Angel:

Your letters are too beautiful. I am speechless, after reading the one I received this morning. Oh darling, you do love me and I am so happy. I have been perfectly miserable without you, sweetheart, and shall continue being so until we are together, holding each other, kissing each other, and making such beautiful love. Oh my sweet, I can't wait. I can't possibly wait six long weeks, maybe more. Oh honey, something must be done. I'm going mad, completely mad. I want to be so close to you always, my love.

Nothing exciting has happened since you left; only I have softening of the brain from working jigsaw puzzles and seeing movies. By the way, honey, if *Rasputin and the Empress* happens to be in the same town with you, do not miss it. It is an excellent film. You will be mad about Lionel, his acting is superb.

Dear Mr. Columbo: Just a line to ask you a few questions. Do you happen to know a little girl who is all alone in N.Y.C. and who loves you more than anything in the world? I think her name is Itta-Ca-pwetch, not—Anzie Panzie—Klein. My, how she adores you, and she is completely lost without you and cries like a little baby over you every night. She told me if you didn't come back soon, she is coming after you. I'm so sincere, sweetheart. I can't possibly go on like this. Kiss me darling— Kiss me and hold me closely.

Honey, honey, you'll never know how much I love you and miss you. Darling, I want you—only you. I worship you, my sweet. Goodnight. Think of me, love me, kiss me every second. Ooh honey, you must kiss me—that was heavenly—All my Love and Kisses to you

Always,

Your Sweetch

P.S. Everytime you look at my picture, please remember I am saying, love me darling, love me, do you hear me—

XXXXXX

Like the romantic hell described in a popular tune, Columbo found himself inside a zombie zone "between the devil and the deep blue sea." Hannah's words were like a Venus flytrap, clasping at his spirit and teething on his brain. After reading her garish description of sleepless nights, he too contracted insomnia:

February 11, 1933 8:30 PM
Mr. Russ Columbo
C/o Hotel Muehlebach, Kansas City, MO

"My Darling"

When you're away both night and day, remember me—honey. I heard that on the air last night and wanted to cry my eyes out. That song brings back beautiful memories. Remember how grand it was at the Park Central, being together, dining together every single night, and listening to glorious music. Oh honey it was heavenly. If only we were doing that now. I miss you so sweetheart. You must hurry back to me. I can't do anything without you.

Despite the miserable weather, this day has been a beautiful one for me. A wonderful letter and wire from my only love. I'm simply mad about your letters. Each one seems to thrill me more and more. I'm going insane sweet, absolutely insane without you. Each time you say, "hold me, kiss me darling, love me until I can't breathe, " I get chills up and down my spine. Oh my angel, we couldn't possibly live without each other. Could we?

I'm terribly worried about your not being able to sleep. Something must be done. You must see a doctor. He might be able to help you. Honey, please don't be stubborn. Go and see what can be done, because you must sleep. Dearest, you will be a nervous wreck. Please, for me.

New York is as dull as ever. Dorothy and myself went to see a mystery play last night. It was simply awful. Poorly acted, not the least bit spooky. So we had a miserable time.

Dearest, you can expect your photograph, that is, my photograph. The one you like in the bathing suit, at the end of the week. Bye Bye for now, my darling. Think of me honey as I think of you every minute of the day.

Love and Kisses,

All my love to you, my angel

Always,

Your Sweetch

Hannah's prose—with its imagery of clinging arms, hysterical sobs, and pillow-pounding fits into the wee hours—bore an uncanny likeness to the popular romance literature of the time.

One example is a tale that appeared in the January 1933 issue of *True Story* entitled "Her Secret Lure," about a female singer who serves as a ghost voice. After hearing her divine piping, a darkly virile actor—who plays the lead for a production called "The Invisible Master"—offers her the job of singing off-stage for the part of his love "Lenore" (played on-stage by his fiancée). But when the fiancée suffers a compound fracture, the girl with the golden voice wins the role and succumbs to the actor's charms on both sides of the footlights. Told as a first-person account by the singer herself, the story's style takes on a Hannah-esque flair while echoing Columbo's previous career as a voice-over:

> "*For the moment, I became the Voice itself—a Voice without flesh or body, whose very existence rode on the wings of sound. In the most dramatic parts, I worked myself into a frenzy of passion. I threw forth my storm of words; tears coursed down my face and my body was racked with the force of emotion... And when the time came for Philip to forgive the contrite Lenore, he crushed me in his arms with a fervor that was not altogether necessary. For a long, blessed moment, I lay in his arms, my heart beating so loudly that I was sure it must be heard beyond the footlights. Then he raised my face and sought my lips eagerly, hungrily, as though he had thirsted long... The night was sweet out there. Summer stars winked above and the fragrance of petunias puffed against our faces.*"[4]

Hannah's variations on love's fragrant language were as convincing for Columbo as similar stories were to faithful romance magazine subscribers. "Romances are rarely practical," so wrote *True Story*'s publisher Bernarr Macfadden. "One rushes into the hectic allurement with little or no thought of the future. The enchantment of the moment is the dominating influence."[5]

All said, even a Western Union telegram from Columbo's mortal beloved could not prevent Valentine's Day from being a lonely affair:

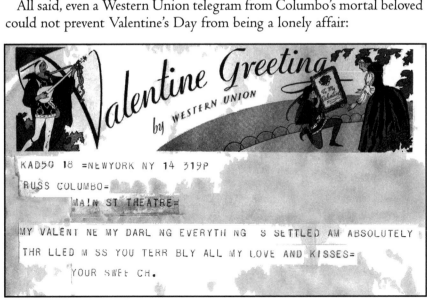

```
KAD50 18 =NEWYORK NY 14 319P
RUSS COLUMBO=
    MAIN ST THEATRE=
MY VALENTINE MY DARLING EVERYTHING IS SETTLED AM ABSOLUTELY
THRILLED MISS YOU TERRIBLY ALL MY LOVE AND KISSES=
    YOUR SWEET CH.
```

February 19th marked Hannah's momentous arrival in Reno. Columbo meanwhile had to fulfill a weekend obligation at Omaha, Nebraska's RKO Orpheum Theater. Once again, the movie following the show bore a foreboding title, this time *Man Against Woman*. Taking a redundant route, he and the band headed back to Kansas City for several days to perform at the RKO Vaudeville Theater before yet another screening of *American Madness*. As the tour bus headed for Minneapolis, Columbo received mixed greetings from his divorcée-in-waiting, who now inhabited The Riverside in Reno with sister Dorothy. Like a crafty seductress who whispers sweet nothings to pique the ears of a third party, Hannah embellished her account of an actual rendezvous with the dexterity usually expected of a *True Story* editor:

> February 23, 1933
> C/o RKO Vaudeville Theater
> St. Louis, MO
>
> My Darling—
> How thrilled I was to see you. Oh honey, to feel your arms around me, to hear you whisper how much you love to love me, to feel you kissing me, our bodies so close together, ooh my angel it was heavenly—heavenly. You looked so grand, I had so many things I wanted to say, but, I don't know honey. I was speechless. I was so happy. I wanted only to look at you, to kiss you, ooh sweet. Your lips were so warm, I get chilled up and down my spine when I think of it. Oh I hated to leave you dearest, after we left. I just sat staring into space thinking, thinking what a fool I was not to have stayed there with you. That's all that matters sweet, our being together—always. It's absolutely criminal our having to be separated for weeks and weeks, it seems endless. I'm going mad, I do love you so my angel.
> Well, honey, here we are in this beautiful City of Reno (not so beautiful). Would you believe it is exactly like Staten Island? You remember how tiny and awful that place was. Really, darling, it is the biggest shock I have ever had, a tiny little Main Street with lots of funny people standing around such as Indians—cowboys. I'm not lying sweet… Dorothy and myself have been hysterical ever since we arrived. We can't possibly stay here six weeks. My attorney tells me it may look small but it is every bit as gay as New York. Gambling, drinks of any kind, funny cafes. Oh well, why talk about it any longer? I am thoroughly disgusted.

Being as there is so little to do in this great big city, I have decided to become a great horsewoman. I'm going to take a lesson every day; we are going out to a dude ranch tomorrow—that should be a little bit exciting. My angel, what am I going to do, without you? You belong to me, so therefore should be with me every second. Everything seems to be all upset, dearest truthfully do you ever think we will be happy? I'm so depressed, sweetheart. It seems everything has to happen to us.

Oh Sweetheart, our love is so beautiful. Nothing shall ever spoil it. I love you, love you, love you with all my heart, body and soul and shall always love you. Believe me, my angel. Your wires have been so beautiful. I read them over and over again. They really are the only things that keep me alive. Dearest, my love, I am counting the hours until I see you again. I'll never want to be away from you again. I love you madly honey—honey. Darling, kiss me, here's a great big one for you. X

Think of me sweet every second and remember—please, darling, above all you are my life, my heart, body and soul. Our love is so beautiful.

Goodnight my Darling,

All my Love & Kisses,

Your Sweetch

Since Nevada law specified that divorce applicants had to establish state residency for at least six weeks, Hannah had plenty of time for horses and "funny people." Columbo left Omaha *en route* to Minneapolis for a show at the RKO Orpheum Theater. The next stop: Chicago's Palace Theater—a one-week stint that included Vaudeville-style comedians, dancing midgets and the Wheeler & Woolsey movie *So This Is Africa*.

On March 4th, a dismayed Herbert Hoover walked off history's stage for Franklin Delano Roosevelt's Inauguration, just a few hours after getting word about the American banking system at tether's end. The next day, Roosevelt prohibited the export of gold and proclaimed a national bank "holiday" to last indefinitely. And like the now ex-President Hoover, Columbo too was in a slump-shouldered mood, depleted as he and the band traveled Ohio-bound for a performance at Cincinnati's Albee Theater.

As the Russ Columbo Orchestra tour headed into the eye of an emotional storm, Gene Krupa had later corroborated on a dramatic account of the tumultuous events during this Cincinnati engagement. It started after an evening's performance, as the boys kicked back in their hotel suite for drinks. Columbo barged into the room, visibly shaken and furious after an apparent telephone altercation with Hannah. She was pitiless, she was unfaithful, and she was leaving him. Hannah turned out to be as hard-hearted as the famous song's namesake. She had been his reason for living, and now it was all over! Twisted by rejection and emboldened by alcohol, Columbo made a dash for the window before his pals restrained him. Russ calmed down and continued breathing, but from that moment on the tour was cancelled and the Russ Columbo Orchestra was dead.

Franklin Roosevelt had promised that the banks would soon reopen, but Columbo, by nature a generous man, was much more forthcoming than the President on his monetary word. He gave his players a two-week severance pay before making arrangements to fly to "The Biggest Little City in the World" and retrieve his "Sweetch." The International News Service soon reported that a fevered Columbo rushed to find out, in his words, "why Reno claimed the only girl I ever loved and why it changes people so." He arrived on March 27th to a friendlier Hannah.

Newspaper photographers, zealous over the couple's reunion, captured them picnicking in the idyllic outdoors. While Russ smiled into the camera looking happy and relaxed, Hannah seemed to be wincing with indigestion. Another photo had them gobbling spaghetti with Hannah's sister Dorothy, who had since married but was about to divorce Columbo's cornet player Jimmy McPartland. Reporters gleaned nuances behind the genial poses, one caption noting that Columbo already had two points against him: neither Hannah's mother nor her sister approved of him as a future in-law.

Hannah and Dorothy also established a new divorce record when they filed simultaneous cruelty charges against their husbands. On April 4th, Hannah emerged from the Washoe County Courthouse with her—to borrow a Winchell term—"Reno-vation"; the next day Dorothy got hers from Jimmy. They may have even kissed one of the white columns where countless other divorcées had left their lipstick traces. Immediately after the ordeal, Hannah and Russ hooked up and traveled back to the dude ranch for another horseback ride. Then, in an outlandish display of media gluttony, NBC's San Francisco office sniffed around for a sponsor to back a proposed soap opera about the Russ Columbo–Hannah Williams courtship. The executives at the Standard Oil Company of California were overjoyed to receive a script entitled "True Romance."

In the end, Columbo could not deny that Hannah Williams, who once declared she was the center of his life, had another life. While Roosevelt lulled the nation into temporary complacency with his "fireside chats" and a New Deal, Columbo got a *raw* deal. The wallop his father gave him years before could never prepare him for the blow he received after learning that Hannah was being wined and dined by Jack Dempsey. After making an inexplicable trip back to New York, Hannah betrayed her chameleonic hues. She stated to the press that she and Columbo "are just good friends" and denied any stories about marrying him.

In his autobiography, Dempsey was a bit self-aggrandizing when re-capping the Hannah deception:

> *Hannah arrived in Reno with her sister Dorothy, who was then married to jazz trumpeter Jimmy McPartland. I stayed out of the picture. Dorothy kept Hannah company while she was establishing residency, and I waited nervously. Russ Columbo flew in shortly after she arrived, convincing many that he was the one she would marry once she had her divorce. After signing the final papers, she changed and disappeared to a dude ranch with Columbo. Later, when everyone was thrown off the track she met me.*[6]

Columbo went to Los Angeles to recuperate, walled himself up in a suite at the Beverly Wilshire Hotel and managed to contract the flu. He could only get sicker after receiving a Postal Telegraph from New York, dated April 14th:

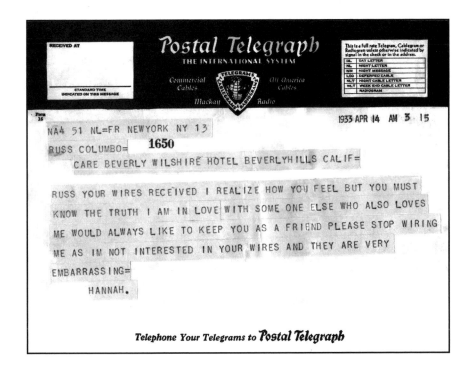

RECEIVED AT

Postal Telegraph
THE INTERNATIONAL SYSTEM

Commercial Cables   *All America Cables*

STANDARD TIME INDICATED ON THIS MESSAGE

Mackay   *Radio*

This is a full rate Telegram, Cablegram or Radiogram unless otherwise indicated by signal in the check or in the address.
DL	DAY LETTER
NL	NIGHT LETTER
NM	NIGHT MESSAGE
LCO	DEFERRED CABLE
NLT	NIGHT CABLE LETTER
WLT	WEEK END CABLE LETTER
	RADIOGRAM

Form 16

1933 APR 14   AM 3 15

NA4 51 NL=FR NEWYORK NY 13

RUSS COLUMBO=   **1650**

CARE BEVERLY WILSHIRE HOTEL BEVERLYHILLS CALIF=

RUSS YOUR WIRES RECEIVED I REALIZE HOW YOU FEEL BUT YOU MUST KNOW THE TRUTH I AM IN LOVE WITH SOME ONE ELSE WHO ALSO LOVES ME WOULD ALWAYS LIKE TO KEEP YOU AS A FRIEND PLEASE STOP WIRING ME AS IM NOT INTERESTED IN YOUR WIRES AND THEY ARE VERY EMBARRASSING=

HANNAH.

Telephone Your Telegrams to **Postal Telegraph**

'' The Same Old Trouble, LOVE. ''

Gee,life is funny, in so many ways,
That sometimes you wonder if it really pays,
To go on struggling and striving for glory and fame
And to fight and just fight , until you are lame;

The question arises, just why do we do it,
But the answer is simple, for there's nothing to it,
Yes, it's all for some woman, she loves you more than life,
And promises faithfully to become your wife;
Well, you know you're in Heaven, and life seems a song,
The world is so beautiful, and you just can't go wrong;
For she is the one you have waited for,
And you love the sweet angel with your life, if not more.,

Ah, but suddenly like a thunderbolt out of the sky,
You feel something has happened, you sit and you sigh,
And for days you don't exist on this earth, so it seems,
And you're beginning to wonder if you're having bad dreams;
But the shock's not for long, the truth finally you know,
She's written a letter and you're afraid, ah, but no,
So you read and you read,then you cease wond'ring why,
When she mentions, she knows she loves some other guy;

So the tears start to fall, and you threaten to quit,
You're thinking of suicide , and you're having a fit,
But you think you'll keep going, tho it kills you inside,
And just say you're a new man, FOR THE OLD GUY HAS DIED.

Unpublished lyrics found in Russ Columbo's personal effects.

THIS COCK · EYED WORLD

In Photorature   •   •   •   •   By Arnold

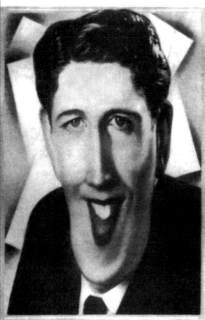

At our upper left we have Mr. Rudy Vallee, who is the oil on the troubled ether waves. At our upper right we have Mr. Paul Whiteman, who believed the story that nobody loves a fat man and who has since been able to reduce to a point where his face resembles an ostrich egg instead of a full moon. At our lower left we have Kate Smith, another weighty problem with the broadcasters. Yes, she bulks large in the air firmament. And at our lower right we present Russ Columbo. We ascribe his long face to chagrin. "If I had started as long ago as Rudy," says Russ, "look where I'd be." If you had started with Rudy, Russ, you might not yet have graduated from Yale.

ETHER MADNESS

It's always open season for crooners!

—Franklin Pangborn, after firing a gun at Bing Crosby, in the Mack Sennett short *Sing, Bing, Sing*.

Radio's influence by the early Thirties was almost supernatural. In 1933, E. B. White declared: "One of the chief pretenders to the throne of God is Radio, which has acquired a sort of omniscience ..."[1] That same year, the Radio Corporation of America announced "The Radio Waves Are Calling!" in a promotional brochure that invited readers to travel the vast United States via the miracle of "dial browsing." Permeating domestic settings just when the country needed a homogenizing force, radio eventually surpassed sheet music, vaudeville and records as a musical disseminator.

Andre Kostelanetz, the light music innovator and CBS radio orchestra conductor, would later state in his memoirs that radio represented a "new age" that promised to "diminish loneliness, open communication, end isolation..."[2] He also emphasized how much the microphone "was the result of our proud and surprising discovery that music was not what was played at all, but rather what people heard—that is, what went through the studio mike into the control room and out over the air."[3]

In a creative effort to advertise its "4-pillar radio tubes," Eveready Raytheon garnished its 1932 pamphlet with a striking icon. An angelic woman hovers in the ionosphere above a small American community. In her hand is a microphone from the period—a round, metallic object resembling an intergalactic transmitter. She is poised to whisper a tune as her billowy blonde hair and gossamer gown ripple along with the space waves. This hybrid of Holy Ghost and Hollywood Goddess captured the soul of radio—a mechanical emanation of disembodied voices floating through electromagnetic heaven.

The Eveready pamphlet provided an impressive account of the company's role in the rise of artists like Vaughn De Leath, Nat Shilkret and other performers heard regularly on WEAF's Eveready Hour broadcasts. Along with photos, it included mini-biographies of airwave luminaries like Rudy Vallee, Bing Crosby, and Morton Downey. There was, of course, the "Valentino of the Air" displayed in flattering profile. Of all the featured artists, Columbo bore the closest psychic affinity to Eveready's ectoplasmic cover girl. Her kindred spirit had already haunted him as the dancing sprite on the Granada Theater stage and had reappeared as a ghost-fiddling alter ego in *Street Girl*.

A columnist writing for the *New York American* in April of 1932 may have intuited a comparable supernal presence when sharing his fond impressions of a Radio Romeo performance: "There was about Columbo, the faint glow of spiritual incandescence often noted among young priests."[4]

This was the splendid side of crooner history. But there was another side, teeming with countervailing forces eager to witness Columbo and his cohorts fall from grace...

A year before Fay Wray screeched inside of King Kong's grip, Russ Columbo and Bing Crosby had already demonstrated the hazards of giant mechanical hands. Proprietors for both the Manhattan and Brooklyn Paramount theaters decided to showcase their two star crooners in a hand-shaped device attached to a crane. If all went according to plan, the singers would break into their opening numbers while swooping over the audience.

During his 1931 New Year's Eve celebration at the Manhattan Paramount, Crosby was supposed to fly above the crowd like a proud songbird. He instead became the prey of inebriated sailors who reached up, held the crane in place, and began taking off his shoes and socks. The crane operator came to the rescue by switching off the power and yanking Crosby back onto the stage just before the sailors removed his pants. As Crosby recalled: "I finished my song in my bare feet, clutching my belt."[5]

A few days later, Columbo was fortunately spared such feral follies, mounting the motorized paw at the Brooklyn Paramount with no mishaps as he opened for a movie called *Reckless Age*. As the theater darkened and the house orchestra played the opening strains to "You Call It Madness," Columbo's face appeared in a sudden spotlight, elevated above the throng. The show may have gone more smoothly, but some in attendance no doubt waited for the hand to goose him at any moment. This colossal claw aroused much media mirth. In his *Daily Mirror* column, a puckish Nick Kenny asked: "Is that the only way these boys can get a hand?"[6]

Whether as objects of worship or sublimated rape, Columbo and Crosby, like many other crooners of their time, played a precarious role. he best among them tried rising above the fray with lofty aspirations of romantic bliss yet were always threatened by the predatory earth's downward pull. Their sonic sugardust trail would soon teem with buzzards in the wake of an unprecedented crooner backlash.

Vallee was among the first to detect an ill wind during a Boston performance in January of 1931. While he and his band did a rendition of "Oh, Give Me Something To Remember You By," a monobrow in the audience took the song's title literally and hurled a grapefruit from the balcony. The projectile just missed. A distraught Vallee, second-guessing his assailant's motives, immediately placated the crowd with "an all-out impression of Al Jolson, theorizing that my previous vocalizing perhaps had been lacking in virility and masculinity."[7]

Testy tabloid scribes, perhaps picking up on Vallee's gender paranoia, took delight in characterizing crooners not as radio's angelic emissaries but as Depression-era demons with limp wrists. By the time Columbo, Crosby and Vallee became America's crooner triumvirate, scores of jealous husbands and other rancorous male competitors bit and clawed back.

An ad for Rudy Vallee's 1929 film *The Vagabond Lover* had already blared: "Men hate him—Women love him!" In 1931, celebrated composers Joe Burke and Al Dubin wrote "Crosby, Columbo and Vallee," a tune crafted to augment these anxieties:

> *Before the radio a married man could throw*
> *Any gigolo out in the alley.*
> *But now who comes into your home and you can't*
> *Say a word?*
> *Crosby, Columbo and Vallee...*

"Crosby, Columbo and Vallee," though never a resounding hit, was soon ingrained in radio listener minds, especially when Eddie Cantor sang it on his Sunday night WEAF coffee hour. Warner Brothers paired the song with a "Merrie Melodies" cartoon that featured dancing Indians on a tom-tom tirade against how "these crooning vagabonds are stealing all our blondes."

Writing about crooners for the *Evening Graphic*, Ed Sullivan claimed: "They do it in pantomime and the amplifiers squeeze it into harmony."[8] *Daily News* critic Ben Gross wrote: "...I do agree with John McCormack that this tremendous fad for crooning is doing more to undermine real singing in America than any other factor."[9] The New York Singing

Teachers Association declared: "Crooning corrupts the minds and ideals of the younger generation." Even radio's pioneer inventor Lee De Forest cited "sickening crooning"[10] as a precipitating factor behind the declining sales of radio sets.

Others attempted to go beyond petty matters of musical taste for more "profound" arguments. In her "Getting Personal" column, the *Evening Graphic*'s Julia Shawell decried crooners and torch singers alike for performing "songs for the half-forgotten recesses, music for the gray hours, lyrics for the lonely depths." She concluded her piece with a schoolmarm's outrage: "Sometimes I wonder if the Tommy Lymans, Helen Morgans, Ruth Ettings, Bing Crosbys, Russ Columbos and their contemporaries realize just how much their music does to people. They've swayed love, switched romance, reversed decisions of parting, awakened old emotions and killed new ones in how many lives?"[11]

At about the time when President Hoover called upon Vallee to help chase away the Depression, another unsporting gal wrote to *The New York Times*, complaining that crooners were contributing a "depression of spirit." She took gleeful note that *Webster's Dictionary* referred to crooning as "a continuous hollow sound, as cattle in pain..."[12]

In their efforts to expose the crooner aura's smoke and mirrors, journalists took their best shots at paid "stooges." The stooge's job was to publicly comment on a crooner's great looks and voice, hoping that reporters within earshot would echo the same sentiments. Columbo, Crosby, Vallee, Morton Downey, and even the earnest earth mother Kate Smith had stooges on their payroll.

"The duties of a stooge in radio are approximately the same as on the stage or in the movies," columnist Walter Wray wrote in the December 3rd issue of *Radio Dial*. "I'm informed that Bing Crosby's stooges are restrained to the use of only three words. They meet Bing when he comes out of theaters, studios, parties, and even hospitals. They clap him on the back, and exclaim either, 'Terrific!' or 'Colossal!' or 'Stupendous!'" Jerry Wald (usually a Columbo supporter) soon put out a shortlist of "stooge titles" that included "Crosbunkers," "Mort Downeighs," "Valliars," and "Russ Columbozos."[13]

Jack Foster, radio editor for the *World-Telegram*, was taken aback by Columbo's abounding stooge entourage: "During the brief period we talked about his set of encyclopedias and what a pity it was he could not bring them along when he moved east, five separate and distinct kinds of stooges appeared. From the casement they came, from the hall, from the dining room, from the kitchen—all ready, if he should glow with a whistle, to shout:—'Terrific! Colossal. Great!'"[14]

An anonymous *Evening Journal* writer sniped: "So much has been written about Bing Crosby and Russ Columbo that fans are asking radio writers whether they're press agents for the battling baritones. I shall dispel at once the possible suspicions of this space's clients by stating that neither of these gents gives me a thrill. As one listener writes in, the throaty baritones remind him of a surgical operation without ether."[15]

The *World-Telegram*'s Elizabeth Clark interpreted the Columbo-Crosby clash as a struggle for ethnic primacy: "Would they choose the blond, blue-eyed, stocky and forthright Bing: a football playing Nordic who broadcasts for Columbia Broadcasting Co.? Or would the laurels go to the suave, smoldering-eyed, smooth-haired Russ, a Latin who croons on NBC, the 'Rudolph Valentino' of the air?"[16]

"I played the Paramount, New York, with Crosby and then the following week I played the Paramount Brooklyn, with Russ Columbo," George Burns would reminisce. "They both sang exactly alike, and they're both stars! I sang entirely different and couldn't get anyplace!"[17]

NBC officials, in the meantime, got into hissy fits over the "Valentino of the Air" moniker. They apparently just caught onto the fact that the silent screen star had passed on, insisting that their network not be associated with anyone dead. The term "Romeo of Radio" also caused a stir when Jerry Baker, a singer appearing regularly on WMCA, claimed proprietary ownership over the title and threatened to sue.

Popular sportswriter and satirist Ring Lardner put his fists into the debate by writing a deathbed column of radio critiques for *The New Yorker*. On crooners, Lardner was predictably punchy as he concentrated his antipathy on Morton Downey, accusing him at one point of being a "soprano." Lardner attributed the Columbo and Crosby cat-fight spectacle to "a universal feminine failing," but his overall feelings for them were much more ambivalent. Assuming the role of a referee, he imagined the Romantic Rivals in a boxing ring:

It is just about a toss-up between the lads in the matter of putting lyrics across... Russ can outsyllable Bing over a distance; for example, Russ, without apparent effort, sings, "Nahight shall be fa-fa-filled with mee-hew-hew-sic, na-hight shall be fa-fa-filled with luh-uh-uh-uhv," or whatever it is. Bing, however, is unbeatable in a sprint, such as the word "you," which he nurses along till you would swear it was spelled yoohoohoohoohoohoo-oo. When Russ repeats a refrain whose lyric bores him, he usually substitutes dee-dee-dee-dum, whereas, in like circumstances, Bing uses da-dee-dee-do.[18]

Portrait of Bing Crosby, Morton Downey and Rudy Vallee, circa December 1931.

Sometimes Columbo and Crosby spoke for themselves. Leona Pell, writing for *Zit's* quoted Crosby: "Russ is an all right singer, but our style is different... Columbo is a sexy, torch singer, while I go for ballads." When asked about Crosby, Columbo countered: 'Different stuff. I can't sing those torchy songs. Ballads and those soft love songs are my specialty."[19]

A January 1932 issue of *Inside Stuff* claimed: "Within a period of six weeks both were in New York, both broadcasting, each for a rival network. Then they started private broadcasting of recriminations. Bing charged Russ was imitating his style; Russ shrugged his shoulders... it's a big world and there is plenty of room for both; Russ charged Bing with trying 'to hog the mikelight'."[20]

Despite the rivers of ink dedicated to their hyped-up feud, Columbo and Crosby were not the only crooners at the hit-making trough. By June of 1931, Morton Downey joined Leonard Joy and His Orchestra to bay at the "Wabash Moon." Shortly thereafter, Gene Austin released a successful version of "When Your Lover Has Gone," while Nick Lucas recorded "When The Moon Comes Over The Mountain." Smith Ballew combined forces with his "Piping Rock Orchestra" for a rendition of "Time On My Hands." He also rode Columbo's coattails by covering "You Call It Madness (But I Call It Love)." Vallee scored three knockouts with "The Thrill Is Gone," "My Song" and one of the first ever recordings of "As Time Goes By." England's Al Bowlly, who avoided a hand-to-mouth existence by becoming a romantic singer, ascended with Ray Noble and His Orchestra to #1 in 1933 with "Love Is The Sweetest Thing."

All considered, Columbo and Vallee (at least as far as the latter was concerned) ended up immersed in the bitterest of crooner rivalries. The Vagabond Lover betrayed signs of resentment toward the Vocal Valentino's skyrocketing success and reportedly fumed over the release of "Crosby, Columbo and Vallee." Nick Kenny, in his *Daily Mirror* column, was wise to the "It Boy": "Certainly no music publisher in his right mind would publish such a song and run the risk of offending Rudy Vallee while Rudy was in the heyday of his career ... I understand that Vallee's sole objection to the song, and a strenuous objection it was, had to do with mention of Columbo."[21]

Seeking redress, and perhaps wishing to promote his own little Irish mafia, Vallee insisted to no avail that the song be changed to "Crosby, Downey and Vallee." Vallee was fit to be tied when he addressed a group from his hometown in Maine, accusing New York circles of being "anglers and parasites." He also uttered lines like: "Hundreds on Broadway are waiting to crucify me."[22]

From *Philadelphia Daily News*, April 16, 1932.

Vallee also saw red over the tender ballad "Good Night, Sweetheart." He had performed it at his nightly engagements, but when the time came to make a record, Victor chose to press an instrumental by waltz maestro Wayne King. The situation worsened when Victor released Columbo's version just around the time that Crosby came out with his interpretation on Brunswick. By October, the Battling Baritones made it to *Billboard's* #3 and #5 respectively.

On December 5th, 1931, the *World-Telegram* tallied up the final results of an opinion poll that compiled the votes of 132 radio editors from around America and even some cities in Canada. The "three foremost male singers of popular songs" were 1) Morton Downey, 2) Bing Crosby and 3) Rudy Vallee, with Russ Columbo trailing a close number four. The top three still did not have an easy time. One satirical cartoonist responded to the poll results with an effeminized caricature of Crosby, Downey and Vallee huddled together as "The Three Graces."

"Rudy Vallee always has said that the radio editors are the ones who have tried to destroy his popularity," the *World-Telegram's* Jack Foster observed. "Yet I find that he is a good third on the team after these two years of trying fame. Morton Downey heads the singers of popular songs and Bing Crosby, now that he has hit his stride, is a fine second. Both of these singers have extensive networks and possibly it's because Russ Columbo has been given only a few stations that he rates such a poor fourth."[23]

Into 1932, while crooners fought among themselves, their critics showed an increasing lack of mercy. *The New York Times* sniped, "Crooners will soon go the way of tandem bicycles, mah jongg and midget golf." Someone in the February 19th *Variety* proclaimed: "Columbo is of the Bing Crosby flash in the pan style of ether exhaler."[24]

The June 5-11 issue of *Radio Guide* passed further judgment in an article titled "Are Crooners Doomed?" The writer in this case was apparently suckered in by fantasies of primitive war gods: "Crooners belong to an age of romance and plenty. They are the successors of the troubadour and the wandering minstrel. They are as much out of place in these times of hard knocks and cold facts as a wandering minstrel on a battlefield."[25] Record sales did not reflect this opinion.

Inquisitors, with pretenses to an even higher authority than journalist ethics, also got into the fray. In January, Cardinal O'Connell complained to members of Boston's Holy Names Society that he could not "turn the dials without getting these whiners, crying vapid words to impossible tunes." A fairy-baiter in cleric's lingerie, O'Connell condemned what he perceived as "whiners and bleaters defiling the air."[26] For him, only wickedness could inspire "a man whining a degenerate song, which is unworthy of any American man."[27]

"Something has happened somewhere at sometime to upset him," Vallee responded with dismay over O'Connell's sanctimony. Vallee also made a gallant attempt to explain crooning aesthetics: "I have found that most of the so-called crooners like myself are able to sing with considerable volume when the occasion demands it. However, we realize that the mechanism of the microphone is such that the voice must be brought down to an extreme softness or pianissimo. This is quite an art, inasmuch as most persons are unable to stay in pitch when singing extremely softly."[28]

Nick Kenny's "Getting An Earful" column offered more insights on the O'Connell controversy that are lengthy but worth reiterating:

> His withering attack on radio crooners in which he called them "whiners and bleaters," and dubbed crooning "a degenerate type of singing" proves to me that Cardinal O'Connell, of Boston, does not understand the problems of radio. Crooning is not a degenerate form of singing. It is merely an adaptation to the dynamics of the present-day microphone. Artists like John McCormack, Lawrence Tibbett and Everett Marshall have so much power and volume that they paralyze the microphone and do not register with the pleasing, soothing effect of the crooners, whose voices are not strong but sweet. The problem of replacing crooners with the trained, higher type of singers is one clearly up to the engineering departments of the broadcasting stations. In order to give full register to this type of singer the engineers would have to install microphones of type used by symphonic broadcasts.[29]

Like protective moms doting over their metallic tots, crooners cooed into their fragile mikes with great care and flair. Sam Coslow even resorted to baby language on a tune he wrote for the 1933 film *Too Much Harmony*. In one scene, as a chorus (including Jack Oakie) joins him on a train ride, Crosby uses bludgeoning irony to advise audiences of the ease with which they could "Boo Boo Boo" their troubles away.

No actor personified the anti-crooner crab better than Lee Tracy. In the 1932 Warner Brothers film *Blessed Event*, he played Alvin Roberts, a shrill and cackling scandalmonger (modeled on Walter Winchell) willing to

David Manners as the temperamental Ted Taylor in *Crooner*.

jeopardize any reputation for the glory of good copy. Throughout the picture, Tracy's character (like some real-life columnists and clerics) expresses a croonerphobia so visceral that it borders on psychosis. He is especially nasty toward a radio star named Bunny Harmon, a part that Dick Powell (in his crooning screen debut) plays to perfection. Razzing Harmon for being a "megaphony" as well as a "pansy," Alvin Roberts flies into a rage when he finds his dear old mother sitting fondly by her radio to hear "that pet canary croon." *Blessed Event* offers stark character contrasts: the aggressive and unattractive cad taking every opportunity to harass his handsome and melodically gifted nemesis.

The best Hollywood document on this ether madness is *Crooner*, a 1932 First National "Vitaphone" feature directed by Lloyd Bacon. It tells the story of Ted Taylor, a bandleader and saxophonist who undergoes a drastic personality change after his musicians draft him to be their star vocalist. With his nice face, pretty voice and charismatic way of holding a megaphone, Taylor soon acquires cult status. Women cluster like lemmings to watch him perform, while envious men register collective disgust. The more he is idolized, the more Taylor assumes dandyish stereotypes. He eventually alienates his friends, his fiancée (Ann Dvorak) and even his fellow band members who proceed to mock his uncontrollable pomposity.

Some reports claimed that Columbo was the first choice to play Ted

Taylor before Con Conrad blighted the deal with gauche demands. The part went instead to David Manners, a judicious choice. Manners was an underrated actor who put character and charm into problematic roles. Known as the dashing and lovable milquetoast in such Universal horror films as *Dracula* and *The Mummy*, he was handsome, genteel and among few male leads capable of compounding a story's terror by coming across more helpless against the monster than his female co-star.

By 1933, America's crooners multiplied on the charts. Little Jack Little came back from his early radio days with a sweet interpretation of "Hold Me." Gene Austin joined the Dorsey Brothers Orchestra for the misty nostalgia of "(Just A) Little Street Where Old Friends Meet." Dick Powell struck up some weak-kneed rapture when he sang "I Only Have Eyes For You" to Ruby Keeler in an outlandish Busby Berkeley sequence for the movie *Dames*.

Composer and erstwhile crooner Sam Coslow, famous for singing through the side of his mouth, adopted a more straightforward tone on "Cocktails For Two," which he co-wrote for the 1934 backstage mystery *Murder at the Vanities.* Danish singer Carl Brisson added European grandeur to the crooner mystique by performing the song in a scene involving top hats, candlelit tables and Martinis. Brisson, who was also a boxer, delivered lines about "some enchanted rendezvous" with the effete diction of a frumpish schoolteacher, an endearing combination of womanly phrasing and manly girth.

Once the big band era formally began in 1935, the inherently fey delights of crooning helped ignite the debate over "sweet" versus "swing" music. The 1937 Warner Bros. movie *Melody for Two* attempted to address this aesthetic quandary. James Melton, a commended tenor of the period, was quite similar to Brisson with his meticulous elocution and highly formalized style. Here, Melton portrays a singer/bandleader, with a reputation for "playing melodic arrangements," who must come to terms with the rising vogue for swing dancing. Slapped with an ultimatum from his club owner to play "hot" music or else, Melton tries to comply but at one point cynically declares: "Swing music is merely jazz rehashed and served up under glass." Nevertheless, the movie's highlighted songs have nothing to do with swing at all. This is especially true of two numbers by Harry Warren and Al Dubin: the film's title song and the everlasting "September In The Rain," which here made its screen debut. Instead of adopting a surly rhythm, Melton performs it as an operatically-inspired, perfumed ballad: he rolls his r's and sings of "raindrops" playing "a sweet refrain" before a background of chiffon blonde violinists.

Some of the crooner criticisms did not go unwarranted. A special breed of detractors suspected—sometimes with good cause—that many crooners were poseurs who candy-coated their lullabies to hide more randy intentions. Coslow, in a more roguish mind frame, brought this paradox to the fore when he wrote "Learn To Croon"—a prescription for smarmy guys who just need to "murmur bu-bu-boo bu-bu-boo" if they want to win their "heart's desire."

Even before gaining notoriety for his blue humor, Vallee gave off an air of preppy prurience when he sang bawdy numbers like his memorable tribute to "Betty Co-Ed." Crosby posed an even more profound contradiction between the singer of love songs and the roué eager to run off for drinks, a round of golf, or some skirt-chasing the moment the recording session ended. His untroubled image was arguably a façade. As crooner historian Ian Whitcomb observes: "This public manner took a private toll. Hotel rooms where Crosby had stayed were littered with broken or chewed pencils."[30]

In the 1933 film *Going Hollywood*, Crosby is a singing playboy who, after falling for Marion Davies, tries to atone for his wicked ways. One liquor-ridden night, he laments in a sleazy nightclub, uttering self-deprecating quips while Davies pleads for him to return to show business and into her arms. "I wanna get away from Hollywood," he blurts out. "It's a fake place, phony people... crooners!" But a heartbroken Davies bites back: "You're really no more sincere than those songs of yours about love and moonlight, or whatever else you've been crooning about. You're just a voice that croons about something that once was real..."

Going Hollywood has an even more important scene when The Radio Rogues (a comedy trio masquerading as film crew engineers) impersonate some of the era's airwave masters. They exude the warmth of a bloated canary on the Kate Smith classic "When The Moon Comes Over The Mountain." Morton Downey fares not much better with the quasi-coloratura chirping of "Remember Me." And Rudy Vallee takes the hardest knocks on the Rockefeller-inspired send-up "My Dime is Your Dime." When it comes time for "Rusty Columbo" to get his share of jabs, however the Rogues break character and deliver "You Call It Madness" with surprising reverence.

Unfortunately, Columbo's recording career took a giant step backwards throughout the year of 1933 when he strangely made no sides. Of the eleven Victor songs he did with his "Russ Columbo Orchestra" in 1932, only one made *Billboard*'s charts. Stymied by past legal wrangling and professional run-ins, a flaky and soon-to-be litigious ex-agent, the "forget me" notes, the Hannah debacle, and his frayed nerves, Russ was in a slump. But a revival was, as Crosby would say, "just around the crooner."

EVERYBODY'S COLUMBEAU!

Say, who's this man passing himself off as me?!

—Russ Columbo talking about his doppelganger in *That Goes Double*

Rising at noon, Russ Columbo looks forward to having his valet read Shakespeare to him. He is fond of cold showers, has an aversion to olives, loves Southern fried chicken, but prefers reading Tennyson to eating.

Though well-mannered and at times even chivalrous, he is not always the best listener. He tends to speak very low, is generally quiet, and recites Longfellow passages when conversation proves tedious.

He is leery about riding in New York City taxicabs, has little sense of direction, limits his strolls to no more than a city block, and is bewildered that an urban jungle like Manhattan would have mounted policemen.

Placid about his newfound success, he is also reticent in crowds, blushes whenever introduced to someone new, and enjoys having photographers tell funny stories to ease his camera shyness.

He is fussy about his hair, has meticulous taste in clothes, prefers blue shirts, never wore a hat until he arrived on the east coast, is rarely seen sporting a coat and hat simultaneously, and is partial to festively colored silk pajamas.

While indisputably handsome and no stranger to the mirror, his good looks ultimately mean little to him. He prefers to spend his remaining days of beatific youth writing love songs till the wee hours.

He has a less than husky constitution but enjoys tennis, is a bit too genteel for his press agents' tastes, telephones his mother at least twice a week, and, of course, sings like an angel.

This Columbo composite—assembled from descriptions in various magazines, newspapers and fan club bulletins—says so much about the man yet widens the mystery chasm. Any biographers facing such a short and all too concentrated life can only imagine the deeper personality recesses that even Columbo himself was too young (and perhaps too mortified) to fathom. In a neatly typed and translated letter sent to his Detroit address during the 1933 Columbo Orchestra tour, his ailing mother reveals that she too was grasping in the dark: "My boy, take care of yourself and be happy always. Write and let me know the truth about yourself."

Others fancied having more than a mother's intuition. An article entitled "The Truth About Him" in the June 1933 issue of *The Illustrated Love Magazine* added Columbo to its study of movie ideals. Among the other stars analyzed were Lewis Stone, pictured in his usual leaden but paternal posture and deemed "the mental and the motive" type. Gary Cooper, sporting riding boots and a sword, was "a splendid example of the keen, stimulating mental type." And Columbo, in white pants, dark jacket, left hand in pocket, and eyes aimed toward an invisible horizon, comprised "the artistic, beauty-loving, musical type."

That following November, Madeline Graw, the co-President of the Russ Columbo Co-Ed Club, published her insights after scrutinizing a hand-written letter Columbo had sent to her. She detected "the strong character, and self-confidence of the writer." She then forwarded the letter to a professional graphologist who returned a slightly more probing diagnosis: "He has the deep imagination of a dreamer and a keen sense of humor. We also learn that he is emotional… which is usually the companion of an artist's in nature."[1]

Columbo also had an artistic fashion sense. Crosby often wore ill-fitting clothes with clashing colors, but Columbo became what one journalist described as "the height of sartorial perfection."[2] More than even Fred Astaire, he personified the dapper evening jacket of a chap. All of the glowing prose about his smart tuxedos, immaculate shoes and Mediterranean pulchritude notwithstanding, "the Gent with the Golden Voice and the Bedroom Eyes" often found himself all dressed up with nowhere to go.

Struggling to get a grip on his identity, Columbo was, at least early on, perplexed about his name. Never comfortable with "Russ," he once toyed with the idea of going under "Roger Russell." He scribbled more titular permutations on a piece of paper that was later found among his belongings—doodlings that suggested fantasies of a moniker merger with Rudy Vallee: "Rudy Valetti," "Russ Valetti's Orchestra," "Roger Valetti's Orchestra," and "Café Valetti."

Russ Columbo's name salad.

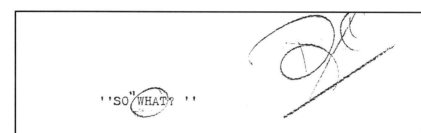

```
                                       ''SO WHAT?''

IF I WERE A POWER TO CONTROL(this beautiful thing
called ) LOVE ,
I WOULD BE A KING RULING THE UNIVERSE.
THE WHOLE WORLD WOULD BOW AND BEG ON ITS KNEES,
AND CRY, SAVE ME , SAVE ME;

WOULDN'T IT BE WONDERFUL TO SIT ON A THRONE,
AND LISTEN TO SOME OF THE CASES I'VE KNOWN,
I'D PROBABLY LAUGH TILL MY SIDES WOULD GIVE IN,
AND ALL I COULD SAY WOULD BE SOxx-OOO---, LIKE ED WYNN
```

Another of Russ' autographed musings.

On his records and radio shows, Columbo's introspective undertones simultaneously conjured the murmurs of a reticent Romeo and a dazed child. This airwave paramour was too immersed in his canorous daydreams to fully comprehend the magnitude of his 2,000-plus weekly fan letters. One insightful critic attended a concert and immediately took a shine to Columbo's lack of protective coating: "He was mottled with bewilderment over the sensation his personal appearance created. A skilled violinist, he is the most versatile and by far handsomest and best dressed of the pack. Ladies sighed over his slumbering eyes and the bird-like flutter in his throat as he mooed. I was especially impressed by his effort to hide a whipping nervousness that created a palsied shake."[3]

Columbo left behind a striking testimony to his amiable awkwardness in a bit of studio test footage. Wearing only swimming trunks and a beach robe, he sat amid sunshine and sand, strummed on a banjo and sang to a pretty but distracted woman reclining beside him on a chaise longue. He seemed to find the situation both amusing and unnerving as he sported a bashful smile and repeated verses from "Between The Devil And The Deep Blue Sea":

> I should hate you,
> But I guess I love you,
> You've got me in between...

The fair-haired object of his serenade fidgeted politely but managed to smile back at Columbo on cue.

Fate seems to give my heart a twist,
And I come running back for more...

Finishing the song, Columbo looked over to her and asked: "How did you like that, Billie?" She replied with dignified distance: "It was wonderful, Russ." Then, a moment of misfired communication followed as the crew gave an off-screen command to start the song over; Columbo stared through the woman in utter silence.

In darker moods, Columbo may have gazed into a void similar to the one his childhood idol Valentino encountered at the height of fame. "Here was a young man who was living daily the dream of millions of other young men," H.L. Mencken wrote in 1926 to commemorate the Sheik's untimely transition to the other side. "Here was one who was catnip to women. Here was one who had wealth and fame. And here was one who was very unhappy."[4]

Unlike Valentino, however, Columbo seemed capable of buoying himself with an inner vigor that surfaced just when life seemed most dire. The aforementioned graphologist also saw in Columbo's longhand "a very strong, dominating personality... We learn too, that he is restless and very excitable; but on the other hand, when the necessity arises, he can be nonchalant, and take what comes, coolly enough."

Somewhat hardened by Hannah Williams' fickle heart, Columbo summoned up his fortitude by the fall of 1933. He waved "Arrivederci" to the east, settled back onto the Hollywood fault line, and rented a house on 509 North Crescent Drive in Beverly Hills. Though Giulia and Nicola, back from their temporary stay in the New York area, returned to the old residence at 1322 Tamarind Avenue, they would often live in with their son.

A photograph taken at approximately this time (and credited to Roy D. MacLean) shows a blissful family portrait inside of an ornate room. Along with his customary white suit, Columbo is clad in a white scarf and shoes, singing and playing at the piano while mom and dad fasten their eyes on his sheet music. Dad looks proud, while Mom stands beside her boy with a radiant smile and arm around his shoulder.

Two other photos, apparently taken at the same time and place, depict Columbo in a more solitary mood, sitting cross-legged on a plush sofa in the identical white outfit, offset by a floral wall rug in the background. In one, he registers mild disgust while gazing into a copy of *Photoplay*; in the

Safe at home with his parents and music.

Waving from his Beverly Hills residence.

other, he exerts a much more satisfied smile, perusing what appears to be one of L. Frank Baum's *Oz* books. These two prints captured Columbo in the "dreamy dreamland" he had eulogized on "Good Night, Sweetheart." This is where he seemed his most comfortable, ensconced in a shelter of satiny, cerebral quietude.

As he took voice lessons from a Los Angeles professor named Pietro Cimini, Columbo started touting his intentions to return to the airwaves as a "straight baritone." He made several appearances on NBC's weekly *Hollywood On The Air* as a "new" Columbo. He fortunately retained all of the charm of his first Victor sessions, with the added advantage of a deeper chest. Broadcast at 8 p.m. (Pacific Time) from KECA, the show paired Columbo's gossamer tones with the kindly strains of Harry Jackson's "Hollywood On The Air Orchestra." He performed a medley of "More Than You Know" and "Time On My Hands," eschewing the perfunctory patter of his erstwhile dance band for a silkier and slower orchestral mood.

With dreams of movie stardom ready to materialize, Columbo signed a contract with Universal Studios at a fifth of the salary he was used to receiving from his stage shows. At the same time, Darryl F. Zanuck at Twentieth Century offered him some parts, the first being a lead role in a

Russ with Dolores Del Rio on the *Hollywood On the Air* soundstage.

splendidly wacky enterprise entitled *Broadway Thru A Keyhole*. Columbo satisfied all parties concerned by agreeing to make a yearly commitment of two films for Twentieth Century and three or four for Universal.

Uplifted, Columbo made a departure from his usual prepared press statements and displayed refreshing candor. Speaking to the *Los Angeles Examiner*'s Ray De O'Fan—on a Hollywood movie lot, no less—he expressed how much he resented the "Battle of the Baritones," lamenting over the unnecessary friction it brought between Crosby and himself. He was also up-front in renouncing his past errors: "It was a case of bad handling all the way around. I was poorly managed, badly publicized. The men taking care of my affairs involved me in fights with the networks and sponsors. They turned down fat contracts for reasons I can't imagine. The publicity put out by my own men did not tend to build me up, but actually created a bad situation."[5]

In October, De O'Fan reported again from the *Examiner*, this time with news that the Romantic Rivals formally "buried the hatchet" when Columbo attended the christening of Crosby's son Gary. The mantra "Columbo's here!" buzzed throughout the crowd that Sunday at Crosby's home. America's two favorite warblers greeted one each other, spoke for a spell and sealed their truce with a handshake worth a thousand photographs. (Snapshots were forbidden on this chaste occasion.) A member of Crosby's press contingent was on hand to tell O'Fan: "Everything is going to be alright between these fellows." Columbo was also reported to be among the last guests to depart. Also present that day was a stupefied Sam Coslow, who declared: "If I hadn't seen it with my own eyes I'd never believe it."[6]

Columbo got the chance to satirize his public image in *That Goes Double*, a Vitaphone short he started making in late 1932 but which Warner Brothers released in 1933. The director Joseph Henabery (who played Abraham Lincoln in D. W. Griffith's *Birth of a Nation*) made several other Vitaphone musical shorts that featured Little Jack Little, Ben Pollack, and a stockyard of terpsichorean showoffs. Here Columbo, instead of dubbing for someone else, had the pleasure of lip-synching to himself in the dual role of a crooner and a flustered clerk named Clarence.

The story opens with Clarence entering his drab office. His mood is already low as he notices some of his co-workers gawking at a newspaper photo of Columbo in an ad for a "Radio Popularity Contest." After barking that he does not like crooners, he gets even more peevish after someone chides him about his resemblance to the radio star: "Say, he's made my life miserable. Everywhere I go, people point at me and say 'There goes Russ Columbo!' They pester me for autographs and photographs and dates and what have you. A lot of phooey! Listen, I'd like to meet that guy face to face. I'd tell *him* a few things!"

A glutton for discontent, Clarence goes to witness Columbo get crowned King of Radioland. The contest officials point him out in the crowd, mistake him for the star, and drag him up to the podium. The "real" Russ Columbo soon appears, draped in a dapper suit with a white carnation, brandishing a walking stick, and acting every bit the fop. He feigns outrage and must prove he is the genuine article by singing a few bars of "My Love." One of the old codger contest judges sighs: "Every time I hear him sing that song, the melody haunts me for days." An exasperated Clarence rolls his eyes and counters: "It should—the way he murders it!"

That Goes Double proceeds with Depression-era satire as an uppity socialite (Charlotte Wynters) gets into a dither while planning one of her "pink teas." With Columbo photos displayed throughout her living room, she is obviously a dedicated fan determined to have him perform for her guests. To get him, she must endure a scenery-munching theatrical agent named Manny Stein who handles "everything from a trained seal to an operatic tenor."

"Russ and I are pals," snaps the Conrad clone as he goes into his stooge-like spiel. "Why, I put Russ in show business. And when Russ chirps a ditty; when he yodels a cadenza; when he gargles an obbligato, he's terrific, dynamic, stupendous, colossal, effervescent, and if I might use another preposition, he's gigantic!"

The crooner and the clerk have meanwhile made peace. Columbo even hires Clarence to do some "doubling" for him at "public functions." Clarence exceeds his job description, however, by treating the party-planning socialite to an impromptu performance of "Prisoner Of Love" after showing up at her penthouse, mouthing to a record as a Victrola grinds outside the window.

When the actual Columbo finally arrives on the scene to expose the hoax, the woman demands to know "Which is which; who is who?" Clarence 'fesses up to the charade but still gets the last laugh. When Columbo hollers, "Say, I'd like to see those other fellows who seem to think they look like me," the icy hostess escorts him to the window. He looks out to a chorus of Columbos, all leering back from several apartments and singing "You Call It Madness (But I Call It Love)" in unison.

Oddly, the supposedly authentic Columbo in *That Goes Double* seems much more an imitation, nothing like the polite daydreamer and forlorn romantic he portrayed along life's proscenium. By 1933, he and Crosby may have outgrown their rivalry, but they still remained stark personality contrasts. Even with a toupee, shoe lifts, shoulder pads, a special glue to hold back his ears, and a corset to shrink his expanding midriff, Crosby managed to pass himself off as the unadorned wild oats sower aspiring to be Mr. Normal. Columbo was more of a mold-breaker—an enigma wrapped inside a press release—who eluded easy classifications and made his insecurities seem endearing.

The Truth about "Him"

NOT long ago a young girl came into my studio in New York with the photographs of two young men in their early twenties.

"Which one," she asked, "shall I marry?"

I looked at the two snapshots—typical, full length, vacation photographs—with each hero arrayed only in his bathing suit.

"I'm sorry," she said, "that the faces aren't clearer."

"I'm sorry, too," I replied, "but I think I can answer your question just the same."

I didn't think—I knew.

For Anatology, which comes from the Greek word meaning bones and the Greek word meaning study, is just as much interested in people below the collar as above. In fact, if your boy friend had lost his head altogether—which, of course, I hope he has done over you!—I could still tell you whether or not he was the man for you to marry.

AS between the two boys in the pictures, who looked very much as Walter Hagen, the golfer, and Lewis Stone, the actor, must have looked at their age, the difference in their characters was indicated in every detail of their fine young bodies.

"Take this young man's hands," I began, referring to the heavier and rounder of the two figures, the one that looked like Hagen. "His hands are square, with medium short fingers, aren't they?"

"Yes, they are. Jack's hands are as wide as they are long. I've often remarked about them."

"Well, Jack needn't be ashamed of that. A man with square hands and short fingers invariably does big things. He chafes at petty details. Notice his thumbs: long, low-set and apparently not pliable. Thumbs like that indicate self-control and practicality. Their owners are usually high-principled. Sometimes they are obstinate."

"I'll say they are!" she laughed. "How about Charlie's hands? What do they show?"

"Charlie's hands are not like Jack's at all. They are rather conical in shape—"

"Comical?"

"No," I smiled, "conical, as an ice cream cone—with rather long fingers, and, I imagine, well developed, sensitive pads. This type of hand, although it suggests the possession of common sense and a fair degree of determination, puts the emphasis on sensitiveness, responsiveness and refinement."

"Right again!" she agreed.

"Now as to their expression—"

"The expression of the hands?" she exclaimed.

"Yes, hands have expressions just as much as faces. See the way Charlie holds his—open. Now look at Jack's"—I showed her the photograph of the heavier of the two boys—"They are closed. I imagine both poses are the usual thing with these boys."

"Come to think of it, they are."

Gary Cooper is a splendid example of the keen, stimulating mental type.

If He is built like Fatty Arbuckle, He, too, is of the entertaining vital type.

In Lewis Stone the mental and the motive types are well combined.

Russ Columbo represents the artistic, beauty-loving, musical type.

Globe

From *The illustrated Love Magazine,* June 1933.

Roughed up by hoods in *Broadway Thru a Keyhole* (Twentieth Century Pictures–United Artists release, 1933)

MERCUROCHROME
AND
MOBSTERS

Take a Peek Thru the Hottest Keyhole in the World and See the Inside of the Big Stem with ITS WOMEN—ITS MEN—ITS SONG—ITS GAIETY.

—Advertisement for *Broadway Thru A Keyhole*

Broadway Thru A Keyhole was a funny, hardboiled, and at times rude movie that exposed some of the Great White Way's blemishes. It was also Columbo's first chance at a starring role that, like many of his life's journeys, tripped along with a caravan of colorful personalities.

The script was based on Walter Winchell's factual story concerning the 1928 love triangle between Al Jolson, Ruby Keeler and legendary mobster Johnny "Irish" Costello. Costello took a shining to Keeler after watching her dance at Texas Guinan's Salon Royal, a club that (like Guinan herself) embodied the decade of the Twenties at its brassiest. Influential and threatening, Costello used his muscle to insure that Keeler became the club's main draw. Soon the two were an item.

Trouble started when Jolson also got a case of the Keeler crazies. The moment he watched her clomp about the stage in a Chicago production of *Sidewalks of New York*, the cackling cantor conducted an elaborate courtship to win her over, resorting to fancy words and gifts of pricey finery. Keeler returned to New York and to a jealous Costello who vied for her affections with a beautiful diamond engagement ring. But Keeler's heart was lost to the ballbuster in "blackface."

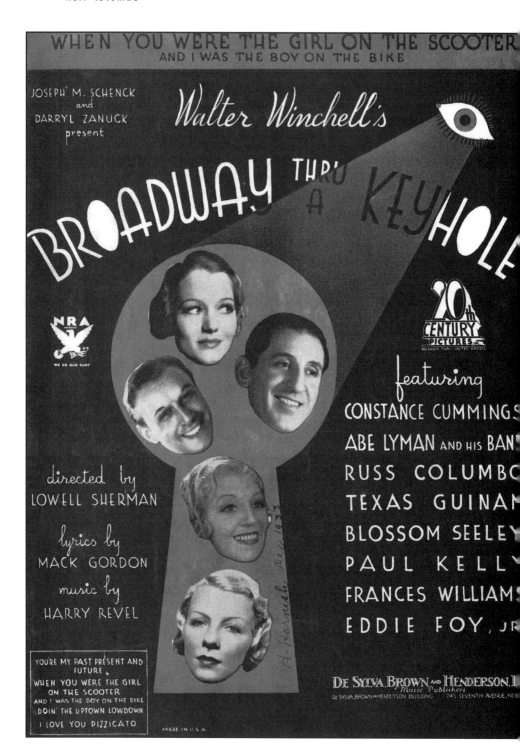

Instead of slicing Jolson into pastrami, Costello stunned everyone by honoring Keeler's wishes and backing off. Costello broke character even more when, instead of taking his ire out on the next available plug-ugly, he (at least according to Neal Gabler's Winchell biography) had a good cry one day outside of Dinty Moore's restaurant.

As Costello's confidante during this crisis of the heart, Winchell knew he had a salient movie treatment on his hands. But Jolson and Keeler, now married, balked at Winchell's cinematic aspirations. The tension culminated when the three parties confronted each other at a Hollywood's Legion Stadium prizefight. After Jolson allegedly punched him out, the "Boswell of Broadway" dusted himself off, secured over $500,000 worth of advanced bookings for the proposed film, and filed a lawsuit against Jolson for the same amount. Winchell also taunted his assailant with requests for a second round, for which he would charge admission and donate the proceeds to charity. Jolson declined.

Art imitated life once again as Columbo played Clark Brian, a sensitive crooner with looks, magnetism, talent, fashion, flair, and the added distinction of being (as one character in the film puts it) "a little screwy." The part offered Russ a tale of romance, a couple of good songs, and another opportunity to show off his quirky charm. For optimum effect, the story set him up against a potent male rival—a poultry racketeer named Frank Rocci (Paul Kelly) who is stone-faced and tough on the surface but tenderhearted underneath. Winchell also had an honorary presence as an on-air narrator, ballyhooing in and out of the story with wisecracks about his showbiz contemporaries.

The film begins with Rocci on a typical business day as he intimidates clients and makes life miserable for potential competitors. Soon an acquaintance from his old Bronx neighborhood arrives at his office, pelting him with a sob story about her mom dying and being left virtually penniless. Rocci's lacquered exterior starts to crack. He agrees to help out her younger sister, an attractive ingénue named Joan Whelen (Constance Cummings) who also happens to be his childhood sweetie.

After getting Whelen a job in a nightclub chorus line, Rocci falls for her all over again. He goes out of his way to make her a star, purchases the nightclub and proceeds to browbeat Whelen's already high-strung dance instructor into making her the show's centerpiece. Rocci approaches Whelen with a successful marriage proposal, but they are forced to curtail any wedding plans when rival gangs nearly decorate him with bullets. For safekeeping, Rocci sends Whelen off to Miami—a cautionary move that backfires when she instantly swoons to Clark Brian's croon.

Word of Whelen's dalliance gets back to Rocci, who immediately orders her flown back home. While Rocci's blood boils, Clark Brian develops a previously nonexistent streak of valor as he trails Whelen to New York and confronts the gangster face to face. Touched by this admitted coward's bravery in the name of love, Rocci thinks the matter over and, contrary to his warring nature, agrees to let Whelen go. This magnanimous gesture goes unrewarded, however, when gang rivals kidnap Whelen on her wedding day and frame Rocci as the culprit.

Broadway Thru A Keyhole's plot might seem a bit formulaic at first glance, but it was an anomaly among backstage musicals—thanks to its peculiar characters and risqué innuendos. Though largely forgotten today, *Keyhole* was nonetheless a curiosity of its time, reflecting the moral and social complications that intensified in the spate between Prohibition's demise and the restrictive 1934 Hollywood Production Code. It was more candid and in some ways more intricate than the hyper-slick Busby Berkeley fare—a story chock-full of hoods, saucy vaudevillians, racy stage revues, off-color but hilarious ethnic jokes, and a few sly references to gender-bending.

Actor turned director Lowell Sherman also deserves credit for the movie's jaded ambiance. Before earning the reputation for being a rogue both on and off the screen, Sherman evolved from a show business family. He made one of his first memorable appearances in 1920, as the lustful fiend out for Lillian Gish's virtue in D.W. Griffith's *Way Down East*. The role established him as a pro at playing self-styled scoundrels, oily-tongued Casanovas and cynical sots. "Be cruel but elegant," he once instructed someone when asked about the art of screen knavery. He doled out other De Sade-inspired aphorisms like: "Consistent virtue on the screen is the very skim milk of monotony."[1] The same year he directed *Keyhole*, Sherman also showcased Mae West's bedroom humor in that more famous 1933 foray into pre-Code mischief, *She Done Him Wrong*.

Sherman embellishes *Keyhole*'s cast with cronies from the speakeasy days. One is Blossom Seeley, a performer who fully understood stardom's demon nectar. She sampled it as a child singer, drank it by the bottle when maturing into a ragtime performer along San Francisco's Barbary Coast, and got hooked by the time she headlined in New York revues. But as vaudeville faded in the wake of talking pictures, so did her limelight. From then on, Seeley was destined to portray *Keyhole*'s Sybil Smith, a character with the spunk of a Minsky's Follies veteran and the bitter wit of a dry drunk.

Facing down Paul Kelly (as the good-hearted gangster).

The great Texas Guinan also appears, this time as a permutation of herself named Tex Kaley. She plays the proprietor of the "Klub Kaley" where Whelen makes her mark. Showing off her glittery gowns, pearly caps and sabertooth fingernails, Guinan relishes the chance to mug for the camera while belching out her own volley of Shermanisms like: "I never lost my voice from saying 'No'; never lost my reputation for saying 'Yes'— I never had it!" She at one point asks Seeley: "What's that? The 'Old Gold Hour' coming in over your bridge work?" Guinan's enthusiasm for the picture waned, however, when she saw Sherman's finished product and griped to the press that her part was so small that she played "the keyhole."

The film's crossover between reality and fantasy continues with Columbo's co-star Kelly. He began as a child star but ended up specializing as mobsters and killers. While still in his twenties, Kelly got involved in his own deadly love triangle with Dorothy MacKaye, who was in the middle of a stormy marriage to actor Ray Raymond. By 1927, Kelly and MacKaye were exchanging love letters while a frantic and out-of-work Raymond indulged in drinking, violent fits and spousal abuse. Kelly, attempting to defend MacKaye, engaged Raymond in a drunken quarrel that degenerated into a deadly fistfight. As a result, Kelly was convicted of manslaughter. He spent over a year in San Quentin, finally married MacKaye in 1931 and eventually became the first convicted killer to win a Tony Award.

With Constance Cummings.

Keyhole also indulges in the ever-trendy "masculine women and feminine men" theme. Character actor Hugh O'Connell (who somewhat resembles Jack Benny) plays Chester Haskins, the Boy Friday to Kelly's Rocci. He assumes a role similar to that of George E. Stone to Edward G. Robinson's "Rico" in *Little Caesar*—a gangster's lackey whose doting attentions border on wifely obsession. In one scene, Seeley's Sybil literally wears the household pants when she disembarks from a plane in male drag, teasing her nurse-maid of a concubine Haskins into kissing her in full view of the press.

Ethnic buffoon Gregory Ratoff rounds out the cast as Max Mefooski, a temperamental and terrified stage manager. As a walking stockyard of Yiddish shtick, he cowers at Rocci's barking orders like a pet schlemiel. And yet, despite Ratoff's caricature, *Keyhole* is more remarkable for playing against the kind of ethnic typecasting that would plague future cinema. Kelly portrays an Italian gangster with a dignified reserve that defies "goomba" pigeonholes.

With musical direction from Alfred Newman, an orchestra conducted by Abe Lyman, and songs by Mack Gordon and Harry Revel, *Keyhole* is a cheerful earful. The songs also manage to rattle the sensibility cage. On the racially charged "Doing The Uptown Lowdown," Frances Williams dons a top hat and tails to join a phalanx of other androgynous lady dancers as she sings about "bankers with their Cinder-relatives listening to those hot, high-yellatives." Eddie Foy Jr. later joins Cummings for "When You Were The Girl On The Scooter, And I Was The Boy On The Bike," a ribald number that starts out facetiously wholesome but slides headlong into the gutter when the surrounding chorines, dressed as toddlers on tricycles, wheel toward the camera with undies in full view.

Keyhole was, in some respects, a Columbo coup, particularly because his character takes the story into a less predictable and more fascinating direction. The narrative pacing gets more dreamlike once Winchell introduces Clark Brian over the radio, the camera dissolving to an exotic club where Columbo leads a hotel orchestra. As Russ' Clark launches into the dreamy ballad "You're My Past, Present And Future," Joan and Sybil sit at their cocktail table, marveling at how he swings his conductor's baton, plays his violin and beams his pearly-whites in their direction.

After the two gals strike up an engaging debate over why he "doesn't look like a crooner," Clark introduces himself. He is amused to discover both he and Joan are entertainers and inveigles her to join him on stage to perform "I Love You, Pizzicato." This ticklish duet about the romance between a harpist and violinist flurries along with lines like: "Tell me Pianissimo that you care for Tissimo/ When our kisses blendo, I feel so darn'd Crescendo..."

The more Joan gets to know him, the more Clark flouts her expectations. Behind the calm, urbane façade is a hypochondriac who cringes at the slightest bruise and "buys Mercurochrome and iodine by the gallon." "We've got to get some Mercurochrome quick!" he moans after getting a splinter on his hand. Whelen tries to assure him that it is "just a little drop of blood," but he scurries away. Clark reappears later that evening in fit form, albeit after gargling all the germs from his throat, swallowing a few pills, and donning red flannels and an overcoat to guard against the Miami breeze.

Keyhole's most captivating interlude occurs when Clark and Joan confide with one another on a private beach. As he takes refuge under an umbrella and inundates his skin with lotion, Clark complains about how he nearly died of sunburn the previous year. He soon delivers some deliciously ambiguous lines: "Joan, I'm going to tell you something I've never dared tell anybody else. I'm a coward... Somehow I don't feel ashamed to tell you... There are a lot more things I ought to tell you...I've been trying for days to say something to your face, but you know my complexes..."

Aware that the conversation is roaming into a raw zone, Joan musters up her maternal instincts to assure him that she doesn't care for "men who talk big and ache with strength" anyhow. In these precious few moments of screen time, Columbo emerges as a prototype for such dark, handsome and fragile heartthrobs as Montgomery Clift and Sal Mineo.

With Constance Cummings, *Broadway Through a Keyhole*.

Columbo's character toughs it out for the ultimate showdown when he struggles for Joan's love. "I can't even believe that I'm standing here talking to you this way," he confesses to Rocci after barging gunslinger-style through the swinging doors of the gangster's nightclub. "I'm not a fearless guy at all. But I would prefer anything else than to go on living without the only thing that gives me the courage to tell it to you straight from my heart." Stalling on his answer, Rocci symbolically wipes the problem from his life by brushing the lint from his pants. He thinks for a moment before blurting: "Okay. Just be good to her!"

On Clark and Joan's wedding day, a rival racketeer (played by C. Henry Gordon) kidnaps the bride. Rocci gets accused of the deed and takes a bullet from the cops while trying to retrieve Joan from a fleabag hotel. Clark and bride presumably go off to their connubial paradise, but the film ends with another kind of romantic finale as the ever-faithful Haskins stands at Rocci's sickbed; at one point even holding his hand. He turns on the radio just as Winchell's broadcast debunks the rumor that Rocci was the kidnapper. Haskins then steps out of the room, leaving Rocci to look out from his hospital window at the Broadway lights that would soon glow for *Broadway Thru A Keyhole*'s New York premiere.

Columbo promoted *Keyhole* for the September 18th KECA broadcast of *Hollywood On The Air*—weeks before the film's official release. Along with actor Bruce Cabot as master of ceremonies and vocalist Estelle Taylor (the former Mrs. Jack Dempsey), Columbo appeared as a guest artist to sing an especially lingering version of "You're My Past, Present and Future." After Russ finished and the applause died down, Cabot returned to the microphone: "...Now Russ Columbo will sing 'Kisses In The Dark,' which Al Dubin and Harry Warren have written for Twentieth Century's new Constance Bennett musical *Moulin Rouge...*"

Not to be confused with an unrelated German silent film of the same name by E.A. Dupont (as well as a Fifties movie Jose Ferrer made about Toulouse Lautrec), *Moulin Rouge* was a slapdash affair, revolving around Bennett playing the dual role of a wholesome American singer and a pretentious French chanteuse. "Kisses In The Dark" was the alternate title for "Coffee In The Morning And Kisses In The Night"—a number Columbo and Bennett perform together in the movie (along with The Boswell Sisters) in front of a cozy cottage backdrop. Singing it over KECA, Columbo accomplished another exercise in phantasmal vowel inflection, the gorgeously slow tempo appreciably different from the swinging and nonsensical film version.

Apart from the Columbo-Bennett duet and the other Warren-Dubin songs, *Moulin Rouge* had one other fascinating aspect. A rumor has persisted through the years involving deleted footage of Russ crooning "Boulevard Of Broken Dreams" as he saunters through the Paris streets. Twentieth Century allegedly thought the scene too depressing and excised it into oblivion.

The fact that Columbo was promoting *Moulin Rouge* right along with *Keyhole* revealed Darryl F. Zanuck's fervor to market both his new star and his new studios. *Keyhole* was, after all, Twentieth Century's second feature. On the day after Columbo's *Hollywood On The Air* appearance, the *Los Angeles Evening Herald and Express* flashed the headline: "June Knight, Columbo Paired." Universal Studios' Carl Laemmle, Jr. finally found the right vehicle in what would soon become *Wake Up And Dream.*

On November 1st, *Broadway Thru A Keyhole* had its gala premiere at Broadway's Rivoli Theater. Posters lined newsstands; Gimbel's and Macy's arranged promotional window displays; a sound truck rolled from block to block playing some of the featured Gordon-Revel themes; and audio snippets from the movie filled the marquee area. Zanuck stressed how much *Keyhole* made *42nd Street* and *Gold Diggers of 1933* "look like a trailer." Famed Chinese Theater owner Sid Grauman, keen to screen it at his United Artists cinemas, declared: "What I need with a picture like *Broadway Thru A Keyhole* is a marquee with about 15 rows of letters and about 20 feet tall."

Mordaunt Hall of *The New York Times* complimented both Columbo and Kelly, walking away from the film with the moral: "Even a thug can show a

A winning publicity shot.

sacrificial streak."[2] Bland Johaneson's *Daily Mirror* review began with the fanfare usually reserved for press agents: "The color, the excitement, the melodrama, the vast sentimentality of Broadway—all are conveyed with ringing accuracy by this new musical movie from the incisive pen of Broadway's Walter Winchell."[3] Rose Pelswick of the *Evening Journal* loved the "excellent cast" and observed that Columbo "looks his best when he has his profile to the camera."[4] The *New York Post*'s Thornton Delehanty felt that Columbo "as the irresistible crooner reminds you both in looks and acting of William T. Tilden."[5]

The Russ Columbo Co-Ed Club newsletter had its matinee idol pegged: "...in addition to the charm of his personality, he has brought to the screen that same feeling of sincerity which distinguished him in radio—an impression of emotional restraint, of power in reserve. He seems to be simply, inevitably following his natural reactions to the situations presented, and *not* acting at all."[6] *Variety*, meanwhile, took note of his "camera shyness" but offered kind counseling: "Surprise of the picture is Russ Columbo. He screens unusually well and suggests a type who, with development and screen tutelage, may go places."[7]

Rob Reel of the *Chicago American* also took the Columbo-Kelly screen confrontation to heart by observing, "...the scene between the bandsman and the bandit is one of the ace sequences of all time in screendom. The

COLUMBO COLUMNS

THE *Russ Columbo* CLUB

Co-Ed

Madeline Graw   Genevieve Fitzpatrick

Price 10 Cents   *130-26 Lefferts Boulevard*   Pub.ished Quarterly
November, 1933   *South Ozone Park, N. Y.*   Vol. I—No. II

FEATURING "BROADWAY THRU A KEYHOLE"

New York Reception

Russ Columbo's first feature-length film, the Walter Winchell story "Broadway Thru a Keyhole", produced by Twentieth Century Pictures, has been nationally released.

On November 1st, amid a fanfare of music from the film, dazzling lights, and a radio description of the scene, the big picture hit the big town, at the Rivoli Theatre on Broadway. For hours and hours, on the opening night, a continuous musical and chatter broadcast from t h e theatre marquee, and a sound truck touring the block, kept the crowds along the Main Stem, conscious of nothing but this flashing tintype of themselves and those who go to make the White Way what it is. The excitement reached its peak at midnight with the personal appearance of those "screen celebs aud stage satellites" that Winchell loves to tell about, and continued through the special chorus girls' showing at 3 A. M.

Russ Columbo in "Broadway Thru a Keyhole"

"Movie Star! What Now?"

Your voice and music won our hearts,—
   A sweet, romantic charm
Bade millions pledge allegiance to
   Sincerity, so warm.

And each new venture seems to leave
   Our fondest hopes quite cold
Your versatility deceives,—
   Surpassing dreams, two-fold.

For now, your magic, from the screen,
   Unmercifully projects
Drama . . . on a defenseless world,
   With light and sound effects.

Our Theatre Party

The New York members of the Russ Columbo Co-Ed Club attended the show the opening night, and at a meeting in the theatre afterward, broadcast, pictorially to Russ Columbo on the Coast, what thev thought of his performance. Need we say that the message, quoted from the picture, was:—

"We think you're swell!"

A thoughtful, air mail, special delivery letter from Russ Columbo to the meeting, read by everyone present, provided additional thrill. Autographs and comments on the picture were collected from members and mailed to Russ. Walter Winchell also sent a note of good wishes to us all. Thank you, Mr. Winchell, and we hope you will have fully recovered from your illness by the time this reaches you.

—◆—

restraint with which it is played ought to make it a candidate for some sort of academy award. A special hand to Lowell Sherman for his direction!"[8]

Sherman also put in some good words by publicly praising his cast, reserving special thanks to his crooner: "I am convinced that Russ Columbo, radio star, has possibilities as great as Rudolph Valentino had. This boy, Columbo, with his gentle, crooning voice, his handsome Latin beauty and lovable personality is headed straight for stardom."

More *Keyhole* ads abounded, one boasting "'Bowery' Is Out, 'Broadway' Is In!" Another announced it as "The Sock Heard Round The World." An ad at San Francisco's United Artists Theater read: "Swaying arms and prancing legs! Flashing thru the whirling madness of Broadway nights!" And at Brooklyn's Loew's Metropolitan, the rave got more personal: "The Story that Caused the Feud between Jolson and Winchell!"

Guilt perhaps seeped into the calluses of Winchell's personality as he watched *Keyhole*'s trailer with sickened alarm. He may have also been skittish about potential lawsuits. Perhaps out of mercy, the studio credited Gene Towne and Graham Baker as the official screenwriters, although Winchell's name appeared on the opening credits. Still, the voice was unmistakable.

This welter of hoopla got stymied just three days following the film's premiere when Texas Guinan, one of its biggest names, died in Vancouver after problems arising from ulcerated colitis. Especially with Guinan's untimely passing, *Broadway Thru A Keyhole* was a swan song to the Jazz Age, arriving just one month before the 18th Amendment (one of Columbo's admitted pet peeves) got nullified, allowing the 1st Amendment to slam Prohibition's coffin shut.

Studio moguls may have been sidling up to him and devotees may have glued their ears to the radio each time he sang, but Columbo always had to keep one eye out for the next boorish surprise. He would have done well to heed *Broadway Thru A Keyhole*'s advisory words when Blossom Seeley's character tells Constance Cummings:

> *I always get a stitch when I hear that old hokum about 'the show must go on' and 'go on out there and knock 'em dead'. Well honey, that stuff was made for hams and stage-struck suckers! And take it from me, dear. Tomorrow will still be Wednesday, whether you're a pancake or a hit. And fifteen years from now, they won't remember you any more than they remember me!*

Moments later, at the blare of the curtain call, Seeley does an about-face and commands Cummings to "Go on out there, be a sensation, knock 'em dead, kill 'em with success, and no matter what happens, the show must go on!"

The "Orchid Lady."

VICTIMS

OF

GRAVITY

With both of us, we're not people. We're lithographs. We don't know anything about love unless it's written and rehearsed. We're only real in between curtains!

—Carole Lombard to John Barrymore, from *Twentieth Century*

"My love for you has always been a faithful, beautiful and sincere love," Russ Columbo once wrote to Carole Lombard. "You wanted it that way—didn't you? At least I thought you did."[1] And so Columbo took yet another picaresque plunge into the gaping jaws of *amore*, this time with Hollywood's fervent and flighty "Orchid Lady."

Columbo's much-touted romance with Lombard remains one of Movieland's finest oddities. Magazine and newspaper articles coated their relationship in Cupid's spew, but Columbo and Lombard usually endeavored to project a less conventional co-dependency. Lost as both were in an infinitely regressing pattern of romance, rejection and more romance, neither could bid the other a definitive hello or goodbye.

Metaphysically speaking, they formed one ideal being. Both were born in the same year, derived mutual delight in commiserating about Hollywood's inherent cruelties, and, judging from various photos of them dining out together, shared an affinity usually reserved for fraternal twins reuniting after separation at birth.

Born Jane Alice Peters in Fort Wayne, Indiana, Carole Lombard became an inveterate tomboy by the time she and her family relocated to Southern California. There, she was left to raise hell in a rowdy environment with two older brothers.

In contrast to Columbo, whose roughhousing met with a parental pounding, Lombard sparred with her brothers and got a reward. Director Allan Dwan, visiting friends who lived next door, was so enthralled to see the lionhearted lass swing her fists that he got her a part as Monte Blue's kid sister in the 1921 drama *A Perfect Crime*.

Lombard's mother, who subscribed to the Baha'i faith and indulged in numerology, was also a sexual equality advocate. Though nurturing her daughter's free spirit, Mrs. Peters retained misgivings about her fifteen-year-old's acting bug.

At the Marian Nolks Dramatic School, Lombard made fast friends with classmate Betty Jane Young (sister to Loretta Young) who later became Columbo's crony Sally Blane. Carole's beauty was already in bloom, but she preferred playing male roles in class, taking special delight in skits requiring her to don trousers and a moustache.

Following a serious auto accident when her face smashed through a windshield and left a scar, Lombard abandoned pretty girl roles for a while. She instead succumbed to pratfalls, pie-tosses and mud-puddle plummets after getting a job as one of Mack Sennett's daffy dames. One of her Sennett co-stars, the hilariously plump Madalynne Fields, soon became Lombard's sidekick and confidante.

Next to Lombard's lean frame, Fields was a perfect comic foil. Sennett himself remarked that they amounted to "my own Laurel and Hardy in drag."[2] Quick to tag her with the affectionate nickname "Fieldsie," Lombard took Fields around with her everywhere. Fieldsie was well-read, an intellectual merit that solidified their friendship. The two had another significant factor in common, what Lombard's biographer Larry Swindell called a "friendly detachment toward men."[3]

Lombard had her share of male dates, some of them arranged by Paramount's publicity machine. Entering the virginal world of the "talkies," she nonetheless felt compelled to protect her pubescent self from an industry fraught with hairy, probing hands. The celluloid cowboys who hung around the set protected her from strangers whenever she played Buck Jones' leading lady, but her brothers had already trained her with a repertoire of intimidating cuss words.

For all her enthusiasm to be seen and to sleep with men of sophistication, Lombard had a distinctly déclassé talent for mouthing off the most offensive expletives imaginable. She would hurl obscenities at dinner parties, on movie sets, on dates, and in diverse public places. When horny wolverines in brilliantine came sniffing her way, she had only to intimidate them with an incisive "Kiss my ass!"[4]

Lombard did accumulate an impressive roster of male "friends" and concubines as she advanced in the studio system. Be it the amorously unavailable Noel Coward or the chronically horny publisher Horace Liveright, Lombard sought to attain stature through osmosis. She liked prestige as well as good looks and gladly snuggled with dignitary directors like Preston Sturges, Rouben Mamoulian and Ernst Lubitsch.

Jane Peters became Carole Lombard partly out of superstition. She took her last name from a surrogate father and friend named Harry Lombard, but accounts of how she embellished her Christian name with the extra "e" vary. One story has her mystically inclined mother consulting a numerologist who thought the name "Jane" accounted for the young girl's habit of stumbling and bumping into various objects. The numerical vibrations for "Jane" were 1-1-5-5, a sum of 12, which, for a girl born on October 6th, amounted to a fatal 3. Platt recommended "Carole" and its more prosperous numerical value of 27.[5]

Another version has Carol encountering a printing error on posters for her 1930 film *Safety in Numbers*. She liked the added "e" and, perhaps goaded by the numerological implications in the movie's title, kept that spelling. Her ambitious publicity department played up the occult angle by touting how this new 13-letter configuration created more positive vibrations and augured a brighter future.

Oddly, Columbo's adopted name was also supposed to have good mystic vibrations. His numerologist friend Trix MacKenzie added up Russ Columbo to the vibration of 9—a number signifying "ambition, generosity and achievement." "In some cases," MacKenzie once wrote to him, "9 gambles everything, loses with a grin or wins with a whoopee party. In all cases 9 will 'take a chance'—will win back speculative ventures—will lend a helping hand to a friend by passing out real money—and in large quantities."[6]

Lombard had already crossed paths with Columbo in 1929, during the filming of *Dynamite*, a time when circumstances were not yet as fortuitous for her as for the crooner. The story goes that Cecil B. De Mille relegated her from a second player to an uncredited extra after she complained that the assigned dialogue was beneath her intelligence.

Like her mom, Lombard practiced as well as preached what would later be called a more "liberated" lifestyle. She bragged about the joys of sleeping in the nude and not wearing a bra. She may have played at being a floozy, but Lombard's prominent forehead suggested an intellect larger than is generally tolerated in pretty blondes. She was sassy and sensitive, whimsical and witty—an excitable little girl spitting through a worldly

Lombard with the supercilous William Powell.

veneer. As *Life* magazine's Noel F. Busch later observed: "She gets up too early, plays tennis too hard, wastes time and feeling on trifles and drinks Coca-Colas the way Samuel Johnson used to drink tea."[7]

Lombard sometimes cultivated fatal friendships. She sacrificed her part as the second lead in the 1930 film *Laughter* by giving it to pal Diane Ellis. When shooting was finished, Ellis married but quickly contracted a fatal exotic disease while honeymooning in India. Another of Lombard's friends was the actor John Bowers (the supposed prototype for *A Star is Born*'s Norman Maine) who failed to make the adjustment from silent to sound pictures and left the world after a one-way stroll into the Pacific Ocean.

Life changed drastically for Lombard in 1931, when she got paired with the supercilious William Powell in the movies *Man of the World* and *Ladies' Man*. Impressed by his air of breeding, debonair moustache, and taste for exquisite cuisine, Lombard had already spun a romantic fantasy about the actor even before she met him. Sixteen years her senior, Powell embodied for Lombard the perks of privilege, the glamour of yachts and country clubs, the grandeur of "high art," and the excitement of a paternal figure to husband her schoolgirl cravings. "When she was assigned to a Powell picture," Larry Swindell writes, "she felt very like Cinderella mistakenly invited to the royal ball."[8] She married him in June of that year.

By spring of 1933, Lombard called her marriage to Powell a "waste of

"...what brought Lombard and Columbo together was a mystery even to some of their friends..."
—Warren G. Harris.

time." It was around this period when Columbo mesmerized her during one of his Park Central performances. Later on, amid the aura-poking confines of a typical Hollywood party, the Romeo of Radio and "America's Madcap Playgirl #1" were lucky enough to navigate through the restless, conniving energy and lock into one another's retinas. Soon they would call each other "Pookie."

Though she would eventually admit that "good people get to know me and then they die,"[9] Lombard provided Columbo with at least the chimera of a foundation over La-La Land's tremors. Boisterous and lewd, beautiful and kind, Lombard would join Lansing Brown as the only other soul Columbo would submit for his mother's approval.

Lombard's nurturing attitude toward Columbo had a cinema counterpart with her role as the anti-heroine in the 1933 Paramount film *White Woman*. Already vexed by a scandalous past, her character has the subsequent misfortune of meeting up with a shady tycoon, whom Charles Laughton plays to hammy perfection. Laughton hoodwinks Lombard into marrying him in exchange for a semblance of security on his Malayan jungle estate. She soon discovers that this "King of the River" is a sadistic lunatic who holds her, and a bevy of other misfits, his prisoner.

The aggressively independent Lombard, who married boors but seemed to long for a graceful man's affections, transferred her conflicts to the screen. *White Woman* gets more intriguing when Lombard befriends a timid and perhaps (in the obtuse "Classic Hollywood" mode) sexually ambiguous Foreign Legion deserter played by Kent Taylor. From the moment they meet, their bond defies movie expectations. There is no instant pounding of the heart, no sweaty leers or mawkish mating calls. Instead, an endearingly unconventional love transpires: mother-son, sister-brother, or one frustrated misfit reaching out toward the other.

While reflecting their atypical relationship, this film had its special pace in the professional lives of the two Pookies. According to Warren G. Harris, in his *Gable & Lombard* biography: "Lombard would often invite Columbo to the set to watch production and pick up pointers that might help his movie career."

Harris has also been mystified by the Pookie chemistry:

> *Though what brought Lombard and Columbo together was a mystery even to some of their friends, each fulfilled a need in the other's life at that time. Lombard required an escort to squire her around to all those parties and nightclubs she enjoyed so much. She also liked to help people when they were down on their luck—as she herself had been after her accident—which might be another reason why she was so drawn to Columbo.*[10]

Tinseltown historian Adela Rogers St. Johns made her own keen observations on the Columbo–Lombard interaction, noting that "he was almost like her child; he woke all that was mother in her; she couldn't bear to see him unhappy." She continued:

> *Russ was a very unusual man—a boy he always seemed to me. Slim, dark, with one of the loveliest voices I have ever heard in my life... In my time I have seen men in love with women, but I have never seen a man as much in love as Russ was with Carole Lombard. There was poetry in it, and music, and sheer romance... That she knew of some dark shadow that hung over young Columbo, just beginning what promised to be a career as brilliant as any we have ever seen on the screen and in radio, there can be no doubt... Her great friend Fieldsie... knew it. Her mother knew it. Perhaps it was the reason she was so tender with him, gave in to his wish never to be separated from her.*[11]

As the maternal half, Lombard complemented the paternal Lansing. Both surrogate parents became friends while doting over their dream child. The child himself would soon extol their virtues to *Motion Picture* magazine:

Just now he [Lansing] is urging me to take advanced singing lessons and put in several hours a day at hard practice. I'm lazy, but Lansa has ambition enough for two... Carole is after me too... She says to me, 'Russ, you can't go on crooning forever. You have a voice and you should study.' Between Lansa and Carole, I guess I shall have to go to work. They want me to study with [Professor] Marafioti. I have already arranged this. If someday I am singing in grand opera, it will be due to them.[12]

Columbo may very well have envisioned Lombard coaching him from the other side of the KECA studio's glass window as he sang Richard Rodgers and Lorenz Hart's "Lover" for the November 16th *Hollywood On The Air* broadcast. After the brassy opening, Columbo follows a cascading clarinet into a soft and slow mood. One can easily imagine his billowy "goddess" guiding him along to the rollercoaster rhapsody as the orchestra shifts from a gallant waltz to a rumbling crescendo, driving home Hart's lyrics about enchanted dances and desperate glances.

For Columbo, Lombard's platinum blonde strands symbolized the lemon chiffon dreamscape he would sometimes conjure to focus away from stress, in contrast to Lansing's handsome, dark and probing face which had enticed him to look inward. Carole represented someone so different from himself, something so other. She helped him get his mind off his mother's health problems, the bad scripts Universal kept sending, and that pervading sense of never being fully comfortable in his own skin.

Not even Lombard could cheer him at the end of December, when Con Conrad made the Yuletide gray. According to an item in the *New York Sun*, Conrad was in New York promoting his latest vocal discovery "Del Campo" when he developed a severe infection of the larynx. The once glib wheeler-dealer could no longer talk and was rushed to the city's Midtown Hospital for an operation. His recuperation proved a debatable fortune when he walked from a hospital bed into his lawyer's office to file a suit against Columbo for, of all things, supposed contract breaches.[13]

Still in the red for the $7,500-plus he owed from the Park Central Hotel proceeds the previous year, Conrad had the temerity to file a suit against Columbo in the Los Angeles Superior Court. His lawyer W.I. Gilbert, a well-known Hollywood attorney who once helped Valentino in his divorce case against June Acker, accompanied him. The suit claimed that Columbo was remiss in his obligations to pay Conrad a third of all performance earnings. Conrad would end up demanding from Columbo ridiculous sums of over $66,000.

The Conrad suit put Columbo in an understandable snit. Even those closest to him could not escape the conspiratorial haze clouding his perceptions. This was more than ever true when Conrad's professional betrayal coincided with what seemed to be Lombard's emotional betrayal. One antagonist in this scary scenario was "Fieldsie," who, no longer salient as an actress, gladly became Lombard's secretary. Her insistence on also being Lombard's personal adviser put Columbo on the defensive. Fieldsie's habit of being a well-meaning but irksome meddler came to a near breaking point on the apparently miserable Christmas Eve of 1933—a night so riddled with angst that he tried to exorcise his misgivings in a letter:

> Dear Carole—
>
> Fieldsie seems to have known quite a great deal about your love for me when she takes it upon herself to say it was merely physical and did I think for one minute that you fell in love with my mind. Well—darling—that's a lot to take from someone else—supposedly speaking your mind or thoughts.
>
> You wouldn't have the least bit of respect for me if I did take it. In other words—as I gathered from Fieldsie—I should have felt perfectly contented to take love as it was and enjoyed it and cherished the sweetness and loveliness when it was all over. Well—that's all nice and lovely —if I had known that you wanted me just that way, but I gathered from our earlier meetings that you wanted me for always...
>
> There was nothing too great or too small that I wouldn't have done for you—I loved you more than anything in this world—this life—You said the same thing to me many times but you proved otherwise...

Lombard's erudite spirit (studied as it may have been) scared Columbo as much as it captivated him. He found her infatuation with older and brainier types intimidating. Powell—Columbo often called him "Bill" or just "B."—remained a problem. This, despite Lombard's insistence that she had grown weary of her ex-husband's hauteur and complained that the "son of a bitch is acting even when he takes his pajamas off."[14] Even after she divorced Powell for being "cruel" and "cross in manner," she started socializing with him again. Columbo adapted to the sickening circumstances by assuming the role of a private eye. He shared his foreboding about this triangle in the same letter:

> You wouldn't have done so many things if you had had such a great and fine love for me. For instance—your spending that week-end at the Beverly House with Bill—You know what resulted. Not satisfied with a

severe lesson you were taught by the Almighty for being unfaithful… I knew right along it happened after that week-end party—especially when Bill called you that one nite one week or two later. I forgave you—because I loved you. I know how you felt about Bill being so unhappy because he had lost you—and that was your opportunity to prove to him that you still cared for him a great deal—so much for that…

Even by Thirties standards, Columbo's ensuing letters to Lombard had a soap opera sheen. It was as if he deliberately embellished them in the event that they fell into another's hands. Take for example his florid desperation six days after Lombard failed to show up on his birthday:

> Jan. 20, 1934
> Letters to my Great Love—
> The Ideal of my dreams—Perfection of woman—she is—at times
> Yet—at times—she is so naughty.
> My Dearest One: My Angel—
> In this world of artificiality and superficiality, it may not seem quite sane to say—
> I worship you as the ancient worshipped their gods and goddesses. I have placed you on a pedestal, yes, and there I shall always keep you in my heart and soul, as my goddess—my infinite ideal. My dream come true. My love for you is so great sometimes—that it almost crushes the very life out of me. It creates a new being inside—a greater and more beautiful soul and sometimes from the spirit of God, I receive a message that you have been unfaithful—I don't exist any more. You crush all—my life and my being becomes dormant as a dead person's.
> If I could express in words, verbally to you how I have known about your doings with him, B., you would doubt me—why do you doubt me and say it is not true when God in my very soul speaks the truth and it is always revealed—without error.
> Remember, my Angel—
> Faithfulness, Loyalty, Truthfulness and Honesty are the "Four Horsemen" of Love.
> —Pookie

Closing with an allusion to the film *The Four Horsemen of the Apocalypse*, Columbo also adopted a literary mode similar to an entry in *Day Dreams*, the famous book of Valentino's verse. In his own copy, Columbo had placed a ribbon mark on "You," a poem Valentino loaded with embraceable lines like: "*You are the History of Love and its Justification. . . The Reality of Ideals. . . Idolatry's Defense. . . The Power of Gentleness. . . Vanity's Excuse. . . The Melody of Life. . . Sanctuary of my Soul. . . Eternity of all Happiness. My Prayers. You.*"[15] Columbo took an equally prayerful approach in a subsequent missive:

> Monday, Jan. 22, 1934
> My Darling—My Angel—
> Why do we have to discuss this thing any further?
>
> You seem to have your ideas about our love as to how it should develop, and the conditions of complication should eventually eliminate themselves. But Angel, don't you realize that you are quite satisfied and content to go on like this and I am not. No two people in love have ever dared to take love as we have. Of course, Angel, not willingly have I stood for this sort of treatment for so long but merely because my love for you is so great that I have overlooked the smaller and, yes, very vital things.
>
> If two people are so madly in love with each other as we are, why can't they be together constantly? For what reason should they be separated? None, my Darling, except for the selfishness on your part of trying to keep your love as well balanced as possible.
>
> You know definitely in your own mind that mentally I do not meet your certain requirements, so therefore you look elsewhere for that. Physically you adore me and love me madly. But Angel, this is not a great love on your part. For if you loved me as greatly as I love you, there would be no requirement that you might demand from me, for a great love between man and woman demands nothing.
>
> It just happens. Two people fall desperately in love. Nothing is too great or too small to sacrifice. If you loved me as you say you do, you would give up this great mental companionship with so and so.
>
> Oh Angel, I do pray to God that you will come to your senses soon and realize that either your love for me must surpass all these little foolish pastimes and give all, or we must go our different ways and I shall forget you.
>
> I love you with my heart, mind, body, and soul. That covers everything, darling. Whatever problem or difficulty that arises that must be worked out or solved, we must do together, dear. We must progress together. We must learn and help each other in different ways and yet be divinely happy in doing so. This is mine and probably the rest of the world's proper idea of a great existing love between two human beings.
>
> Oh, I do pray that you will see it God's way. That is the only way it should be.
> —Pookie.

As she tutored Columbo for his upcoming movie parts, Lombard prepared for what would become one of her most important and successful roles. Paramount had loaned her out to Columbia Pictures to star opposite John Barrymore in Howard Hawks' *Twentieth Century*. Ben Hecht and Charles MacArthur based the script on "Napoleon of Broadway," a stage play that Charles Mulholland penned to commemorate his days working for the despotic theater producer David Belasco. Lombard plays a former salesgirl who, after submitting to Barrymore's iron fist, assumes all of the affectations expected of a grand actress. Despite Hawks' insistence that she improvise and appear as "natural" as possible, Lombard's every line and gesture took on a comic flair achievable only through zero spontaneity. As the following letter shows, Columbo, who likely assisted her with reading her lines, could not help but detect how much Lombard got fused to her part.

> Friday, Jan. 26
>
> Oh my Angel—
>
> I'm not exactly sober but always know what I'm doing, and the brain is always alert and active.
>
> I finally concluded and confirmed my own thoughts about the carryings on with B—I know, darling, exactly why you're so attentive and charming to him.
>
> I realize and have known for quite some time that you are quite extravagant and live rather lavishly, and a bit too luxuriously for the amount of money you earn, and so you must get it elsewhere.
>
> Don't misunderstand me if I say merely that you are playing with B. very wisely and always to protect your own self and what's more—security and good security.
>
> That is why it is so difficult for you to choose between love and an assured, comfortable, and luxurious living. That is why I said tonight that this certain quality that you have must be hereditary. It is not the beautiful and divine Carole that I love, but the superficial and artificial person that does not even exist in my heart and soul for a minute.
>
> —Pookie.

With such displays of devastation, Columbo could have very well made Lombard haughtier by revealing her power over him. "His love for me was of the kind that rarely comes to any woman," she would later tell reporters. "I never expected to have such worship, such idolatry, such sweetness from any man. He had no life apart from me. He was lost if we were not together."[16] Facilitating this primacy game, Columbo wrote on:

Sunday, Jan. 28

Oh My Darling—

Why do you make it so difficult? You know exactly what I mean when I say that we are so unlike other lovers.

From now on it has to be different. I must see you every nite and there must be a stop put to all this unreasonable amount of foolishness and selfishness on your part. All I ask is that you be fair and return the love I give to you.

We must be together always—every day—darling—as lovers should be, together constantly.

I do pray and hope you will see it this way—the only way.

I don't want to do anything drastic during one of my idiotic and depressed moods—and probably go off and marry someone just for the hell of it.

We're not being fair to each other by just carrying on as we have been in the past. I must be near you and see you every day—and nite. Is that asking too much of one whom you love so dearly with your heart and soul? I think not, my darling, and I'm sure you will see it my way, the right way.

—Pookie.

Among his letters to Lombard, Columbo apparently retained at least one that the doyenne of screwball comedy had written to him. It has no specific date, but the tone suggests that she reached a point when she needed to clarify her nurturing role:

Oh my loved one.

I have just received your beautiful letter and poems would fail to express how full of love my heart is. So full that I am crying for joy. I love you my angel, with a great love. Dearest, I know you must think me insane and you are quite right. Your love for me has made me happier than anything. I am so grateful.

You see dear—I know that beautiful soul of yours. At times I may seem caustic and petulant. But as you said in your letter, you could express your thoughts—so much better on paper. Believe me darling, your letters and messages of love are so inspiring. They are truly great and express the real you. Sweet, I am filled with such eagerness for you to let that come forth orally. I know what it will do for you.

Dearest, I never want to hurt. On the contrary, I want only to give you love, understanding and help. I am like a mother at times. Completely filled with love, ambition wanting you to be perfect. Guarding and protecting you from being hurt. (Sweet, I wish you were here this second to kiss me, I miss you so.) I love you always with all my heart and soul.

Sweet, I am giving you this band ring and I want our love to be a complete circle of perfect harmony and understanding.

God bless us both and may we always see his light and follow it.

I love you
Your angel—

The Pookies staged for themselves a drama of affective despair followed by sentimental binging. Within a week, all calm would be restored before the next wave of emotional cannibalism. Some might call it love; some might call it madness. Perhaps an anecdote from Oscar Wilde's *The Picture of Dorian Gray* puts the Columbo and Lombard story in better perspective, as the hyper-cynical Sir Henry Wotton marvels at the final irony committed by a paramour he once spurned. After railing to him about how he had ruined her life and how she threatened to end it, the wronged woman proceeded to gorge herself on a full-course meal.

THE
TREMBLING HAND

Everything seems to point to the fact that it just had to be. There is a thread running all through this that we cannot understand. But some day we will know why this had to be.[1]

—Virginia Brissac, Russ Columbo's secretary

KITTIES IN PERIL

On an otherwise miracle-deficient afternoon in Beverly Hills, guests at Russ Columbo's patio on Roxbury Drive marveled as their host emerged from his swimming pool—a sight no less mystical than Venus rising from her half-shell. His dark eyes sparkled as the refracted sunlight grafted a halo around his wet hair, the water pouring like pearls of amniotic effluvia from a chlorinated incubator. Clark Warren, a visiting journalist from *Screen Play* magazine, had to do a double take.

The rapturous poolside atmosphere soon switched into a panic mode as Columbo's anxious mom ran across the patio to drape a bathrobe over her chill-prone hatchling. Russ then displayed his own maternal mania as he scurried around the yard looking for his cat's missing kittens. All the while he hollered at the clumsy Alaskan husky that Lombard had given him—also named "Pookie." Fortunately, the dog did not lunch on the felines, but the kitties-in-peril incident worked Columbo up into what *Screen Play* would describe as "the sentimental, highly emotional mood so characteristic of the Russ Columbo his intimates know."[2]

Once Columbo stopped fluttering, he allowed Mr. Warren to fire some questions. All the while Russ watched his mother, who was now in the kitchen brewing a pot of coffee to help prevent her Ruggiero from catching cold. Russ made a point of proving his fealty by giving her a loving pat each time she passed. Mist glazed over his eyes as he leaned toward Warren and hummed: "My mother. God bless her!"

Sipping his java, an upbeat Russ paused to reflect on how the day's crazed events captured his life in all of its discord and glory. He chatted about his rebounding career, his ongoing opera and tennis lessons, and how much he looked forward to playing a lead in the movie *Wake Up and Dream*. Puzzled by his father's desire to shackle him to a wife, Columbo expressed relief that his wiser mom preferred to see her last-born shrink-wrapped against matrimonial spoilage.

Clark Warren had already witnessed the mother-son symbiosis a few weeks earlier at the Columbo manse during the first interview. Entering through the kitchen, he discovered what resembled a living Pieta as Ruggiero and Giulia wept in each other's arms. The fret session started when Columbo discovered his mother shaking and sobbing over a recent news story. The item concerned a little girl from Tucson, Arizona named June Robles who had been kidnapped, shackled, crammed into a box, and finally rescued from a pit in the desert where her captors had ditched her. Not since the Lindbergh baby was kidnapped a couple of years before did America get so wrapped up in the fate of an endangered child.

How ironic that, while wringing her hands over the suffering of a distant bambina, Mama Columbo remained somewhat less cognizant of the hazards affecting the runt of her own brood. This was because Columbo, terrified of giving her a stress-induced coronary, kept mom in the dark regarding certain matters. Preventing her from watching his movies, Russ assumed that she would forget it was all a flickering illusion and perish from the horror of viewing her baby depicted in any kind of distress.

Columbo's mom did not have to languish inside a movie theater, however, to sense vandals invading her nursery. Her son most likely took extreme measures to hide the fact that the former landlady of his previous 509 North Crescent Drive residence was a reputed psycho who did not like him—a notorious anti-mom named Charlotte Shelby.

At least according to Sidney D. Kirkpatrick's controversial book *A Cast of Killers*, Shelby was a spiteful harridan who imposed such tyranny over her daughter—the silent star Mary Miles Minter—that she (a former child actor herself) perfected the "stage mother" stereotype. Kirkpatrick also portrayed her as a financial and psychological grifter who hoarded her daughter's loot while coveting most everyone else's. Flirtatious toward men with whom she sought favor and vindictive toward those she could not win through blackmail or bribery, she was reported to have no qualms about exploiting every possible legal avenue to boost her matriarchal ambitions.

Shelby allegedly threatened some on her hate list with the wrath of a .38 caliber revolver. Those who believed her capable of pulling the trigger were somewhat vindicated when she became a prime suspect for the 1922 shooting death of director William Desmond Taylor. The proposed motive? She believed that Taylor defiled her little Miss Minter's purity. Coupled with Fatty Arbuckle's deadly rape scandal a year earlier, this sensationalized homicide shamed the Hollywood community into pseudo-Draconian feats of self-censorship. The identity of Taylor's killer remains a mystery, but some true crime enthusiasts still get a whiff of murderess musk whenever hearing Shelby's name.

So, just twelve years after the smoking gun had cooled, Columbo managed to kick off 1934 by getting on Shelby's bad side. When he packed up to vacate her property after leasing it for only three months, Shelby took offense not only at her tenant's abruptness but also for what she claimed were unpaid back rent, bills and damage to the premises. To remedy the situation, she instinctively filed a lawsuit with the Los Angeles court. Worse, when itemizing her defaced belongings, she included the luckless detail of a broken mirror.

POOKIE IN THE DOGHOUSE

Barely fazed by Shelby's antics, Columbo was preoccupied with, what he at least perceived as, more crucial matters. He had to adjust to his new address; get in touch with the Packard company about his ever-ailing auto; phone his clothier Boyer's about the faulty collars on his blue shirts; undergo costly scalp treatments for his receding hairline; keep tabs on the maneuverings of Conrad's lawyer W.I. Gilbert; work through his power struggles with the studios; play telephone tag with Lansing; and make sure to write down the limousine numbers of Carole's various chauffeurs waiting outside of William Powell's home.

Thanks to these niggling events—all jotted in his laconic but illuminating 1934 "Year Book"—Columbo's subsequent days on the planet transpired with the tragedy of grand opera and the bathos of a Mack Sennett clown chase. Columbo's ritualistic minutiae gained madcap momentum on Tuesday, January 9th, when he called his lawyer Milton T. Hunt, Jr. to discuss details of the upcoming courtroom showdown with

Conrad. That same day, before taking his rattling Packard into the shop for repairs, he wrote down Pookie's car #87937 as it stood outside Powell's place at approximately 8 a.m.

"Only God knows how many times this same thing has happened," Columbo would soon write to Lombard on Beverly-Wilshire Hotel stationery. "I've tried oh-so hard not to believe it but after sitting in my car and almost dying from a broken heart—watching the Beverly House after the lights all went out—Oh—I thought you were the one girl I could faithfully believe in and trust..."

> *Thursday, January 11: Check for Miss Shelby; Call Bullock's—robes, bedroom slippers, suspenders, garters, tennis shoes, tennis socks.*

> *Sunday, January 14, 1934: My birthday today, I am 26—well! No Pookie, on my birthday (nice going).*

"You'll never know the wound you have carved in my very heart," the jilted birthday boy continued in the same letter. "...Oh, why was I born, dear God, to live to see the only thing I ever wanted in this world and life—before my very eyes—stay with another man. Well, maybe God is punishing me for taking you away from him—now you must lie to me to see and be with him... God—oh God—my heart is breaking—and I pray with these tears from the very depths of my soul—spare me in this life any further sorrow—May I never have to feel like this again for I'd rather not live than go through this awful and most heartbreaking experience I have ever known..."[3]

Had Universal Studios given him the chance to express such sentiments in a screen monologue, Columbo might have held a candle to someone like Colin Clive, the accomplished British actor and angst champion who jolted the world just three years before with his frenetic role as "The Man Who Made A Monster" in Universal's *Frankenstein*. Radiating much of Clive's dashing demeanor and neurotic charm, Columbo hoped that his talent agent Phil Berg would negotiate for more creative and distinctive parts. Instead, Universal offered him the lead in something called *Glamour*, where he would play a character named "Lorenzo Valenti."

> *Friday, January 26: Refused to do picture "Glamour." Saw Pookie.*

Although Glamour (directed by William Wyler) would have put him opposite Constance Cummings and Paul Lukas, Columbo balked. Universal replaced him with Philip Reed and, starting on January 27th, had discharged Columbo temporarily without pay. Louella Parsons reported that Columbo was "warring with Universal on account of he feels this company hasn't kept its word to let him sing in film musicals... Rather than play in parts he finds uncongenial, Columbo has stepped out and is asking for his release."[4]

Superstitious thoughts may have slinked across Columbo's mind upon discovering that his work schedule and future payment hinged on the completion of Universal's satanic shocker *The Black Cat*, starring Boris Karloff, Bela Lugosi and David Manners.

Thursday, February 1: Pookie—Preview of picture "Bolero" in Santa Barbara; Script of "Bachelor Wife" (bad).

Friday, February 2: Call Berg about "Bachelor Wife"; Shirt back to Boyer's—no hole for cuff link. Pookie—dinner.

Tensions mounting and legal ledgers piling, Columbo continued to purchase toilet water, polo sweaters, swimming tights, jock straps, and Pookie's gardenias. He also sought release by strengthening his tennis elbow. Besides taking lessons from champion Eleanor Tennant, he relished the opportunity to lob and serve on the courts with Gilbert Roland, actress Leila Hyams, Pookie, and Pookie's brother Stuart Peters. But the psychic war with William Powell accelerated. Whenever deprived of Pookie Time, Columbo got more sullen. Lombard, in turn, seemed to grow more cavalier each time Columbo sported another worry wrinkle.

Alluding to his personal struggle through the airwaves, Columbo highlighted one of his KECA shows with a Lew Brown tune called "I've Got To Pass Your House (To Get To My House)." Crosby recorded it with Jimmie Grier's Orchestra at about the same time, but the Vocal Valentino turned the song into a melodic document of his days as a Lombard sleuth:

> *I'm wondering who is sitting with you*
> *And doing the things that I used to do.*
> *I have to close my eyes,*
> *When they meet your eyes,*
> *For in your eyes I see,*
> *No longing for me, just sympathy,*
> *A message that says, "It just has to be..."*

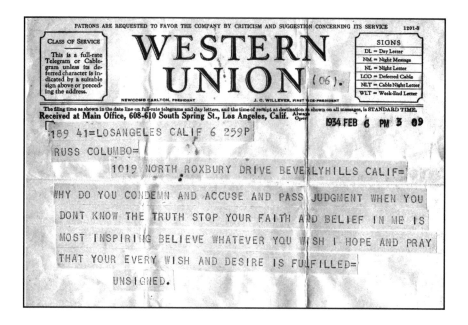

PATRONS ARE REQUESTED TO FAVOR THE COMPANY BY CRITICISM AND SUGGESTION CONCERNING ITS SERVICE   1201-8

WESTERN UNION (06).

CLASS OF SERVICE

This is a full-rate Telegram or Cable-gram unless its de-ferred character is in-dicated by a suitable sign above or preced-ing the address.

NEWCOMB CARLTON, PRESIDENT   J. C. WILLEVER, FIRST VICE-PRESIDENT

SIGNS
DL = Day Letter
NM = Night Message
NL = Night Letter
LCO = Deferred Cable
NLT = Cable Night Letter
WLT = Week-End Letter

The filing time as shown in the date line on full-rate telegrams and day letters, and the time of receipt at destination as shown on all messages, is STANDARD TIME.
Received at Main Office, 608-610 South Spring St., Los Angeles, Calif. Always Open   1934 FEB 6 PM 3 09

189 41=LOSANGELES CALIF 6 259P

RUSS COLUMBO=

1019 NORTH ROXBURY DRIVE BEVERLYHILLS CALIF=

WHY DO YOU CONDEMN AND ACCUSE AND PASS JUDGMENT WHEN YOU
DONT KNOW THE TRUTH STOP YOUR FAITH AND BELIEF IN ME IS
MOST INSPIRING BELIEVE WHATEVER YOU WISH I HOPE AND PRAY
THAT YOUR EVERY WISH AND DESIRE IS FULFILLED=

UNSIGNED.

Monday, February 5: Pookie—flowers; Watson's—all suits refitted; [see] Boyer's about shirts—some bad; Pookie with Bill—12 to 6 a.m. <u>All nite</u>. I <u>Know</u>.

Tuesday, February 6: Fight with Pookie.

In between chiropractic appointments, missed engagements with Lansing, and emotionally upended dinner dates with Lombard, Columbo endured the clown shows of litigation. Along with Shelby's claims, there was the backwash of Lew Erwin, his former talent agent, who was now intent on collecting an allegedly overdue commission for booking Columbo into the Woodmansten Inn in the summer of 1932. A courtroom confrontation for the ongoing Rusco suit occurred on or about February 9th. Columbo's lawyer Hunt argued before the judge that Conrad failed to represent his client in good faith. Russ was also pressured to dig back into his records to July of 1932 in order to account for his earnings. He also consulted with Hunt about (what he listed in his date book as) a "bankruptcy idea."

This was messy and frightfully unromantic stuff—a knuckle-dragging gambit involving money, bluster, deceit, and more money! How utterly unfit for a crooner who sang about "living in dreams"!

Saturday, February 10: Pookie's party for [Norman] Taurog & Co.—Not invited.

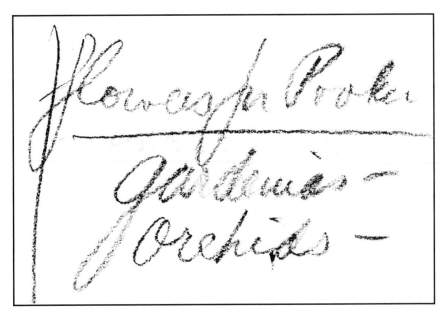

From Russ' 1934 "year book."

Sunday, February 11: Get dog from Pookie; saw Pookie—all beautiful again.

With only the letter "P" etched across the middle of the page for his February 14th entry, Columbo was enigmatically silent about Valentine's Day. But whenever he scrawled the lonely words "No Pookie" on subsequent pages, he left behind an almost fragrant sense of life in the doghouse.

According to a Columbo "character study" issued through the Universal Studios press department: "One of the paradoxes of his life is that although thousands of women have fallen in love with him, he has been highly unsuccessful in his personal love affairs. The women with whom he becomes enamored of always seem to be in love with someone else."

In public, Columbo almost always bucked up to insinuations of being a romantic failure. "I have just one object now. Save my dough," he soon told journalist and (so she claimed) friend Ruth Biery. "I have a little house for Mother and Dad. I'm living with them. I'm back here and I don't believe I'll ever leave. The big world looks marvelous when you have never seen it. Marry?—No. I like all the girls now. Sally Blane, Loretta Young, Carole Lombard—they're all great sports. They're pals. I'm through with love. I'm glad to be back. I want to work hard—and save my money!"[5]

Ernst Udet, the German ace, was the honor guest at Junior Laemmle's party, attended by more than two hundred. Left to right, standing: Edward Everett Horton, Russell Simpson, Neil Hamilton, Ernst L. Frank, Chester Morris, Mabel Marden, Russ Columbo, Harold Lloyd, Joe E. Brown, Charles Murray, Hugh Enfield, Carl Laemmle, Jr., and John Farrow. Seated, From left to right: Anita Page, Mary Brian, June Knight, Madge Bellamy, Benita Hume, Mary Carlisle, Dorothy Burgess, Gloria Stuart and Maureen O'Sullivan.

Wednesday, February 28: Call Roy Turk about lyrics; Tennis with G. Roland... No Pookie.

Saturday, March 3: See Junior; cash settlement on 6 mo.—1 yr. Temporary release; Call Roland about Racquet...

When mentioning "Junior" in his date book, Columbo referred to Carl Laemmle, Jr., the Universal mogul who continued haggling with him over the right movie vehicle. All the while, Russ acceded to Universal's constant shooting postponements and endured the humiliation of applying, likely at the studio's request, a gunky preparation called "Gro-Hair." Perhaps to purge himself of the abounding psychic debris, not to mention unwanted body weight, he tried rooting (literally) into the bowels of his dilemma— as his subsequent references to "internal" and "intestinal" baths indicate:

Monday, March 19: Toilet water; license for dog; get copy of "Anthony Adverse"...

Monday, March 26, 1934: Call Hunt about insurance policy—making out will; See [Walter] Lang at studio; Quinine and cod liver oil for dog; Internal bath; Call Lansing about place... Pookie at Bill's.

Tuesday, March 27, 1934: Internal bath; occulist, ears blown; pack clothes for trip.

One moment Columbo would be on top of the world during his weekend breaks with Lombard at Lake Arrowhead; the next he would feel as dejected as he did on Fieldsie's birthday (April Fool's Day) after Pookie nixed plans for a get-together and snuck over to Powell's place again.

Wednesday, April 11: Flowers for Pookie; ... Check on battery in car—noises in gears, rattles and squeaks; Appointment for eyes...

When Crosby starred opposite Lombard in the screwball comedy *We're Not Dressing*, Columbo could have easily found himself at loggerheads with his crooner foil. During the shooting of one crucial scene, however, he may have been sore enough at Pookie to live through his Romantic Rival vicariously.

Crosby, according to script specifications, had to slap Lombard across the face. Extremely phobic about physical abuse since childhood, Lombard did not take kindly to the situation. She tried intimidating Crosby, telling him how unmanly it would look for him to hit a woman. But director Norman Taurog demanded that the scene stay. When time finally came for the blow, Lombard went on a tear. In Crosby's own words: "I didn't want to hit her back, but she kicked me in the belly, knocked off my toupee, wrecked my make-up and tore my clothes."[6]

Along with the internal cleansings, the tennis appointments and countless bouquets to Pookie, Columbo's world remained a projection board for the press' matrimonial pipe dreams. On Friday the 13th, the *New York Evening Journal* announced: "Russ Columbo and Sally Blane, after an on-and-off romance of many months, will take the Long March in June—with cameramen present, of course."

Saturday, April 21: Mom's birthday.

Sunday, April 22: Finally P. decides not to see B. anymore.

Tuesday, April 24: Call Hunt about Erwin—settlement—hear from Conrad— 5:30 tomorrow. Call Hunt when news comes; P. at B.'s, last time I hope...

Wednesday, April 25: Pookie's broadcast with Louella at 10:15 a.m.; Dinner with Pookie at Stuart's; Expect to hear from Conrad 5:30 p.m. regarding Erwin settlement...

By April, Lew Erwin's case finally ended, leaving Columbo in arrears of over a thousand dollars in overdue commissions. He also faced a Superior Court order to render up his accounting books and various other documents of earnings accrued between June 28, 1933 and April 20, 1934. The Rusco case was off the docket until mid-August, but Conrad still planned to file an amended claim for bigger damages. And like a proud cat that licks itself in times of distress, Columbo confronted this pettifogging by fussing over his appearance all the more, particularly over his finery:

> *Saturday, April 28: White shoes; Call sox man; Shirts—low Barrymore collars; Toothpaste, razor blades, Milk of Magnesia; Ask Phil Berg for release; Hunt re: Erwin and Conrad; Carole's Ford at Bill's—4:30 p.m.—said she was talking business...*

Columbo's date book entry for Sunday, April 29th was a drastic departure from the usual terse passages:

> *B. must be a vital thing in her life when she is willing to give me up if she cannot see him again: Oh, such a selfish and spoiled child—always must have her own way. She wants both of us—argued with Pookie about B. again. This time it was definitely understood that she will always see B. in matters of business, etc. Oh—such a tragic scene. He must be very vital in her life.*

> *Monday, April 30: [Call] Universal about starting. (Raise Hell). No Pookie—out with B.?* [Here Columbo crossed out an entry that reads, "Send Pookie gardenias every day."]

> *Wednesday, May 2: B. called Pookie—Truth revealed—Thing definitely off between—Bill taking it pretty hard—P. a bit upset???. Looks the definite end of the Riptide...*

> *Thursday, May 3: Tennis balls, slave bracelet for Pookie... Flowers for Pookie?*

On May 9th, for an afternoon banquet sponsored by the Los Angeles Junior Chamber of Commerce, Columbo sang "Going To Heaven On A Mule." Al Jolson had to perform the Harry Warren–Al Dubin tune with a face full of burnt cork for a climactic spectacle in the movie *Wonder Bar.* Russ, however, avoided minstrel makeup and still got plaudits from the *Los Angeles Times* for his "stirring rendition."[7]

The movie offers and critical praises seemed at times too good to be true. When the doubts got intense and he needed a heart and an ear, Columbo got Lansing to join him for soul-searching moonlight drives. "I am a friendly person, but I have few friends," Columbo would tell *Motion Picture* columnist Rilla Page Palmborg. "The little taste I have had of popularity has taught me the difference between friendship and acquaintance. I had to have several experiences with so-called friends, using their so-called friendship with me to try to get into pictures or touch me for money, before I learned it. Lansing has never wanted anything from me, except just to help me. I don't know three people qualified to understand a friendship like ours."[8]

But just as in the song "Just Friends," when he sang of "two friends drifting apart," Columbo might have suspected that Lansing—his best buddy, adviser, and Pythias to his Damon—had abandonment issues of his own. After all, Columbo's repeated statements about Lansa always being there in times of need suggested a co-dependency that was a bit lopsided.

Thursday, May 10: Check with Hunt about N.B.C.—sustaining; Eyes examined. Hair washed with new cream. Teeth cleaned. Call Lansing. Call Mom...

Friday, May 11: Eyes, teeth, and internal bath. Tennis—Pookie.

Sunday, May 13: Mother's Day. Flowers for mom. Flowers for Mrs. Peters, Mrs. Lansing Brown; Pookie, Fieldsie, Stuart for tennis, 10:00 a.m. Polo matches—Pookie.

Columbo's next film, which seemed to take forever to start, underwent several title permutations. Originally called *Love Life of a Crooner*, it later became *Tonight's The Night*. Close to the time production commenced, Universal finally settled on *Wake Up and Dream*. Actual filming, slated to begin by the end of May, got postponed again.

Monday, May 14: Call Hunt; Studio about script. Tennis—Pookie 1:30–2 p.m.; Call Lansing, Call Mom.

Saturday, May 19, 1934: Had intestinal bath today. Pookie—dinner. Pookie—ill.

Tuesday, May 22, 1934: P. didn't call me at 4:30. Had me worried to death. Finally saw her at 8:30. Said she got tied up with wardrobe.

Into June, as he prepared for another NBC sustaining program, Columbo was more eager than ever to present himself as a new, improved "straight baritone." He acquired this stature by pursuing (on the joint advice of Lansing and Carole) regular opera lessons with the esteemed Professor Mario Marafioti.

There is a curious omission in Columbo's date book for June 8th. His old flame Dorothy Dell, who was also prone to worry over cosmic numbers, grew wary after attending the recent funerals of two fellow stars, Lilyan Tashman and Lew Cody. One of her friends recalled Dell saying, "The old theater superstition says death strikes in threes. I wonder who'll be next?"[9] A week later, just past the June 8th midnight hour, the nineteen-year-old actress rode home from a party in Altadena. After her car skidded out of the lane, bounced off a tree, landed in a ditch, and crashed onto a huge boulder, Dell became the third martyr.

Columbo's new NBC program started on June 10th. It would begin each Sunday evening at 8:15, broadcast from KECA coast-to-coast. The first show featured luminaries like Jean Harlow, Walter Winchell and, of course Jimmy Fidler. Russ' second broadcast on June 17th commanded a much eerier dignity, opening with the customary bars of "You Call It Madness" and proceeding with Cecil Underwood's prim introduction: "Good evening, ladies and gentlemen. For the next fifteen minutes, the National Broadcasting Company presents the Romeo of Song, Russ Columbo, in songs to delight your ears and heart… And now friends, sit back and enjoy Russ Columbo's enchanting voice as he sings 'The House Is Haunted'…"

A piano twinkled with fragile hesitation as Columbo intoned:

> Lights are soft and low tonight,
> Summer breezes flow tonight,
> And to think that we're apart.
>
> Knowing you refuse to love
> Someone that you used to love,
> There's a chill within my heart.
>
> I hate to be alone when evening falls,
> I'm so afraid of all these empty halls, doors and walls…
> The house is haunted,
> By the echo of your last goodbye…

Billy Rose and Basil G. Adlam had freshly penned this amorous monody for the *Ziegfeld Follies of 1934*, but Columbo was born to brood to its dirge about unrequited passion. Being among the very first vocalists to introduce it to the public, Russ was virtually married to the song and might have in due course adopted it as another signature theme.

Columbo completed the program that day with a relatively tame rehash of "Time On My Hands" and a slightly uptempo version of another new song about dearly departing lovers called "Easy Come, Easy Go." Though his voice was at its richest and most controlled, Russ grew disenchanted with the "Hollywood On The Air Orchestra" and was most likely seeking to make Jimmie Grier his new arranger and conductor.

Monday, June 18: Supposed to start picture today—but no start.

Saturday, June 23: Script from Universal; call Berg; Call [sister] Anna— Doctor about mom's liver—examinations.

Sunday, June 24: Third broadcast; Orch.—not good.

Friday, June 29: Call [Jimmie] Grier; Possibly see make-up man about piece—etc., try to pencil in also before taking pictures; Pookie to bed 8:00—but drunk.

On July 1st, Columbo opened his *Hollywood On The Air* segment with a very misty reading of the brand new Mack Gordon and Harry Revel tune "With My Eyes Wide Open, I'm Dreaming." Dorothy Dell had coincidentally sung it in her last film *Shoot the Works* (which already had its theatrical premiere on June 29th). He followed with "Star Dust."

WAKE UP AND DREAM

By July, Columbo moved for the third time in a year's span. Now he sought refuge in the Hollywood Hills—a Spanish-style manor at 1940 Outpost Circle. On his July 8th broadcast, he sang "True" as well as the Harry Revel–Mack Gordon composition "She Reminds Me Of You" (a number that Crosby also happened to have performed in *We're Not Dressing*). On the next day, Columbo embarked on a new phase.

Monday, July 9, 1934: Picture definitely to start today—and it did.

From July 9th on, Columbo's 1934 Year Book remains blank. On the first day of the *Wake Up and Dream* production, Columbo took a course that looked so promising, yet his mood was likely shaken when he received a cautionary letter—postmarked that same day—from his numerologist friend Trix MacKenzie:

> *Your Astrology is going to be pretty bad during the next month. You have Mercury against you; so don't quarrel any more about written stuff, stories, news items and such. These items will probably flourish along about Wednesday and Thursday this week, as you will have the moon against you too; so watch out for worry and despondency over these things. Guard your health especially well beginning Saturday and over the weekend as the sun is opposing your sun. Don't take any chances at that time. I'll tell you more next week about Mars and Venus which are not yet opposing...*

Wake Up and Dream was nowhere near as racy as *Broadway Thru A Keyhole*. It had a more cuddly formula, with Columbo as the brooding baritone Paul Scotti. Co-star Roger Pryor played his likable pal and chump Charley Sullivan, while dancer (and ex-concubine to Max Baer) June Knight played Toby Brown—a pert and good-hearted female counterpart for whom both men in the story hold a torch.

While less challenging than his previous role, Columbo's part has some great, melodious moments. Musical Director Sam K. Wineland and Hollywood composer Howard Jackson provide the background score. *Wake Up and Dream* is most essential for being Columbo's creative showcase, featuring three wonderful songs that he composed and performed. With lyricist Grace Hamilton, he wrote "Let's Pretend There's A Moon" and also collaborated with Bernie Grossman and Jack Stern on "When You're In Love" and "Too Beautiful For Words."

The story opens with Columbo and his pals in Atlantic City, trying to sneak off the stage after performing in a poorly-attended vaudeville show. But, thanks to the extortionate threats of the theater owner, Columbo and June Knight must go out to perform the final number, a doe-eyed duet of "Let's Pretend There's A Moon." Columbo, sporting a mariner's cap, is all smiles as he takes the vocal helm, betraying no outward signs of duress as he sings and sighs about "a lovely night to spoon." In the wings, Pryor's character is left with the less glamorous task of trying to authenticate the song's "spell of moonlight bliss" by holding up a prop crescent slapped together with cardboard and glitter.

With June Knight and Roger Pryor in *Wake Up and Dream*.

The lonesome threesome soon gets turned out from one variety house after another, forced to scrimmage for change while living on frankfurters and false leads. Sullivan, the least inhibited of the trio, attempts to hijack one show by kidnapping its besotted star singer (Gavin Gordon) and tricking the producer to hire Scotti as a replacement. This sets Columbo up to audition with "Too Beautiful For Words," the tune that lingers throughout the narrative and plays no less than four different times. The words may be romantically optimistic, but the tone is again ghostly and sad:

> *You're like a lover's dream in the spring,*
> *A song that's as free as the birds,*
> *You're just a lovely love song,*
> *Too beautiful for words...*

Wake Up and Dream's skeletal plot leaves room for some charming byways, with a supporting cast of eccentric character actors who sometimes overshadow the principal players. Jane Darwell has a cameo as a shanty Irish landlady. Clarence H. Wilson is a diminutive, squinty-eyed detective named Hildebrand, hired by Sullivan's alimony-hungry wife to keep tabs. Andy Devine plays Joe "Egghead" Egbert, the blundering boozer of a bodyguard to Catharine Doucet as the flighty fortuneteller Madame Rose.

The rotund Paul Porcasi also appears briefly as Polopolis, a showbiz impresario with an exasperating facial tic.

Wini Shaw (who would later introduce "Lullaby Of Broadway" in *Gold Diggers of 1935*) shows up as a gold-digging nightclub singer named Mae La Rue, joining Columbo for dreamy duets when not trying to break up his competing romantic interest. The real scene-stealer, however, is Henry Armetta who plays Cellini, Scotti's old friend who has just arrived from Italy. As an ethnic caricature, Armetta was to Italians what Barry Fitzgerald was to the Irish—a walking catalog of folksy mannerisms laced with a triple-layer accent.

One notably quirky scene transpires in a Southwest Indian-themed cocktail lounge housed inside a Santa Fe bus terminal. As Columbo and Knight take the stage to duet on "When You're In Love," the creamy sweet melody proves so contagious that the club's patrons sway gently to the beat: a cocktail waiter digresses into a soft-shoe while holding a tray, Catharine Doucet tries seducing Armetta by chomping on a banana, and two ersatz Indians (one parodying Ramon Novarro's role in *Laughing Boy*) look on in deadpan amazement.

There is a very special moment in the movie in which Columbo's soul gets emblazoned on celluloid. As he and his three cronies take their bus trip from New York to Los Angeles, the camera captures Russ gazing in a slightly off-kilter direction. He could be eyeing the shifting landscape outside the window or yearning for Knight, his script's pre-arranged love interest. But, in an otherworldly moment with movie script bleeds into real life, he also appears to be contemplating an indescribable void, maybe lost in thought over his numerologist's scary foresight.

"...TWO LOVERS IN A LAND APART..."

On July 15th, Columbo got a bit of relief from the shooting schedule with another—and final—radio show. He began with a Mack Gordon and Harry Revel novelty called "Rolling In Love" (from the 1934 W.C. Fields feature *The Old-Fashioned Way*). Cecil Underwood returned to the mike to announce: "Music, romance and Russ Columbo. They go together like sunrise and dawn. Russ Columbo sings, 'I've Had My Moments', from *Hollywood Party...*" This Walter Donaldson and Gus Kahn melody (echoed a bit later in George and Ira Gershwin's "A Foggy Day") inspires sweet reflection, even with the impish interplay of clarinet and piano that characterized Columbo's former dance band.

On a cross-country bus trip in *Wake Up and Dream*, Russ appears to be contemplating an indescribable void.

With actor Andy Devine to his lower right, Russ entertains fellow cast members on the *Wake Up and Dream* set.

Columbo ended the program with "I'm Dreaming," the type of shuffling tune (in the Hoagy Carmichael mode) written for huckleberry friends to whistle on a river raft. The style was nothing like Russ' usual dream ballads, but he did stamp his personality on the memorable line, "I like to ramble on a road that never ends…"

Once filming was over by mid-August, Universal's honchos felt overly confident about *Wake Up and Dream*'s forthcoming success, announcing plans to cast Columbo as Gaylord Ravenal in a new film version of *Show Boat*. Other major studios courted this far more fetching alternative to Crosby. Word got out that MGM wanted him to star alongside Nelson Eddy and Jeanette MacDonald in *Naughty Marietta*, while RKO arranged for him to be in something called *Down to Their Last Yacht*. NBC also dangled more promises of an upcoming radio show to be called *Russ Columbo from Hollywood*. As the professional offers poured in, Russ hired a personal secretary, an aspiring actress named Virginia Brissac to help make sense of all the fan mail and phone calls.

Despite his relative success, Columbo still resented William Powell's looming presence and balked at constantly having to compete for screen roles with the likes of Clark Gable. Lombard's past and future husbands ended up starring together that summer in *Manhattan Melodrama*, with Powell as the straitlaced district attorney and Gable his crooked but loyal

While a chorus reaches out but never touches him, Russ focuses on his true love, his music, in this publicity shot from the set of *Wake Up and Dream*.

childhood pal. Assuming he even took the time to see the film, Russ may have cringed during a key scene when the two moustaches chat while attending a championship fight—the conspiratorial décor of a Dempsey poster looming in the background. The movie was not a good omen for John Dillinger either as he viewed it on July 22nd at Chicago's Biograph Theater. As America's favorite fugitive exited the cinema lobby, FBI agents chased him into a nearby alley and gunned him down.

Vultures instinctively wait for bodies to croak before swooping down for their repast, but Con Conrad proved an inverted scavenger as he pounced on relatively happy and healthy prey. He tried again in August to rain on Columbo's parade by upping damage charges and demanding that the singer give the Court a full accounting of all performance profits since January 1st of 1933. The Court, in a munificent gesture, granted Columbo the option to contest the claim within fifteen days. He now had until September 5th to prove that Conrad never lived up to his end of the Faustian accord.

Despite having to haggle with Conrad over money, with Universal over roles, and with Lombard over quality time, Columbo still enjoyed, perhaps for the first time, the rush of a self-made victory. Like Crosby, who ended up employing his brother Everett to handle his business, Columbo now relied on John Colombo to take charge of his accounts and career management.

Other than that, he was more or less on his own and, in this independent humor, was more adamant about marshalling his creative integrity.

Columbo expressed this invigorating resolve in a Universal press release: "At 26, I find that I have just about everything I want from life and am pretty happy the way things have turned out for me." One evening, he decided to celebrate fate's turning of the worm by inviting close friends to his home, primarily to show off his recent opera training. But he picked an odd piece to express his glee: the "Prologue" to the quintessential tragedy about love, betrayal and crimes of passion, *Il Pagliacci*.

Still imbued with the spirit of a tempered Caruso, Columbo dedicated most of Friday, August 31st to what would be his final set of recordings. This time he was on the Brunswick label and backed (to his delight) by Jimmie Grier and His Orchestra. He sang new and wonderful versions of the songs he wrote for *Wake Up and Dream*, but ended the session with a ballad by Allie Wrubel and Mort Dixon called "I See Two Lovers." Warner Brothers aborted Dick Powell's performance of the tune in the 1934 film *Flirtation Walk*. Helen Morgan torched it a year later in the movie *Sweet Music*. But no matter who attempted to capture this swansong to ideal love, Columbo once again claimed aesthetic ownership over a melody that seemed written especially for him:

> *I see two lovers in a land apart,*
> *Heart to heart, what bliss;*
> *And in my loneliness I see them start*
> *One heavenly kiss.*

Columbo infused "I See Two Lovers" with a deep, low and incantatory power, making timely shifts to the higher notes with a clean, smooth and sublimely unaffected conviction that must have made Professors Cimini and Marafioti proud:

> *Heavenly music, gorgeous perfume,*
> *Voices of night, a silv'ry light chasing the gloom;*
> *Soon a sweet picture comes into view,*
> *And my heart is still, before a thrill I never knew.*

> *I see two lovers, while alone I stand,*
> *By the sand and sea,*
> *I wonder when I'll find the trembling hand,*
> *Fate intended for me...*

Ending on the ominous "trembling hand" image, Columbo now had to curb his fatalism as he prepared to hook up with Lombard that evening. They sneaked into the Pantages Hollywood Theater for *Wake Up and Dream*'s official sneak preview. Sitting anonymously in the same movie palace where he once performed with Slim Martin's band, Russ was teary-eyed to see his name get top billing. Yet, two bees buzzed in his bonnet: 1) his mother's worsening health and 2) the conspicuous absence of Lansing. That same night Mama Giulia suffered a stroke.

The next day, after driving to Santa Barbara for another preview of the film and with mother on his mind, Columbo repeatedly phoned Lansing to no avail. The two men could have conceivably crossed paths in a parallel place and time, since Lansing also traveled to Santa Barbara on the afternoon of September 1st to conduct a photo shoot for a wedding. He planned to spend the night there since the ceremony was not scheduled until 7 p.m. but, after taking the required pictures, decided to avoid the reception and return home.

Lombard, frazzled after working on so many movies in so short a time, heeded her doctor's advice and joined Fieldsie for another Lake Arrowhead rest cure. Russ stayed behind to oversee mom's stay at Santa Monica Hospital. With Lansing still unavailable and the telephone exchanges from Lombard's wooded resort shut down for the night, Columbo had to brave the "empty halls" of his own haunted house—all those "memories that refuse to die…"

Lansing finally got back home and retired at around three in the morning. He rose at 11 a.m., about the time Columbo awakened to feel the closing grip of his mother's aorta. Wanting to see Lansing before paying mom another visit, Russ dressed in a mad flash. He drove over to the cozy little bungalow on 584 North Lillian Way, where Lansing and his parents were just finishing breakfast.

At roughly 12:30 p.m., Columbo arrived to join the Browns over Sunday coffee. Russ and Lansing then went into the library at the front of the house. As Lansing settled behind his big mahogany desk, Russ took the facing chair in front of a large mirror and initiated the conversation with his usual litany of worries: his ailing mom, reservations about Carole's loyalty, unpredictable career shifts, and sundry misgivings about the "dreamy dreamland" of the near future.

As always, Lansing played both the sounding board and sage. But on this otherwise godless ordinary day, he felt fidgety. He could not stop fumbling with his hands as he finished one cigarette and reached for another, finally grabbing one of the two antique Civil War dueling pistols he always kept on his desk for paperweights.

When Russ asked why he was a no-show at the Pantages preview, Lansing seemed distracted as he peeked into the gun's ball-and-cap mechanism, lithely replying something to the effect that he was busy that night. He looked upon the Valentino of Song who had in many ways been his protégé. Russ may have flown along a trajectory to stardom, but to Lansa he was still the moody kid who always looked to him for an emotional safe haven. Though blurry and enigmatic to many, Russ was, to Lansing, always in focus.

Today, however, Lansing's thoughts and Russ' presence lacked their customary clarity. Since neither man had a good night's sleep, the conversation took on an increasingly delirious tone. Lansa's mind grew more absent and his hands got jumpier. He kept pulling and clicking the pistol's hammer, nodding in sympathy as Russ chattered away. Pulling out another cigarette, he lit the match with his left hand and started waving the pistol around with the right.

Maybe Russ and Lansa were looking at the *Los Angeles Examiner*'s morning edition, giggling over its two-page spread depicting Crosby out to gun Columbo down. Maybe they thought it would be a hoot to re-enact such a campy photo essay.

As Lansa's gun pointed toward the desk blotter, the afternoon's events became a convoluted time fugue. The present was no longer real. Cause and effect became nothing more than a vague backdrop of cloudy motives. Whatever transpired in Lansa's library became indistinguishable from the forlorn recollections he shared with *Motion Picture* magazine[10] several weeks after the post-mortem.

> *... All of a sudden, there was a deafening explosion. You have no idea how terrific it was...*

Lansa dropped the gun once the bullet ricocheted off the desk's surface. He waited a moment, thinking Russ was once again up to that old play-dead pantomime they used to enjoy whenever a car backfired.

> *There wasn't a thing Russ did that I didn't know about. I am going to miss that dependence. It was as much a part of my life as anything could be... It shouldn't have happened to Russ through me... The one person I have protected all these years—kept everything unpleasant away from.*

Lansa gently shook him and pleaded for the joke to end, but Russ just stayed slumped over in the chair, letting out only a pained murmur.

If the bullet had struck Russ only a fraction of an inch higher, instead of pene-trating the opening in his eye, it would have not been fatal. And why couldn't I have picked up the other pistol? It had no slug... I want people to realize the awful loss I have and not think of how much I am going to suffer...

Russ looked at Lansa and forgot about all of the scheming press agents, fair-weather friends, deceptive flatterers, religious charlatans, and cotton-candy blondes. He was like the proverbial deer caught in the headlights—shocked yet servile at eternity's tactless flash. Through his shattered safety bubble, Russ Columbo now gazed into the face of unadulterated love.

There is one thing I want to say... Yet I hesitate. It sounds so theatrical. It is about the way I felt at the inquest. If Russ ever was with me, he was with me there—seeing me through. Just as sure as you are sitting here, he was with me.

Powerless to stop the blood, Lansa screamed, "Mother!"

The home of Lansing Brown.

Lansing arrives at the police station after the accident accompanied by Lt. Joseph A. Page. Page, the detective who had investigated the scene of the shooting, holds the cursed dueling pistols.

MONDAY MORNING.

SHOT KILLS SONG STAR

Wound Fatal to Russ Columbo

Relatives at Hospital When End Comes as Crooner Awaits Operation

Friend Says Civil War Pistol Fired by Match and Slug Glanced Off Table

(Continued from First Page)

and father, at 1940 Outpost Circle, Hollywood. One of his sisters is Mrs. Joseph Benedetti of 1606 Court street.

RADIO AND FILM SINGER

Columbo had been an active member of the screen colony since his arrival here about a year ago to take up motion-picture work. He had established a reputation as a radio and night club singer, gaining ascendency with Bing Crosby and other radio stars.

He was unmarried and was recognized as one of the most popular of Hollywood's eligible bachelors. Since his arrival in Hollywood his name had been linked in a romantic way with various stage and screen actresses.

Columbo, christened Ruggiero Columbo, was born in San Francisco on January 14, 1908, the youngest of twelve children. He received his grammar school education in the northern city and later attended Belmont High School in Hollywood.

FEATURED ON RADIO

Young Columbo, eager for a career as a musician, quit school in 1925 and toured the country as a concert violinist. Later he studied under Alexander Bevani, operatic coach, and was subsequently featured as a crooner with Prof. Moore's orchestra at the opening of the Roosevelt Hotel in Hollywood.

It was Prof. Moore who launched Columbo on the career which was to lead him to fame and fortune as a radio artist and later as a screen actor. Moore featured Columbo on his radio programs and within a short time practically every important orchestra leader in the West was bidding for the young singer's services.

JOINS ARNHEIM

Columbo, however, decided to remain in Los Angeles until he was sure of his success. He left Moore and joined Gus Arnheim's orchestra at the Cocoanut Grove and remained one year, during which he made thousands of friends and increased his popularity as a radio artist.

A friendly rivalry sprang up be-

Tells Shooting of Columbo

Lansing V. Brown, Jr., Hollywood portrait photographer, whose attempt to strike a match with the hammer of an old-style Civil War ball-and-cap dueling pistol cost the life of his friend, Russ Columbo, radio and film singer.

Here is a demonstration of the manner in which Lansing said he held the match and lowered the hammer of the pistol to ignite it. The flare of the match exploded a percussion cap in the pistol and sent a bullet into Columbo's brain.

WELCOME
TO
CROONER PURGATORY

So now, dear friends, I am not dead,
But live a glorious life instead.
The form upon the bier you see,
And strew with flowers so tenderly,
Is but the image that I wore,—
A house in which I live no more.

— "I Have Not Died," by C.F. Holland

From the book, *Poems for the Wayfarer on the Path of Life*, bearing the handwritten inscription: "*To Russell Colombo from the author (per Howard Coombs) Christmas 1926.*"

Crooner Purgatory is a spectral world with its own acoustical laws. Its inhabitants comprise a floating society of wandering souls who, famous for singing sentimental ballads in previous lives, glide on as melodic thought-forms. Flashing, hovering and swirling in sometimes gorgeous, sometimes terrifying patterns, each crooner commands colors, contours and textures unique to his personality quirks and unresolved emotional snags.

Bing Crosby, just as nonchalant in the afterlife as he was on both sides of the silver screen, projects a groany gray haze to offset the night-blue and day-gold backdrop of his famous theme. The acoustically sublime Perry Como is always ready to purify the ether with his fuzzy sweater of a voice, inviting all the restless sprites to dream along with him under the blanket of a starry sapphire sky.

Crooner Purgatory is redolent with *true* crooning and therefore cleansed of the fluorescent fungus associated with those "swinging" Vegas pseudo-croon-ers. Here, the otherworldly entertainers are also versatile enough to weave phantasmagoric duets. As Ricky Nelson's "Lonesome Town" congeals into melancholy but agreeable clouds of aquamarine, the renegade Jim Morrison, always more congenial to ballads about summer romance than themes of incest and patricide, tosses in a few streaks of his own deep-throated ocher.

The vibrancy is tenfold when two crooner luminaries from an extreme generational divide transform "Are You Lonesome Tonight?" into a rose-colored repartee. Little Jack Little, among the song's original avatars, whisks in with his powdered pinks, while Elvis Presley disgorges a thick crimson residue—a much more pleasing reminder of the detritus of jollity "The King" had left behind on his empty and bare parlor chairs.

The melancholy Little Jack Little took his own life in 1956 and is among those special emotional castaways—a crooner pioneer whose unseemly demise emits rarefied shades not indexed among Crooner Purgatory's official color codes. Al Bowlly, who supposedly wept in the studio while recording some of his Thirties ballads, also sets off an indescribable kaleidoscopic buzz whenever he slips into "When That Man Is Dead And Gone," the last record he made before becoming an unwitting target for a bomb that crashed into his flat during the London Blitz of 1941.

"Whispering" Jack Smith reported to limbo in 1951 and radiates the same bluish, snowy glow of the television set he expired in front of while marooned in his New York apartment. Rudy Vallee also traversed the other side while the television flickered. Whenever launching into another rendition of "My Time Is Your Time," he decorates his niche on the crooner continuum with a halo of giddy green waves.

Without question, Russ Columbo's rhapsody in turquoise is the envy of the ectoplasmic circuit. Murmuring "Good Night" to his sensorium of imaginary sweethearts, he manipulates his high baritone into arabesques of azure offset by sparks of incendiary red. Compared to his light show, all of the surrounding recitals appear dimmer. His is the color of romantic yearning, the luminosity of doubt, the shape of introverted rage.

These visions from the astral kingdom are not entirely the product of mere mystagoguery. They are inspired clues from another item Columbo had left behind, a pamphlet of spiritual observations by a young J. Krishnamurti entitled *At the Feet of the Master*. In it, the adept declares:

The astral body has ITS desires—dozens of them; it wants you to be angry, to say sharp words, to feel jealous, to be greedy for money, to envy other people their possessions, to yield yourself to depression. All these things it wants, and many more, not because it wishes to harm you, but because it likes violent vibrations, and likes to change them constantly. But YOU want none of these things, and therefore you must discriminate between your wants and your body's.[1]

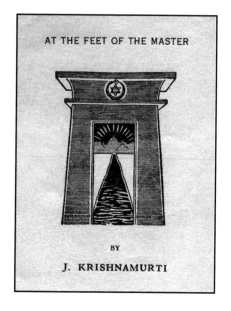

AT THE FEET OF THE MASTER

BY

J. KRISHNAMURTI

Most *terra firma* skeptics would simply scoff at Krishnamurti's hollow sanctimony, but Crooner Purgatory's denizens find it outright infuriating. Unresolved desire is, after all, the philosopher's stone of their eternal passion play. Even the inevitable prospect of contemplating away their character imperfections seems boring compared to the magnificent fireworks that erupt whenever they concentrate on past life traumas. Like theme-park patrons watching a simulated apocalypse, they cannot look away from the pain.

One can imagine Russ Columbo feeling every bit as frustrated as poor Emily Webb in Thornton Wilder's *Our Town*. After dying while in childbirth, she crosses over to a vast cemetery that is cluttered with the preoccupied faces of countless others long deceased—all lingering in wait for a final resting place. Emily, reluctant to wean herself from the friends and places she knew, teleports back to one of her childhood birthday parties but can only plead and scream to a family now oblivious to her invisible ghost.

Columbo, likewise, has the option to wander through both sides of the mystical gauze that separates two worlds. He is especially prone to revisit his death day, watching himself slumped in the chair as Lansing leans over him. He is helpless to turn back the clock or to rearrange fate as Lansing and his parents fail to resuscitate him. They soon arrange for an ambulance to wheel him on a stretcher to the Hollywood Receiving Hospital, where his vigilant brother John Colombo waits.

Virginia Brissac, Columbo's secretary is shown when she identified his body. From *Los Angeles Examiner* archives, courtesy Los Angeles Public Library.

As the doctors decide on a specialized operation, Columbo follows his former self being transferred to the Good Samaritan Hospital. The attendants around his deathbed shudder as the physician declares the wound far too delicate for surgery. Fast-forwarding past the five or so hours of struggle before his surrender to the dying light, Russ watches his face change from that of a disfigured victim to a fallen angel in repose. Soon, his spectral double buoys from the bed to the ceiling, looking down as stalwart friend Sally Blane cries beside his shell.

From the halls of the hospital, Russ passes into the Hall of Justice and to the Inquest that took place on September 4th. A crowd consisting mostly of dour-faced women crams into the courtroom to hear of the shooting. His dedicated secretary Virginia Brissac has the unenviable task of being the first witness, weeping behind blue eyes as she identifies him by name, the town of his birth and his age. The mood is still when a shattered Lansing takes the stand. As the ballistics expert holds up the black metal ball retrieved from his brain, Russ can only whisper "Lansa..." over and over again as his poor, befuddled pal recounts their last conversation together and how the future was aborted in a flash.

Up to this point in Columbo's astral journey, the tinctures of love and sorrow flow to the surface like streams of pent-up bile. Gray smoke soon envelops the vista as he looms among the mourners gathered for his funeral at the Blessed Sacrament Catholic Church on Sunset Boulevard. Unlike the disorderly crowd at Valentino's funeral a decade earlier, the 3,000-plus visitors arriving to pay respects keep their composure as Bing Crosby, Gilbert Roland, Zeppo Marx, Lombard's brother Stuart Peters, and the other pallbearers lift his body from the hearse into the church. His sister Anna, looking so frail, nearly collapses while walking up the church steps. As his brother John and brother-in-law Joseph hold her up, she cries, "No one will ever know how much we loved him."[2]

In conjunction with the ceremony, the personnel on the Universal studio lot honor Columbo with five minutes of silence. Still, all of the movie star trappings he once took so seriously appear ephemeral. Carl Laemmle, Jr. now looks like one of the village mourners in one of his Universal vampire films as he places a cross-shaped flower wreath beside the body's candle-lit altar. Looking down at himself laid out, Russ smiles at how well the bullet gash on his face had been concealed—thanks to the wonderwork of Universal's make-up chief Jack Pierce, the same man who assembled the famous horror faces of Dracula, the Frankenstein monster and the Mummy.

Columbo's pallbearers included Bing Crosby (second from right), Gilbert Roland, Carole Lombard's brother Stuart Peters, director (and Fieldsie's spouse) Walter Lang and Sheldon Keate Callaway. Zeppo Marx was a last-minute replacement for Lowell Sherman whose mounting illness forced him to cancel.

Left to right: Albert Columbo, brother-in-law Joseph Di Benedetti, John Columbo, grieving sister Anna Di Benedetti and Delmar Smith.

With hand to face, Carole Lombard departs from the funeral after leaving her trademark gardenias.

Columbo's loyal friend Sally Blane mourns with her mother.

Roger Pryor (Columbo's *Wake Up and Dream* co-star) and Ann Sothern attending the last rites.

Carole Lombard arrives to make an indelible impression and atones for not coming to the deathbed in time. Her postures of grief bear an eerie resemblance to those of Pola Negri when Valentino lay in state. The service, dutifully performed in Latin, prompts her to weep and totter as Crosby offers solace. In much the same manner that Negri covered Valentino's coffin with roses, Lombard drapes Columbo's bronze casket with gardenias, while the choir breaks into an *a cappella* rendition of "Lead, Kindly Light."

Amid this pageantry, Columbo's gaze inevitably gravitates toward the back of the church, to the pew where the ever-sorry and ever-trembling Lansing kneels. Russ stretches his transparent hand out to his earthly soul mate, assured that Lansing would eventually detect his presence and maybe feel a little better. It is usually at this juncture when Russ redirects his sojourn to Forest Lawn Memorial Park. He wanders down the marble studded corridor of the Sanctuary of Vespers and pays his respects to brother Fiore's wall crypt. He then looks across the way to his own crypt, pleased that those kind and special souls who continue to remember him still place flowers. In an instant, he is gone, leaving the scattered and often frustrating remnants of his existence for posterity to interpret...

EPILOGUE

After Valentino died, tabloids had published doctored photos of him in heaven, socializing with other white-toga-attired figures like Enrico Caruso and Madame Blavatsky. Columbo, adhering to his idol's example in death as in life, exuded enough ectoplasm to inspire his own amazing tales. Singer Rosemary Clooney, who later moved to Columbo's former Roxbury Drive address, claimed the singer returned as a pissed-off poltergeist, so angry for having died there that he terrorized her and her children. Even though Columbo was killed on North Lillian Way, Clooney had adhered to her story. Perhaps she mistook Columbo's ghost for that of George Gershwin, since the composer had spent his final days writing his last two songs at the Roxbury residence.

Much of Columbo's posthumous legend is more mundane. His only subsequent screen contribution was some uncredited stock music for the 1935 Universal release *A Notorious Gentleman* that starred Charles Bickford. Some of the earthbound demons that dogged Columbo were even more tenacious after his passing, especially the crabby creditors who pursued him past the graveyard and into the courts. Charlotte Shelby, for one, continued her demands for chump-change "damages" that finally amounted to a little over $100. Even though he had reinstated his life insurance policy shortly before dying, Russ never had the chance to make out a final will— an omission that invited a flurry of claim-seekers.

The Colombo family members bickered among themselves. John managed Russ' estate and, on July 22, 1948, rendered to the Court a "First and Final Account Report" to the Supreme Court of the State of California that claimed his brother died with estate assets totaling $13,133.72 and not enough to pay Federal income taxes. Official court records listed Columbo's appraised assets to include two violins at $250, one $350 star sapphire ring, one $125 Vacheron wrist watch, four studs totaling $120, a $200 "diamond-encrusted" cigarette case, a trunk full of miscellaneous clothing valued at $15.00, and unpublished songs sacrilegiously logged at having "no value."

Meanwhile, Albert (Alfonso) had long ago filed a petition in Superior Court to have John removed as administrator. And when Albert died in August of 1946, his widow Hazel "Columbo" pressed on with the suit. Shown clutching at her record books on the front page, Section B, in the December 6, 1948 issue of the *Los Angeles Evening Herald and Express*, insisted that the inventory was undervalued. She, on behalf of her daughter Sally, pressed the Court for more money, claiming that the crooner left $56,200 and that John had "maliciously refused to marshal all of Russ' assets."[3]

Mrs. Carmela Tempest and John Columbo, sister and brother of the late singer, Russ Columbo, are shown as they appeared in court.

Among the items Albert and Hazel added were a $20,000 Stradivarius violin, government bonds of $10,000, $7,500 in miscellaneous jewelry, a $750 ring from Lombard, along with $600 in clothing that included 45 suits, 90 shirts, 30 pairs of shoes and 200 pairs of socks. Hazel deemed another item "of great value"—the supposed diary in which Lombard allegedly kept intimate details. "Everybody in the family knew it existed," Hazel declared to the *Los Angeles Examiner*. "Carole asked for it after Russ' death, but members of the family refused to give it to her. Now they say it never existed."[4]

There was also the case of the mysterious opal ring that Pola Negri had supposedly transferred from the finger of Valentino to Columbo. One story has a cousin of a cousin in the Colombo lineage named Del Casino inheriting the ring, getting spooked by its curse, and throwing it into New York's East River.

By the time the Court settled the final account and left Columbo's surviving heirs to divide the estate among each other, there was hardly any meat on the bone to justify the courtroom carnage.

Columbo's immediate family members have all since passed on to their respective Purgatories: Father Nicola succumbed to pneumonia in May of 1942. The siblings faded gradually: Anna (Colombo) De Benedetti died in 1940, Albert in 1946, Anthony in 1965, and John in 1967. Carmela, who adopted the last name Tempest by marriage, tried to maintain her memorabilia collection and remind the world of her famous brother's accomplishments but died in 1986.

According to the July 22, 1948 Superior Court records, Con Conrad added $6,433.35 to his previous $60,000 Rusco suit. But Columbo's brother John had already rejected these claims in November of 1935. Conrad had backed down and concentrated on the progression of events leading to September 28, 1938, when he died in Van Nuys, California from a long and ultimately incapacitating illness. According to several obituaries, including one in the October 5, 1938 issue of *Variety*, The Superior Court of the State of California got involved once again. Leona Conrad (his subsequent wife) filed for a divorce on April 13th of that year, citing her husband's extravagant expenditures and fits of rage. Despite his propensity to get tangled up in nasty litigation, Conrad left behind many sensitive love songs and was inducted into the Songwriters' Hall of Fame. He also co-wrote "The Continental" for the 1934 Fred Astaire and Ginger Rogers film *The Gay Divorcee*—the first tune ever to win a Best Song Oscar.

Lowell Sherman, who was already convalescing on the day of Columbo's funeral, experienced sudden convulsions at his Beverly Hills home and met his maker in December of 1934. Various reports cite either pneumonia or larynx cancer as the cause. He may have appeared the roué to the world but, like Columbo, stayed attached to his mother and lived with her till the very end.

Virginia Brissac returned to performing in a few movie character roles that included "Mother Zombie" in *The Ghost Breakers*, a psychiatric administrator with a hearing problem in *The Snake Pit*, and James Dean's domineering grandmother in *Rebel Without a Cause*. She died in 1979.

Madeline Graw, the Russ Columbo Co-Ed Club Co-President, still held a torch for the singer's memory until her passing in March of 2000. Shortly after his death, she wrote a special commemoration in her *Columbo Columns* about *Wake Up and Dream* and its tragic aftermath:

> *We thought it would be a trying ordeal, but anyone who knew Russ or ever saw him in person couldn't help recognizing those charming little mannerisms, the natural Latin courtesy, the grace of his walk and every move, the strong character in his face, the wonderful smile, the deep dreamy eyes which told so much of what he was thinking and veiled so little of what was in his heart...* [5]

Sally Blane married actor-director Norman Foster in 1937, retired from the screen in the late Thirties but made a brief return in the 1955 Cold

War thriller *A Bullet for Joey*. She raised two children and enjoyed a good, long existence until passing in 1997. Blane's son Robert Anthony Foster shares a Columbo-related anecdote:

> My mother was with Columbo's friend Lansing when he bought this antique flint-lock at a store. Brown had this affinity for antique firearms, but she did not really approve of it and thought that having firearms was completely irresponsible. She said it was a complete freak accident because Brown would never have pointed a gun in Russ' direction. But she also told me she thought it was a bad foreboding, that it was somehow predetermined that he would die so young. That experience haunted her. I remember my father buying me a flintlock souvenir from Spain. She hated whenever I played with it. I'd tell her it wasn't loaded, but she'd reply, "You'll never convince me that guns aren't loaded anymore."[6]

In the 1964 Walt Disney feature *The Moon-Spinners*, Pola Negri had one more screen triumph as Madame Habib, an eccentric jewel thief with a pet cheetah. Toward the end of the movie, when the authorities finally catch up with her, she utters a stirring, semi-autobiographical declaration: "I lived through two wars, four revolutions, and five marriages, but nothing —nothing like this!" Her shadow of a former self finally faded in 1987, when she achieved the peaceful sleep undreamt of in her dire prophecies. She left behind an autobiography that fails to give Columbo even a passing mention.

According to Jack Dempsey's autobiography, Hannah Williams fell off another matrimonial wagon in 1943 when Dempsey, ever suspicious of adultery, hired a detective to retrieve photos of her carousing at nightclubs. After coming home one night to find a semi-dressed man asleep on the couch, he soon filed for a divorce. Hannah, though hindered by another nervous collapse, found the stamina to file a countersuit. By the court date, she proved fit enough to take the stand, but Dempsey, the former "Man-assa Mauler," wimped out in the first round of Hannah's knockouts. She cussed in his direction, accusing him of slapping her around, making her bleed and putting a gun to her head. Though he got his divorce and cus-tody of his two daughters, Dempsey later admitted he had "absorbed a worse battering than I had ever had in the ring."[7] Sometime in the fifties, Hannah suffered major burns after her cigarette ignited a Los Angeles hotel room. She, like another phoenix, survived the flames but led a sub-sequently inscrutable life (and death?).

Carole Lombard found her feet again soon after Columbo's interment. Proving to the world that she was over her motherly ways, Pookie started romancing Clark Gable in 1936 and married him two years later. He was the second of two bulky matrimonial bookends, between which Columbo must have offered volumes of poetry. The accident-prone sweetheart of screwball comedy consummated her tenuous relationship to gravity on January 16, 1942, crashing into Nevada while flying back from a War Bonds promotional tour. Tinseltown lore included a story of séance socialites being stunned when a psychic claimed to have visited Lombard's former Hollywood Boulevard home and saw her spirit "descending the stairs in a red gown and greeting a dark-haired man."

Crosby thrived for four more decades as a crooner, variety show habitué and frozen orange juice mogul. Through the years, his voice mellowed from the rascally, jazzier style of his early days to that of a tempered balladeer. He, along with Perry Como, inspired both Pat Boone and Elvis Presley to crooner pursuits. In 1977, Crosby's heart attacked him under the Madrid sky and spared him from ever having to see his son Gary's Daddy Dearest pathography.

Lansing retreated to a sanitarium for a spell in the wake of what had happened. Though he never truly recovered, he had the good sense to vacate the godforsaken confines of North Lillian Way. World War II—that reformer of previously directionless lives—helped him sharpen his camera eye when he served as an Army photography instructor. He purportedly dedicated most of his later life to traveling and had even been a European tour guide for Sally Blane's niece Judy Lewis—the self-proclaimed lovechild of Clark Gable and Loretta Young.

Lansing kept the studio at 3301 Wilshire Boulevard, the haven of Columbo's youth, but spent most of his remaining days as a resident of Los Angeles' posh Hancock Park area. He stayed in a converted carriage house in back of the same stylish Victorian mansion that was later used for location scenes in William Castle's 1964 horror film *The Night Walker*. Never married, Lansing devoted the rest of his life to photography until his death in 1962. His assistant Beatrice Fox inherited and continued to run the studio until the wrecking ball leveled the building in the late Seventies. Perhaps as symbolic proof that the Colombos forgave his role in their bambino's death, Lansing's ashes were laid to rest in an unmarked Forest Lawn crypt near the graves of Russ' parents.

The most astounding Columbo legacy involved the "merciful deception" that Lombard and Columbo's family survivors had maintained for his infirm mother. Since Giulia's heart condition was severely compromised, her attending physician, Dr. Blodgett, advised that knowledge of her last-born's death would probably kill her. For several years afterward, they all agreed to keep her believing Columbo was still alive and pursuing a prosperous career in London and other parts of Europe. They took the elaborate steps of forging letters from him, each touting one success after another.

Every week, a new letter would arrive. Even relatives from Italy joined the charade, sending greetings with news of Russ' spectacular Continental reception. On special occasions, flowers would come to Giulia with her son's name attached. She also received a monthly check of $398, money she believed Ruggiero was sending her from his earnings. The funds really came out of a double indemnity life insurance policy that Columbo had taken out toward the end.

Mama Giulia may have complained from time to time about not being able to see her boy but somehow the conspiracy of kindness kept her pacified. Being practically blind, she would have the letters read to her in Italian. (Why someone would even bother forging actual letters is a fair question.) An existing date book, presumably kept by John Colombo, includes a "Record of Russ letters to Ma," handwritten entries of the days and months when some of the letters were sent—from September 17th, 1934 through July 10th of the following year.

This was the ultimate delusion in a story that, from the time of Columbo's birth, was predicated on protective scenarios shielding the vulnerable from harm. As deceitful (and somewhat twisted) as it seems, there is something edifying about the manufactured happiness contrived on Mama Giulia's behalf. A mother and son were safeguarded from ever witnessing each other die—a rosy picture on which very, very few can ever rely.

Still, Giulia Colombo's final will, dated August 26, 1944 (just four days before her death), bore a curious omission. It was apparently written out by a witness with tenuous grammar matched only by Giulia's shaky signature: "I like to leave $500 to my son Tony Columbo, $500 to Alfonso Coloumbo, $500 Carmela Tempest. Rest I leave to John Coloumbo."

The converging forces and creepy coincidences surrounding Columbo's death have prompted various Columbologists to try and cast gauche grids of conspiracy theory over otherwise unexplainable events.

Some believe that others had been involved in Russ' killing, pinned the rap on Lansing and threatened to kill him if he ever revealed the truth. Not being an ideal businessman and prone to the professional fracas, Columbo was vulnerable to a fatal grudge or two. Was it the gun-happy Charlotte Shelby or even the litigious Conrad? Could it have been the shortchanged Jack Gordean, who settled his suit against Columbo out of court for a sum that was much less than his original claim? Or was it the Duffy Gang and the other hoods connected to Russ' run-in at the Millbourne, Pennsylvania casino? Was it possible that, besides failing to return the $11,000 he owed, Columbo's scandal irked the casino proprietors all the more because they had to close up shop permanently? Following such trains of thought, one might have to recast Lansing as a programmed assassin, a type of Manchurian Candidate following out someone else's will.

Some have guessed that an unhappy Lansing made a gesture to shoot himself that day and simply misfired. There are others who, in a desperate attempt to domesticate Columbo and vilify Brown, imagine that Lansing killed Russ in a jealous rage after discovering that the Pookies were soon to announce a wedding engagement. But no subsequent records indicate that Russ and Carole ever truly planned to marry. On the day after the shooting, the *Los Angeles Times* quoted Lombard saying that she and Russ were "just very good friends."[8]

As Max Pierce, creator of the *Russ Columbo Remembered* website, shrewdly observes: "It seems that everyone wanted Russ to be engaged at the time of his death, which made heart-wrenching good copy in the papers." And according to biographer Warren G. Harris, Carole held no malice toward Lansing and greeted him at Columbo's funeral as a comforting friend: "Don't be silly. I know you loved Russ. I don't blame you. It was an accident. Russ would want us to go on being friendly, and of course we will."[9]

Those not happy with the "accidental death" scenario have pointed out a few inconsistencies in Lansing's testimony. At one point, he supposedly told investigators that he had only "planned" to light the pistol's trigger in Russ' presence as a practical joke. The Columbo obituary in the *Los Angeles Times* claimed: "Brown said, while he was toying with one gun and Columbo with the other, he accidentally dropped a lighted match on the percussion cap of the gun in his hand."[10] Other reports had Lansing contradicting himself by claiming he had the pistols for seven years and then saying he had just purchased the guns. But not one of these tenuous claims—issued from a deeply confused and distressed man—proved suspicious enough to jeopardize Lansing's declared innocence. Even Columbo's family deemed the killing "an act of God."

As Autopsy Surgeon A.F. Wagner declared in his official "Cause of Death" report from the Good Samaritan Hospital:

> ... said gunshot wound we find to have been inflicted at 584 North Lillian Way, Hollywood, California on September 2nd, 1934, by an old dueling pistol being accidentally discharged while in the hands of one Lansing V. Brown, Jr., and we further find this to have been an accidental shooting and we exonerate the said Lansing V. Brown, Jr., from any blame.

An even wilder theory has Crosby (a reported gun-owner) taking the "Battle of the Baritones" to a literal showdown. The Masonically minded have been curious over how Columbo had been murdered through the eye—an alleged process of ritual blood sacrifice preferred by Freemasonry's more ardent practitioners. The death of Russ Columbo does bear the symbolic trappings of a Masonic assassination—the killing of the "King of the Crooners" followed by a shadowy transfer of power. After 1934, American listeners coped with a new world order of sorts by surrendering their romantic identities to the romantically deficient Crosby.

As stated in the previous chapter, this book suggests another scenario. Russ and Lansing, given their taste for somewhat morbid jokes, may have been so amused over that day's *Los Angeles Examiner*'s photo essay depicting Crosby aiming a pistol toward Columbo, that they decided to play out the parts themselves. That may explain why Lansing, presumably taking the role of Bing, had been fiddling with the pistol in the first place. When they got tired of their prank, Columbo continued chatting about the future while Lansing sat back down behind his desk to unwind, listen and light more cigarettes.

Regardless of the many interpretations Columbo's "accidental death" invites, the only smoking gun is the smoking gun. His story does not have the tidy finale of an Agatha Christie novel when the police inspector ties all the loose ends. Even the photograph (again from the *Examiner*) showing a diagram of the pistol ball's ricocheting path—while Detectives D.R. Patton and Joseph Page enact "the death scene in the room where the tragedy untimely happened"—serves as just an eerie forensic formality. Those attempting to solve the riddle with neat explanations must eventually face the fact that they, like Columbo, are too enraptured by life's abounding hall of mirrors to glean a larger view of the funhouse.

Not long after his death, Columbo seemed to have almost faded from memory, but the Romeo of Song's spirit rebounded during the final days of the Second World War. In the 1945 war film *A Walk in the Sun*, ex-Dead End Kid Huntz Hall shows up as one of the soldiers trudging through the battlefield. He gabs with a combat mate about how nice it would be to hear music again. "You know Russ Columbo?" Hall asks as if resuscitating a shard from ancient history. "My sister used to be nuts about Russ Columbo. She stayed in her room all the time the day he died."

Then, in 1946, when America's war heroes starting marching back home to start a new era of consumerism, Perry Como emerged with his megahit version of "Prisoner Of Love." Backed by the Andre Kostelanetz Orchestra, he intoned Columbo's knee-creeping ballad with a commanding respect. Up until then, Columbo was usually remembered for "You Call It Madness (But I Call It Love)," but it took Como to transform "Prisoner" into the Vocal Valentino's ultimate theme. That same year, a recovering American soldier had heard Perry's song and jumped for joy from his military hospital bed, thinking for a misbegotten moment that it was Columbo's voice on the air.

While Columbo projected insecurity, Como became the fatherly figure in the cardigan sweater with a contoured delivery to reassure television audiences. Como's recording also inaugurated the postwar era in pop singing that spawned the eminent likes of Vic Damone, Al Martino, Johnny Mathis, Bobby Vinton and Andy Williams. These cloud-sweeping serenaders demonstrate what could best be defined as the Easy-Listening Paradox: the intricate art of wrapping dreamy sonic contours around songs that tell of troubled hearts. Unlike hardcore blues and jazz singers, the so-called "middle-of-the-road" balladeers enunciate the lyrics more clearly and give their songs more emotional strength through understatement. They invite listeners to probe beyond the sugar-spun exterior to the eternal themes of love gone lame that haunt most souls. A tormented Russ Columbo hides behind Bobby Vinton's satin pillows.

Columbo was so heroic in his pursuit of the romantic melody that he also inspired more ballad-friendly jazz singers to put a sweeter and more sentimental sheen over their work—much to the chagrin of "purists." In 1946, both Billy Eckstine and The Ink Spots climbed to Billboard's Top 10 with their "Prisoner Of Love" renditions. Eckstine and Nat "King" Cole also recorded hit versions of "You Call It Madness (But I Call It Love)" that same year.

From the early Fifties and onward, several singers, including Eckstine and Gordon MacRae, recorded versions of "I'm Yours To Command," another less-known Columbo composition that once again dramatizes a supplicating swain's thrill and anguish:

> My life and my love dear
> I place in your hand.
> They're yours and yours only,
> I'm yours to command...
>
> I love you so madly,
> And here where we stand,
> I give myself gladly,
> I'm yours to command...

On the day after Columbo's tragedy, radio commentator Rush Hughes offered some of his own honey-glazed observations: "I cannot help but wonder if his death is sad, or a triumph, a triumph for a boy who knew the joys of victory, but didn't have to stay to know the shabbiness of defeat, the bitter days of striving to hang on to a glory that eventually slips away and eludes all men."[11]

Fond of writing parodies on the love songs he otherwise treasured, Columbo left behind the following verse:

> Gee, life is so funny—peculiar it seems,
> You're cursed with illusions and too many dreams,
> You struggle and strive and you try to attain
> A (certain) goal that may be, perhaps, something to gain;
> But when you have reached this imagined domain,
> What happens: Unhappy? Yes, almost insane;
> So you struggle and strive so much more till it hurts,
> And keep calling it madness, or should I say—Nuts!

There he is—the prisoner of love who slipped an occasional mickey into his love potion; a very strange, enchanted man-child whose inner vision eventually triumphed over the bitterness. Notwithstanding all of its tribulations, the religion of romance still kept him believing. Russ Columbo was a beautiful dreamer who, drifting one day on a street where old friends meet, got caught dreaming with his eyes wide open.

> And now sweetheart, you know my little story,
> But dear, before the closing chapter's through;
> My heart may ache,
> My heart may break,
> Still I know I'll always love you.

—"That's My True Story" (1931)
Lyrics by A.J. Neiburg, Music by Russ Columbo

RUSS COLUMBO: A MOVIE IN PROGRESS

In 1945, Paramount Pictures had touted the idea of doing a Columbo life story with Andy Russell as the lead. Russell, a ballad singer of Mexican descent, got hired as a drummer for Gus Arnheim's band in 1939. Arnheim heard him croon, Anglicized his first name from Andres to Andy and gave him the Russell surname in homage to his voice's unmistakable Columbo lilt.

The most obvious choice would have been Perry Como—the singer whom Carmela preferred above all others. When Maurice Duke's agency had made false promises about securing Como for the part, Carmela began her grievance against the agency.

Lee Mendelson Film Productions—a Northern California company— had also planned a Columbo documentary, with singer Johnny Desmond as a host-narrator. After learning that the Maurice Duke Agency (which was handling the project) considered Tony Martin over him for the role, Desmond soon joined Columbo's sister Carmela in a fight with the Duke agency over the project's proper handling. Out of spite, Desmond claimed to have bought the rights to all of Columbo's hit songs, in an attempt to prevent the company from going ahead with its plans. Arguments, suits and counter-suits involving "breach of contract" and "slander"—with large dollar sums—were finally settled out of court. For all the bother, not even a workable movie treatment had surfaced.

In 1955, singer Alan Dale was also considered for a Russ portrayal. His vocal affinity with the Vocal Valentino was evident on the 1955 hit "Sweet And Gentle." He instead ended up playing a washed-out crooner in the 1956 teenage feature *Don't Knock the Rock*.

Louella Parsons reported in 1959 that Tony Curtis had purchased the rights to do a television movie for the Ford Star Theater based on Columbo's life and death. Screenwriter Joseph Stefano (who has specialized in horror films) was supposed to write the story. Then, Robert Alda reportedly teamed with fellow actor Jack Carson to clear rights to do his own Columbo biopic, with Alda playing Russ and Carson acting as the project's independent producer.

By mid-February of 1965, Variety reported that producer Barry Shear had optioned for the film rights "from the Columbo family and singer Johnny Desmond." Before he abandoned the venture, Shear had planned "either a theatrical feature or two-part TV special."

In the early 1990s, Tom Cruise (believe it or not) was rumored to star opposite Michelle Pfeiffer in a film based on the so-called "romance" between Columbo and Lombard. Once again, the movie never happened.

NOTES

THE ALTAR BOY AND THE THUG

1. Johaneson, Bland, *NY Daily Mirror*, 18 November 1931.

2. Giddins, Gary. *Bing Crosby: A Pocketful of Dreams*. Boston, New York: Little, Brown and Company, 2001, p. 265.

3. Tiny Tim, Notes to *Prisoner of Love: A Tribute to Russ Columbo*, Vinyl Retentive, 1995.

4. Slide, Anthony. Notes to *Russ Columbo: Save The Last Dance For Me*, Take Two Records, 1994.

THE THIRTEENTH CHILD

1. Churchill, Edward, "America Discovers Columbo," *Screenplay*, December 1933, p. 60.

2. Quoted from a Universal Studios press release entitled: "A General Interview with Russ Columbo: Universal Featured Player."

3. Harris, Warren G. *Gable & Lombard*. New York: Simon and Schuster, 1974, p. 46.

4. Palmer, Mildred, "Meet Your Neighbor," *The Midtowner*, 25 February 1932.

5. James, Rian, "Names Make News!," *Brooklyn Eagle Magazine*, 29 November 1931.

MOOD MUSIC FOR POLA NEGRI

1. Palmborg, Rilla Page, "Friends," *Motion Picture (combined with) Golden Screen*, December 1934, pp. 47, 74-5. This is an actual quote from Lansing Brown.

2. Negri, Pola. *Memoirs of a Star*. Garden City, New York: Doubleday & Company, Inc., 1970. p. 19.

3. Negri. Pola, Ibid., p. 84.

4. Negri, Pola, Ibid., p. 341-2.

5. Negri, Pola, Ibid., p. 273.

6. Miano, Lou. *Russ Columbo: The Amazing Life and Mysterious Death of a Hollywood Singing Legend*, p. 15. [Incident also cited in "Getting Personal," by Julia Shawell, *Evening Graphic*, 2 December 1931.

7. Negri, Pola, Ibid., p. 288.

8. Ramsey, Walter, "The Tragic Death of Russ Columbo," *Radio Stars*, December 1934, pp. 84-5.

9. Palmborg, Rilla Page, Ibid., pp. 47, 74-5.

PRISONER OF THE COCOANUT GROVE

1. Ramsey, Walter, "The Tragic Death of Russ Columbo," *Radio Stars*, December 1934, p. 89.

2. Miano, Lou, Russ Columbo: *The Amazing Life and Mysterious Death of a Hollywood Singing Legend*, p. 23.

3. Palmborg, Rilla Page, "Friends," *Motion Picture (combined with) Golden Screen*, December 1934, p. 74.

4. "Ah! Russ Columbo Prefers Blondes," *Philadelphia Bulletin*, 28 April 1932.

LANGUID LOVE STUFF

1. Whitcomb, Ian. Notes to *The First Crooners: Volume Two: 1930–1934*, Take Two Records, 1995.

2. "Dr. De Forest and Miss Leath In Program Over Columbia," *Brooklyn Daily Eagle*, 24 January 1932.

3. Ford, Henry, "Jewish Jazz Becomes Our National Music," *The International Jew*, Boring Oregon: CPA Book Publisher, 1995, p. 165, 167, 170.

4. Slide, Anthony. Notes to *Little Jack Little: You Oughta Be in Pictures*, Take Two Records, 1984.

5. Cited in Slide, Anthony, Ibid.

6. Crosby, Bing (as told to Pete Martin). *Call Me Lucky*. New York: Simon & Schuster, 1953, p. 33.

7. Crosby, Bing. Ibid., p. 47.

8. Miano, Lou. *Russ Columbo: The Amazing Life and Mysterious Death of a Hollywood Singing Legend*, p. 26.

9. From a personal interview with Buddy Bregman.

ROMANTIC DEPRESSION

1. Palmborg, Rilla Page, "Friends," *Motion Picture* (combined with) *Golden Screen*, December 1934, p. 74.

2. Vallee, Rudy. *Let the Chips Fall*. Harrisburg, Pennsylvania: Stackpole Books, 1975, p. 92.

3. Goode, Mort. *Russ Columbo* (RCA Records, 1976), p. 3.

4. Wald, Jerry, "Columbo Fame Flickers—Wald Tells Inside," *NY Evening Graphic*, 26 February 1932.

5. Giddins, Gary. *Bing Crosby: A Pocketful of Dreams*. Boston, New York: Little, Brown and Company, 2001, p. 285.

6. Coslow, Sam. *Cocktails for Two: The Many Lives of Giant Songwriter Sam Coslow*. New Rochelle, New York: Arlington House Publishers, 1977, p. 116.

7. Coslow, Sam. Ibid., p. 117.

8. Goode, Mort, *Russ Columbo* (Booklet from RCA Records, 1976), p. 3.

9. Miano, Lou, *Russ Columbo: The Amazing Life and Mysterious Death of a Hollywood Singing Legend*, p. 33.

10. Pell, Leona, "A Little Boy—Russ Columbo," *Zit's* [approximately February 1932].

11. Vallee, Rudy. *Let the Chips Fall*. Harrisburg, Pennsylvania: Stackpole Books, 1975, p. 92.

12. Vallee, Rudy (with Gil McKean). *My Time is Your Time: The Story of Rudy Vallee*. New York: Ivan Obolensky, Inc., 1962, p. 96.

13. Vallee, Rudy. *Let the Chips Fall*. Ibid., p. 94.

FOREPLAY SERENADES

1. Grannis, Robert, "Here & There," *NY Evening Graphic*, 7 December 1931.

2. Wald, Jerry, "Not On The Air," *NY Evening Graphic*, 23 December 1931.

3. Miano, Lou. *Russ Columbo: The Amazing Life and Mysterious Death of a Hollywood Singing Legend*, p. 48.

4. Gracyk, Tim (with Frank Hoffmann). *Popular American Recording Pioneers: 1895–1925*. New York: The Haworth Press, 2000, p. 293.

5. Gracyk, Tim (with Frank Hoffmann). Ibid., p. 298.

6. Wald, Jerry, "Not On The Air," *NY Evening Graphic*, 2 November 1931.

7. Wald, Jerry, "Not On The Air," *NY Evening Graphic*, 25 November 1931.

8. Wald, Jerry, "Not On The Air," *NY Evening Graphic*, 2 November 1931.

9. Porthos, "Reviewing Radio," *Radio Guide*, 10 December 1931.

10. Finson, Jon W. *The Voices That Are Gone: Themes in 19th-Century American Popular Song.* New York: Oxford University Press, 1994, p. 68.

LOVE AND LISTERINE

1. Wald, Jerry, "Not On The Air," *NY Evening Graphic*, 23 November 1931.

2. "Guests at Mrs. Hearst Dinner Fill Milk Bottles with Donations; Stage, Screen, Ring Stars Attend," *NY Evening Journal*, 12 November 1931.

3. "Friends Honor Mrs. Hearst Tonight," *NY Evening Journal*, 18 November 1931.

4. Murray, Richard, "Rich Man's Folly," *Standard Union*, 27 November 1931.

5. Wald, Jerry, "Not On The Air," *NY Evening Graphic*, 1 December 1931.

6. "New Tallulah Bankhead Film Features Week's Screenings," *Brooklyn Eagle*, 13 December 1931.

7. "New Listerine Program With Russ Columbo," *Radio Guide*, 5 December 1931.

8. Air Scout, "Radio Reviews," *Zit's*, 25 November 1931.

9. Gross, Ben, "Listening In," *NY Daily News*, 9 December 1931.

10. Bratton, David, "Outside Listening In," *Brooklyn Times*, 8 December 1931.

11. Foster, Jack, "Opera Felicitations," *World-Telegram*, 26 December 1931.

12. *Star Dust*, January 1932.

13. Landry, Bob, "Disc Reviews," *Variety*, 15 December 1931.

14. Sobol, Louis, "The Voice of Broadway," *NY Evening Journal*, 21 December 1931.

GRAND HOTELS

1. Sullivan, Ed, "Ed Sullivan Sees Broadway," *NY Evening Graphic*, 23 December 1931.

2. Palmborg, Rilla Page, "Friends," *Motion Picture* (combined with *Golden Screen*), December 1934, p. 47.

3. Sobol, Louis, "The Voice of Broadway," *NY Evening Journal*, 4 January 1932.

4. Paris, Barry. *Garbo: A Biography*. New York: Alfred A. Knopf, 1995, p. 215.

5. Winchell, Walter, "On Broadway," *NY Daily Mirror*, 4 January 1932.

6. Wald, Jerry, "Not On The Air," *NY Evening Graphic*, 7 January 1932.

7. Coslow, Sam. *Cocktails for Two: The Many Lives of Giant Songwriter Sam Coslow.* New Rochelle, New York: Arlington House Publishers, 1977, p. 119.

8. Miano, Lou. *Russ Columbo: The Amazing Life and Mysterious Death of a Hollywood Singing Legend*, p. 66.

9. Goode, Mort. *Russ Columbo* (Booklet from RCA Records, 1976), p. 5.

10. Coslow, Sam, p. 119.

11. Winchell, Walter, "On Broadway." *NY Daily Mirror*, 6 January 1932.

12. Wald, Jerry, "Not On The Air," *NY Evening Graphic*, 7 January 1932.

13. Kenny, Nick, "Getting An Earful," *NY Daily Mirror*, 8 January 1932.

ROMEO ROULETTE

1. "Inner-Views," *Jersey Journal*, 27 April 1932.

2. Goode, Mort. *Russ Columbo* (Booklet from RCA Records, 1976), p. 5.

3. Marafiotii, P. Mario, M.D. *Caruso's Method of Voice Production: the Scientific Culture of the Voice.* New York: D. Appleton and Company, 1933, p. 192-3.

4. Wald, Jerry, "Not On The Air," *NY Evening Graphic*, 27 January 1932, p. 25. A special thank you to author Lou Miano for providing this source.

5. Wald, Jerry, "Not On The Air," *NY Evening Graphic*, 4 February 1932, p. 29. A special thank you to author Lou Miano for providing this source.

6. "Russ Columbo Sued By Agent," *Zit's*, 27 February 1932.

7. Mortimer, Lee, "Columbo Crooning Stirs Court Suit By His 'Discoverer'," *NY Daily Mirror*, 18 February 1932.

8. "Agent Would Put Silencer on Columbo," *NY Evening Graphic*, 8 February 1932.

9. Liebling, A.J., "Russ Columbo, 'Slob Ballad' Singer, Is 'Something Like Vallee, but Lower,'" *World-Telegram*, February 1932.

10. "Pola Negri, Wan and Ill, Arrives in New York for Film Opening," *Newark Star-Eagle*, 21 January 1932.

11. "Russ Columbo Coming to Shubert," *Newark Evening News*, 18 February 1932.

12. Perkins, Elizabeth, "Pola Negri Plans This Year A Picture, a Play and Marriage," *Newark Star-Eagle*, February 1932.

13. Shafer, Richard O., "George Jessel's Show Proves To Be Genial Entertainment," *Newark Star-Eagle*, 23 February 1932.

14. "Columbo As Example," *Variety*, 8 March 1932.

15. *Baltimore Post*, 26 March 1932.

16. "Columbo Croons on Mastbaum Bill," *Philadelphia Inquirer*, 16 April 1932.

17. "Russ Columbo at Mastbaum; Warner Baxter Stars at Fox," *Philadelphia Record*, 16 April 1932.

18. "Radio Star Heads Bill at Mastbaum," *Philadelphia Public Ledger*, 16 April 1932.

19. "It's in the Air," *Philadelphia Daily News*, 15 April 1932.

20. "Interesting to the Woman Reader," *Philadelphia Daily News*, 15 April 1932.

21. "Guard Russ Columbo After $11,000 Loss At Dice," *Philadelphia Daily News*, 22 April 1932.

22. "Inner-Views," *Jersey Journal*, 27 April 1932.

23. "Two Seats on the Aisle," *Jersey Journal*, 23 April 1932.

TEARS WITHOUT MEASURE

1. Basinger, Jeanine. *Silent Stars*. New York: Alfred A. Knopf, 1999, p. 252.

2. Hammond, John (with Irving Townsend). *John Hammond On Record: An Autobiography*. New York: Summit Books, 1977, p. 61.

3. Ward, Geoffrey C. & Ken Burns. *Jazz: A History of America's Music*. New York: Knopf, 2000, p. 205.

4 Wald, Jerry, "How Columbo Discovered America and Vice-Versa!" *Modern Screen*, December 1933, p. 32.

5. Pullen, Glen C., *Cleveland Plain Dealer*, August 1932, as cited in Lou Miano's *Russ Columbo: The Mysterious Life and Mysterious Death of a Hollywood Singing Legend*, p. 93.

6. *Variety*, 13 September 1932.

MY CRUMMY VALENTINE

1. Ramsey, Walter, "The Tragic Death of Russ Columbo," *Radio Stars*, December 1934, p. 91.

2. From an interview Max Pierce had conducted with Ms. Graw in December 1998— posted on his *Russ Columbo Remembered* website.

3. Wald, Jerry, "How Columbo Discovered America and Vice-Versa," *Modern Screen*, December 1933, p. 32.

4. "Her Secret Lure," *True Story*, Vol. 27, No. 6, January 1933, p. 105-106.

5. Macfadden, Bernarr, "Can a Romance Be Practical?" *True Story*, Vol. 27, No. 6, January 1933, p. 9.

6. Dempsey, Jack (with Barbara Piatelli Dempsey). *Dempsey*. New York: Harper & Row, 1977, p. 239.

ETHER MADNESS

1. Lewis, Tom. *Empire of the Air: The Men Who Made Radio*. New York: Edward Burlingame Books, 1991, p. 231.

2 Kostelanetz, Andre (with Gloria Hammond). *Echoes: Memoirs of Andre Kostelanetz*, New York and London: Harcourt Brace Jovanovich, 1981, p. 51.

3 Kostelanetz, Andre, Ibid., p. 68.

4 McIntyre, O.O., "Day by Day," *New York American*, 11 April 1932.

5 Crosby, Bing (as told to Pete Martin). *Call Me Lucky*. New York: Simon & Schuster, 1953, p. 62.

6 Kenny, Nick, "Getting an Earful," *NY Daily Mirror*, 13 January 1932.

7 Vallee, Rudy (with Gil McKean). *My Time Is Your Time: The Story of Rudy Vallee*. New York: Ivan Obolensky, Inc., 1962, p. 91.

8 Sullivan, Ed, "Ed Sullivan Sees Broadway," *NY Evening Graphic*, 17 November 1931.

9 Gross, Ben, "Listening In," *NY Daily News*, 28 November 1931.

10 Lewis, Tom. *Empire of the Air: The Men Who Made Radio*. New York: Edward Burlingame Books, 1991, p. 242.

11 Shawell, Julia, "Have A Torch Yourself," *NY Evening Graphic*, 22 November 1931.

12 Cited by Ian Whitcomb in "The Coming of the Crooners," Introduction to *The Rise of the Crooners*, Lanham, Maryland: Scarecrow Press, Inc., 2001, p. 33.

13 Wald, Jerry, "Not On The Air," *NY Evening Graphic*, 8 December 1931.

14. Foster, Jack, "Stooges Dog Heels of Radio Celebrity Wherever He Goes: Hear Sad Story of Russ Columbo, Who Only Wants to Read His Encyclopedias," *World-Telegram*, [approximately January/February 1932].

15. *NY Evening Journal*, 15 November 1931.

16. Clark, Elizabeth, "Two Rivals for Vallee Crown," *World-Telegram*, 24 October 1931.

17. Thompson, Charles. *Bing: The Authorized Biography*. New York: David McKay Company, Inc., 1975. p. 51.

18. Yardley, Jonathan. *Ring: A Biography of Ring Lardner*. New York: Atheneum, 1984, p. 364-5.

19. Pell, Leona, "A Little Boy—Russ Columbo," *Zit's*, March 1932.

20. "Crosby Bings Columbo," *Inside Stuff*, 29 January 1932.

21. Kenny, Nick, "Getting An Earful," *NY Daily Mirror*, 8 December 1931.

22. Wald, Jerry, "Not On The Air," *NY Evening Graphic*, 31 December 1931.

23. Foster, Jack, "How They Voted," *World-Telegram*, 5 December 1931.

24. "Columbo on Straight Percentage Terms," *Variety*, 9 February 1932.

25. "Are Crooners Doomed?," *Radio Guide*, 5-11 June 1932.

26. Ranson, Jo, "Radio Dial-Log," *Brooklyn Daily Eagle*, 12 January 1932.

27. Giddins, Gary. *Bing Crosby: A Pocketful of Dreams*. Boston, New York: Little, Brown and Company, 2001, p. 203.

28. Kenny, Nick, "Getting an Earful," *NY Daily Mirror*, 12 January 1932.

29. Kenny, Nick, Ibid.

30. Whitcomb, Ian, "The Coming of the Crooners," Introduction to *The Rise of the Crooners*, Lanham, Maryland: Scarecrow Press, Inc., 2001, p. 37.

HE'S EVERYBODY'S "COLUMBEAU"

1. Graw, Madeline, *Columbo Columns*, The Russ Columbo Co-Ed Club, November 1933, Vol. 1, No. 11, p. 3.

2. Bronson, Harry, "Behind The Mike," *Jackson Heights Herald*, 14 January 1932.

3. McIntyre, O.O., "New York: Day by Day," *NY American*, 11 April 1932.

4. Mencken, H.L., *The Vintage Mencken*, New York: Vintage Books, 1955, p. 174.

5. De O'Fan, Ray, "Russ Columbo, Now in Pictures, Planning Early Return to Air Networks," *Los Angeles Examiner*, September 1933.

6. De O'Fan, Ray, "Bing Crosby and Russ Columbo, Rival Crooners, Bury Hatchet," *Los Angeles Examiner*, 11 October 1933.

MERCUROCHROME AND MOBSTERS

1. Katchmer, George A., "Cruel, but Elegant: The Legacy of Lowell Sherman," *The Silents Majority: On-Line Journal of Silent Film*, 1997.

2. Hall, Mordaunt, "Thru a Keyhole," *The New York Times*, 2 November 1933.

3. Johaneson, Bland, *NY Daily Mirror*, 2 November 1933.

4. Pelswick, Rose, "Broadway Thru A Keyhole," *NY Evening Journal*, 2 November 1933.

5. Delehanty, Thornton, "The New Film," *New York Post*, 2 November 1933.

6. "Dreams Come True," *Columbo Columns*, Vol. 1, No. 11, November 1933, p. 2.

7. "B'way Thru a Keyhole," *Variety*, 7 November 1933.

8. Reel, Rob, "Winchell Film Captures New York Heartbeats," *Chicago American*, November 1933.

VICTIMS OF GRAVITY

1. From Columbo's handwritten letter, dated Christmas Eve 1933.

2. Swindell, Larry. *Screwball: The Life of Carole Lombard*. New York: William Morrow and Company, Inc., 1975, p. 58.

3. Swindell, Ibid., p. 63.

4. Swindell, Ibid., p. 77.

5. Busch, Noel F., "A Loud Cheer for the Screwball," *Life*, 17 October 1938, p. 62.

6. MacKenzie, Trix, "Numerology As I See It," the draft of an article attached with a personal letter to Columbo, dated July 9, 1934.

7. Busch, Noel F., Ibid., p. 48.

8. Swindell, Larry. *Screwball: The Life of Carole Lombard*. New York: William Morrow and Company, Inc., 1975, p. 103.

9. Swindell, Ibid., p. 95.

10. Harris, Warren G. *Gable & Lombard*. New York: Simon and Schuster, 1974, p. 46.

11. *Great Stars of Hollywood's Golden Age*. New York: A Signet Book, 1966, pp. 203 & 205.

12. Palmborg, Rilla Page, "Friends," *Motion Picture (combined with) Golden Screen*, December 1934, p. 74.

13. "Conrad Under Knife," *New York Sun*, 19 December 1933.

14. Harris, Warren G., Ibid., p.44.

15. Valentino, Rudolph. *Day Dreams*. New York: Macfadden Publications, Inc., 1923, p. 67.

16. Note: This quote is from two sources: Harris, Warren G., Ibid., p. 47; and Lou Miano, Ibid., p. 134.

THE TREMBLING HAND

1. Palmborg, Rilla Page, "Friends," *Motion Picture* (combined with) Golden Screen, December 1934, p. 74.

2. Warren, Clark, "Russ Columbo is Mama's Boy," *Screen Play*, June 1934, p. 44.

3. From a personal letter to Lombard, dated February 5, 1934.

4. Parsons, Louella O., "Russ Columbo Battling Universal Because They Won't Let Him Croon; Asks Release," *Los Angeles Examiner*, 5 February 1934.

5. Biery, Ruth, "I'm Through With Love!," *Photoplay*, February 1934.

6. Thompson, Charles. *Bing: The Authorized Biography*. New York: David McKay Company, Inc., 1975, p. 71.

7. *Los Angeles Times*, 10 May 1934.

8. Palmborg, Rilla Page, Ibid., pp. 74-5.

9. Golden, Eve, "Dorothy Dell: The Last Ziegfeld Girl," *Classic Images*, November 1998.

10. Palmborg, Rilla Page, Ibid., pp. 74-5.

WELCOME TO CROONER PURGATORY

1. Krishnamurti, J., *Inspirations from Ancient Wisdom: "At the Feet of the Master," "Light of the Path," "The Voice of the Silence."* Wheaton, Illinois: Quest Books, 1999, p. 10.

2. Ramsey, Walter, "The Tragic Death of Russ Columbo," *Radio Stars*, December 1934, p. 91.

3. "Russ Columbo Estate Fight," *Los Angeles Examiner*, 6 December 1948.

4. Ibid.

5. "Wake Up and Dream," *Columbo Columns*, Autumn, 1934, p. 3.

6. From a personal interview with Robert Anthony Foster.

7. Dempsey, Jack (with Barbara Piatelli Dempsey). *Dempsey*. New York: Harper & Row, 1977, p. 260.

8. "Carol [sic] Lombard Shocked by Russ Columbo Death," *Los Angeles Times*, 3 September 1934.

9. Harris, Warren G. *Gable & Lombard*. New York: Simon and Schuster, 1974, p. 48.

10. "Russ Columbo Dies from Accidental Gun Wound," *Los Angeles Times*, 3 September 1934.

11. Ramsey, Walter, Ibid., p. 36.

BIBLIOGRAPHY

ARTICLES:

"Agent Would Put Silencer on Columbo," *New York Evening Graphic*, 8 February 1932.

"Ah! Russ Columbo Prefers Blondes," *Philadelphia Bulletin*, 28 April 1932.

"Are Crooners Doomed?," *Radio Guide*, 5-11 June 1932.

Biery, Ruth, "'I'm Through With Love!'" *Photoplay*, February 1934.

Bratton, David, "Outside Listening In," *Brooklyn Times*, 4 December 1931.

Busch, Noel F., "A Loud Cheer for the Screwball Girl," *LIFE*, 17 October 1938.

Churchill, Edward, "America Discovers COLUMBO!," *Screenplay*, December 1933.

Clark, Elizabeth, "Two Rivals for Vallee Crown," *World-Telegram*, 24 October 1931.

"Columbo on Straight Percentage Terms," *Variety*, 9 February 1932.

"Conrad Under Knife," *New York Sun*, 19 December 1933.

"Crosby Bings Columbo," *Inside Stuff*, 29 January 1932.

De O'Fan, Ray, "Bing Crosby and Russ Columbo, Rival Crooners, Bury Hatchet," *LA Examiner*, 11 October 1933.

De O'Fan, Ray, "Russ Columbo, Now in Pictures, Planning Early Return to Air Networks," *LA Examiner*, September 1933.

Golden, Eve, "The Opportunist: Pola Negri on Her (More or Less) Centenary," *Classic Images*, December 1997.

"Guests at Mrs. Hearst Dinner Fill Milk Bottles with Donations; Stage, Screen, Ring Stars Attend," *New York Evening Journal*, 12 November 1931.

Hall, Mordaunt, "Thru a Keyhole," *The New York Times*, 2 November 1933.

James, Rian, "Names Make News!: Russ Columbo," *Brooklyn Eagle Magazine*, 29 November 1931.

Katchmer, George A., "Cruel, but Elegant: The Legacy of Lowell Sherman," *The Silents Majority: On-Line Journal of Silent Film*, 1997.

Liebling, A.J., "Russ Columbo, 'Slob Ballad' Singer, Is 'Something Like Vallee, but Lower,'" *World-Telegram*, February 1932.

McCracken, Allison, "'God's Gift to Us Girls': Crooning, Gender, and the Re-Creation of American Popular Song, 1928-1933," *American Music*, Winter 1999.

Mortimer, Lee, "Columbo Crooning Stirs Court Suit By His 'Discoverer'," *NY Daily Mirror*, 18 February 1932.

Murray, Richard, "'Rich Man's Folly': Mr. Bancroft Scowls Meanly and Mr. Columbo Voices Torchy Songs for Paramount Audiences," *Standard Union*, 27 November 1931.

"New Listerine Program With Russ Columbo," *Radio Guide*, 5 December 1931.

Palmborg, Rilla Page, "Friends," *Motion Picture (combined with) Golden Screen*, December 1934.

Parsons, Louella O., "Russ Columbo Battling Universal Because They Won't Let Him Croon; Asks Release," *Los Angeles Examiner*, 5 February 1934.

Pelswick, Rose, "Broadway Thru A Keyhole," *NY Evening Journal*, 2 November 1933.

Pierce, Max, "Russ Columbo: Hollywood's Tragic Crooner," *Classic Images*, April 2000.

"Radio's Valentino: Russ Columbo Now First In Hearts of Women Fans," *Radio Guide*, 5 December 1931.

Ramsey, Walter, "The Tragic Death of Russ Columbo," *Radio Stars*, December 1934.

"Russ Columbo Coming to Shubert," *Newark Evening News*, 18 February 1932.

"Russ Columbo Estate Fight," *Los Angeles Examiner*, 6 December 1948.

"Russ Columbo Fatally Wounded As Friend Shows Him Old Pistol," *The New York Times*, 3 September 1934.

"Russ Columbo Has Bodyguard As Gamblers Nick Him for Alleged $11,000 Dice Loss," *Philadelphia Daily News*, 22 April 1932.

Schallert, Edwin, "Universal Considers Russ Colombo in 'Show Boat,'" *Los Angeles Times*, 25 August 1933.

Sobel, Louis, "Romances That Made Pola Negri the Queen of Tragedy," *American Weekly*, 1941.

Shawell, Julia, "Have A Torch Yourself," *NY Evening Graphic*, 22 November 1931.

Starr, Jimmy, "Andy Russell, Star of Russ Columbo's Story," *Evening Herald-Express*, 9 August 1945.

"The Truth About 'Him,'" *The Illustrated Love Magazine*, June 1933.

Wald, Jerry, "Columbo Fame Flickers—Wald Tells Inside," *NY Evening Graphic*, 26 February 1932.

Wald, Jerry, "How Columbo Discovered America and Vice-Versa!" *Modern Screen*, December 1933.

Warren, Clark, "Russ Columbo is Mama's Boy," *Screen Play*, June 1934.

BOOKS & BOOKLETS:

Allen, Frederick Lewis. *Since Yesterday: The 1930s in America*. New York: Perennial Library, 1939, 1972.

Basinger, Jeanine. *Silent Stars*. New York: Alfred A. Knopf, 1999.

Collier, James Lincoln. *Benny Goodman and the Swing Era*. New York: Oxford University Press, 1989.

Coslow, Sam. *Cocktails for Two: The Many Lives of Giant Songwriter Sam Coslow*. New Rochelle, New York: Arlington House Publishers, 1977.

Crosby, Bing (as told to Pete Martin). *Call Me Lucky*. New York: Simon & Schuster, 1953.

De Mille, Cecil B. (edited by Donald Hayne). *The Autobiography of Cecil B. De Mille*. (Donald Hayne, ed.) Englewood Cliffs, New Jersey: Prentice-Hall, Inc., 1959.

Dempsey, Jack (with Barbara Piatelli Dempsey). *Dempsey*. New York: Harper & Row, 1977.

Firestone, Ross. *Swing, Swing, Swing: The Life & Times of Benny Goodman*. New York: W.W. Norton & Company, 1993.

Finson, Jon W. *The Voices That Are Gone: Themes in 19th-Century American Popular Song*. New York: Oxford University Press, 1994.

Gabler, Neal. *Winchell: Gossip, Power and the Culture of Celebrity*. New York: Alfred A. Knopf, 1994.

Giddins, Gary. *Bing Crosby: A Pocketful of Dreams*. Boston, New York: Little, Brown and Company, 2001.

Goode, Mort. *Russ Columbo* (Booklet from RCA Records), 1976.

Gracyk, Tim (with Frank Hoffmann). *Popular American Recording Pioneers, 1895–1925*. New York: The Haworth Press, 2000.

Great Stars of Hollywood's Golden Age. New York: A Signet Book, 1966. (Original article taken from *Liberty* magazine, February 1942)

Hamm, Charles. *Yesterdays: Popular Song in America.* New York: W.W. Norton & Company, 1983.

Hammond, John (with Irving Townsend). *John Hammond On Record: An Autobiography.* New York: Summit Books, 1977.

Harris, Warren G., *Gable and Lombard.* New York: Simon and Schuster, 1974.

Heimann, Jim. *Out With The Stars: Hollywood Nightlife in the Golden Era.* New York: Abbeville Press, 1985.

Holland, C.F. *Poems for the Wayfarer on the Path of Life.* Los Angeles: Grafton Publishing Corporation, 1923.

Jessel, George. *Elegy in Manhattan.* New York: Holt, Rinehart and Winston, 1961.

Inspirations from Ancient Wisdom: "At the Feet of the Master," "Light of the Path," "The Voice of the Silence." Wheaton, Illinois: Quest Books, 1999.

Kirkpatrick, Sidney D. *A Cast of Killers.* New York: E.P. Dutton, 1986.

Kostelanetz, Andre (with Gloria Hammond). *Echoes: Memoirs of Andre Kostelanetz.* New York and London: Harcourt Brace Jovanovich, 1981.

Kovan, Florice Whyte. *Rediscovering Ben Hecht: Selling the Celluloid Serpent.* Washington, D.C.: Snickersnee Press, 1999.

Lax, Roger and Frederick Smith. *The Great Song Thesaurus* (2nd Edition). New York: Oxford University Press, 1989.

Lewis, Tom. *Empire of the Air: The Men Who Made Radio.* New York: Edward Burlingame Books, 1991.

Marafioti, P. Mario, M.D. *Caruso's Method of Voice Production: The Scientific Culture of the Voice.* New York: D. Appleton and Company, 1933.

Miano, Lou. *Russ Columbo: The Amazing Life and Mysterious Death of a Hollywood Singing Legend.* New York: Silver Tone Publications, 2001.

Negri, Pola. *Memoirs of a Star.* Garden City, New York: Doubleday & Company, Inc., 1970.

Paris, Barry. *Garbo: A Biography.* New York: Alfred A. Knopf, 1995.

Pitts, Michael and Frank Hoffmann. *The Rise of the Crooners.* Lanham, Maryland: Scarecrow Press, Inc., 2002.

Powell, A.E. *The Astral Body and Other Astral Phenomena.* Wheaton, Illinois: Quest Books, 1927, 1996.

Shulman, Irving. *Valentino.* New York: Trident Press, 1967.

Swindell, Larry. *Screwball: The Life of Carole Lombard.* New York: William Morrow and Company, Inc., 1975.

Thompson, Charles. *Bing: The Authorized Biography.* New York: David McKay Company, Inc., 1975.

Valentino, Rudolph. *Day Dreams.* New York: Macfadden Publications, Inc., 1923.

Vallee, Rudy. *Let The Chips Fall.* Harrisburg, Pennsylvania: Stackpole Books, 1975.

Vallee, Rudy (with Gil McKean). *My Time Is Your Time: The Story of Rudy Vallee.* New York: Ivan Obolensky, Inc., 1962.

Ward, Geoffrey C. & Ken Burns. Jazz: *A History of America's Music.* New York: Knopf, 2000.

Whitburn, Joel. *Pop Memories—1890–1954: The History of American Popular Music.* Menomonee Falls, Wisconsin: Record Research, Inc., 1986.

Whitcomb, Ian. *After The Ball: Pop Music from Ragtime to Rock* (2nd Edition). New York: Limelight Editions, 1994.

Yardley, Jonathan. *Ring: A Biography of Ring Lardner.* New York: Atheneum, 1984.

RUSS COLUMBO RECORDINGS

The following is a list of legitimate vocal recordings Columbo made from the late Twenties up until two days before his death on September 2, 1934. They are entered by date, title, catalog and matrix number.

WITH GUS ARNHEIM & HIS AMBASSADOR HOTEL COCOANUT GROVE ORCHESTRA:
Recorded in Hollywood:

April 12, 1928

"I Can't Do Without You" (with Arnheim vocal trio) (OKeh—41057) 400582

"If I Can't Have You (I Want To Be Lonesome, I Want To Be Blue)" (OKeh –41037) 400583-C/D

April 14, 1928

"Back In Your Own Backyard" (OKeh—41037) 400584-B

"Feelin' Good" (OKeh—41057) 400585-C

January 10, 1929

"Glad Rag Doll" (OKeh—41208) 4002244

(Though he was credited as the vocalist on a British CD compilation, but there is reason to suspect it is not Columbo's voice and that he played only the violin for this track.)

June 18, 1930
"A Peach Of A Pair" (Victor 22546) PBVE-54835-4

THE VICTOR SESSIONS
Recorded in New York:

July 1931—November 1932

Please Note: Matrix numbers (which indicate sequential order of songs as they were recorded) follow catalog numbers:

July 2, 1931
With Con Conrad on piano:
"Out Of Nowhere" (Victor audition test record—unissued and lost) BRC-470

September 3, 1931
With Nat Shilkret & His Orchestra:
"I Don't Know Why (I Just Do)" (Victor 22801-B) BS-70210-1
"Guilty" (Victor 22801-A) BS-70211-1
"You Call It Madness (But I Call It Love)" (Victor 22802-A) BS-70212-1

September 9, 1931
With Nat Shilkret & His Orchestra:
"Sweet And Lovely" (Victor 22802-B) BS-70224-2

October 9, 1931
With Nat Shilkret & His Orchestra:
"Time On My Hands" (Victor 22826-B) BS-70281-1
"Good Night, Sweetheart" (Victor 22826-A) BS-70282-1
"Prisoner Of Love" (Victor 22867-B) BS-70283-1

November 18th, 1931
With Nat Shilkret & His Orchestra:
"You Try Somebody Else" (Victor 22861-B) BS-70953-1
"Call Me Darling" (Victor 22861-A) BS-70954-2
"Where The Blue Of The Night (Meets The Gold Of The Day)" (Victor 22867-A) BS-70955-1

December 29th, 1931
With Nat Shilkret & His Orchestra:
"Save The Last Dance For Me" (Victor 22903-A) BS-71207-1
"All Of Me" (Victor 22903-B) BS-71208-1

January 12, 1932
With Nat Shilkret & His Orchestra:
"Just Friends" (Victor 22909-A) BS-71218-1/2
"You're My Everything" (Victor 22909-B) BS-71219-1

April 6, 1932
With Leonard Joy & His Orchestra:
"Auf Weidersehn, My Dear" (Victor 22976-B) BS-72243-1
"Paradise" (Victor 22976-A) BS-72244-1

With the studio version of the Russ Columbo Orchestra:
Note: RCA Victor files indicate that Russ Columbo was the Musical Director on the following eleven sessions (other sources cite Marlin Skiles).

June 16, 1932
"Just Another Dream Of You" (Victor 24045-A) BS-73017-1
"I Wanna Be Loved"—(Rejected) BS-73018-1
"Living In Dreams" (Victor 24045-B) BS-73019-1

August 3, 1932
"My Love" (Victor 24077-A) BS-73148-1
"As You Desire Me" (Victor 24076-A) BS-73149-1
"Lonesome Me" (Victor 24077-B) BS-73150-1
"The Lady I Love" (Victor 24076-B) BS-73151-1

November 23, 1932
"Street Of Dreams" (Victor 24194-A) BS-73995-1
"Make Love The King" (Victor 24195-A) BS-73996-1
"I Called To Say Goodnight" (Victor 24195-B) BS-73997-1
"Lost In A Crowd" (Victor 24194-B) BS-73998-1

Columbo unfortunately made no known commercial studio recordings in 1933.

THE BRUNSWICK SESSION
Recorded in Hollywood:

August 31, 1934
With Jimmie Grier & His Orchestra:
"When You're In Love" (Brunswick 6972-A) LA-200
"Too Beautiful For Words" (Special Editions 5001-S) LA-201-B
"Let's Pretend There's A Moon" (Brunswick 6972-B) LA-202-A
"I See Two Lovers" (Special Editions 5001-S) LA-203-A

RADIO AIR-CHECKS
What follows is a list of existing recordings of air-checks from Columbo's NBC shows that have been available, with compromised sound quality, on vinyl through the years:

NBC BROADCASTS:
With Harry Jackson & His Orchestra:

HOLLYWOOD ON THE AIR:
June 5, 1933
Medley: "More Than You Know" / "Time On My Hands"

September 18, 1933
"My Past, Present And Future"
"Kisses In The Dark"

November 16, 1933
"Lover"

WEEKLY JIMMY FIDLER PROGRAM:
June 17, 1934
"The House Is Haunted"
"Time On My Hands"
"Easy Come, Easy Go"

July 1, 1934
"With My Eyes Wide Open, I'm Dreaming"
"Star Dust"

July 8, 1934
"True"

July 15, 1934
"Rolling In Love"
"I've Had My Moments"
"I'm Dreaming"

OTHER AIRCHECKS (Dates Not Determined):
"I've Got To Pass Your House (To Get To My House)"
"I'm Sorry Dear"
"How Long Will It Last?"

RUSS COLUMBO COMPOSITIONS

Formally trained, Columbo had composed various pieces of music—both songs and concert works. Some have shown up as hits, semi-hits, movie tunes, incidental movie music, and in-person recitals. Throughout his songwriting and singing career, Columbo was inconsistent with the spelling of his last and sometimes his first name. His songwriting credits list him alternately as Colombo and Columbo, although the material he had filed with the Library of Congress Copyright Office lists "Colombo."

Music and Lyrics by Russ Columbo (Russell Colombo) are listed by either copyright date (where indicated) or publication year:

1. "My Wild Irish Colleen"—words and music by Russell Colombo
Received at Copyright Office September 2, 1924. Entry: Class E, XXc., No. 596940 (Please note that this very early (possibly first) Columbo composition was received ten years prior to the date of his death.)

2. "That Old Fashioned Mother Of Mine"—words: Howard Coombs and Russell Colombo
Received at Copyright Office December 3, 1925. Entry: Class E, XXc., No. 628979

3. "Just For You" (Piano)—listed as "by Russell Colombo"
Received at Copyright Office September 30, 1925. Entry: Class E, XXc., No. 621266 (Please note that subsequent sheet music with a 1926 copyright lists: "Words by Howard W. Coombs and Russell Colombo." The song is also identified as a "Waltz Ballad." Algonquin Music, Inc. renewed the copyright in 1951).

4. "Valse Petite" (Piano)
Received at Copyright Office November 17, 1925. Entry: Class E, XXc., No. 626794

5. "Italian Boat Song"—words and music by Russell Colombo
Received at Copyright Office January 9, 1926. Entry: Class E, XXc., No. 32307

6. "If I Should Lose You"—words: Howard Coombs
Received at Copyright Office May 18, 1927. Entry: Class E, XXc., No. 664629

7. "La Passione Tango" (Piano)
Received at Copyright Office May 18, 1927. Entry: Class E, XXc., No. 664631

8. "Russian Love Song" (Melody with Piano)
Received at Copyright Office May 18, 1927. Entry: Class E, XXc., No. 664630

9. "Spanish Moonlight" (Tango Fox-Trot)—words: K. Bertram Carruth
Received at Copyright Office October 24, 1927. Entry: Class E, XXc., No. 675044

10. "Three Words" (1929) (Instrumental)

11. "(What Good Am I) Without You?" from *Hello Sister* (1930)—words: Jack Gordean

12. "Happy (I Found Somebody To Love)" (1930)—words: Jack Gordean and Russell Colombo
Received at Copyright Office May 13, 1930. Entry: Class E, unp., No. 21720

13. "Yesterday's Dreams (Of You)" (1930)—words: Jack Gordean

14. "You Call It Madness (But I Call It Love)" (1931)—words: Gladys Du Bois, Paul Gregory, Con Conrad, Russ Columbo

15. "Prisoner Of Love" (1931)—music: Russ Columbo and Con Conrad; words: Leo Robin

16. "That's My True Story" (1931)—words: Al J. Neiburg

17. "Only A Voice On The Air" (1931)—words: Al Dubin

18. "Jeanette (Love Theme)" (Dedicated to Miss Bebe Daniels) (Instrumental)

19. "Just Another Romance / Now I Know It's Love" (1931)—words: Al J. Neiburg

20. "Is It Love?"—from *Hell Bound*—words: Howard Coombs
Received at Copyright Office January 2, 1931. Entry: Class E, unp., No. 32662

21. "Beggar Of Love" (1931)—words: Howard Coombs
Received at Copyright Office January 19, 1931. Entry: Class E, unp., No. 33368

22. "What Did I Get For Loving You" (1931)—words: Al J. Neiburg

23. "My Love" (1931)—words and music by Russ Columbo

24. "Until Eternity" (1931)—music (and possibly words) by Russ Columbo

25. "You Captured My Heart" (1931)—music (and possibly words) by Russ Columbo

26. "Let's Pretend There's A Moon" (1934)—from *Wake Up and Dream*—words: Grace Hamilton, Jack Stern

27. "Too Beautiful For Words" (1934)—from *Wake Up and Dream*—words: Bernie Grossman, Jack Stern

28. "When You're In Love" (1934)—from *Wake Up and Dream*—words: Bernie Grossman, Jack Stern

29. "I'm Yours To Command" (original year not determined)—(Please note that Algonquin Music, Inc. renewed the copyright in 1951. The Algonquin sheet music indicates "Words and Music by Russ Columbo.")

30. "So This Is Paradise" (original year not determined)—(Please note that Algonquin Music, Inc. renewed the copyright in 1951. The agreement indicated that Robert Milton was a co-writer.)

31. "What's To Become Of Me?" (original year not determined) (Please note that when Algonquin Music, Inc. renewed the copyright in 1951. The agreement indicated that Robert Milton was a co-writer.)

QUOTED SONGS—Listed Alphabetically by Title, Publishing Year and Composer(s):

All Of Me (1931) (Seymour Simons, Gerald Marks)
As You Desire Me (1931) (Allie Wrubel)
Auf Wiedersehn, My Dear (1932) (Al Hoffman, Ed G. Nelson, Al Goodhart, Milton Ager)
Between The Devil And The Deep Blue Sea (1931)(Harold Arlen, Ted Koehler)
Call Me Darling (from German song "Sag' Mir Darling") (1931) (Bert Reisfeld, Mart Fryberg, Rolf Marbet, Dorothy Dick)
Crosby, Columbo and Vallee (1931) (Joe Burke, Al Dubin)
Good Night, Sweetheart (1931) (Ray Noble, Jimmy Campbell, Reginald Connelly, Rudy Vallee)
Guilty (1931) (Gus Kahn, Harry Akst, Richard A. Whiting)
House Is Haunted, The (1934) (Basil G. Adlam, Billy Rose)
How Am I To Know? (1929) (Dorothy Parker, Jack King)
I Called To Say Goodnight (1932) (Joe Young, Werner Bochmann, Con Conrad)
I Don't Know Why (I Just Do) (1931) (Roy Turk, Fred E. Ahlert)
I Love You, Pizzicato (1933) (Mack Gordon, Harry Revel)
I See Two Lovers (1933) (Mort Dixon, Allie Wrubel)
I Surrender, Dear (1931) (Gordon Clifford, Harry Barris)
I'm Yours To Command (year unknown) (Russ Columbo)
Is It Love? (1931) (Russ Columbo, Howard Coombs)
I've Got To Pass Your House (To Get To My House) (1933) (Lew Brown)
Just Another Dream Of You (1932) (Benny Davis, Joe Burke)
Just Friends (1931) (Sam M. Lewis, John Klenner)
Let's Pretend There's A Moon (1934) (Russ Columbo, Jack Stern, Grace Hamilton)
Living In Dreams (1932) (John W. Green)
Lost In A Crowd (1932) (Bob Rice, Joe Krechter, Con Conrad)
My Love (1932) (Russ Columbo)
Only A Voice On The Air (1931) (Russ Columbo, Al Dubin)
Paradise (1931) (Nacio Herb Brown, Gordon Clifford)
Peach Of A Pair, A (1930) (George Marion, Jr., Richard A. Whiting)
Prisoner Of Love (1931) (Russ Columbo, Leo Robin, Clarence Gaskill)
Save The Last Dance For Me (1931) (Frank Magine, Walter Hirsch, Phil Spitalny)
Sweet And Lovely (1931) (Gus Arnheim, Harry Tobias, Jules Lemare)
That Old Fashioned Mother Of Mine (1925) (Russ Columbo, Howard Coombs)
That's My True Story (1931) (Russ Columbo, Al J. Neiburg)
Time On My Hands (1930) (Harold Adamson, Mack Gordon, Vincent Youmans)
Too Beautiful For Words (1934) (Russ Columbo, Bernie Grossman, Jack Stern)
(What Good Am I) Without You? (1930) (Russ Columbo, Jack Gordean)
You Call It Madness (But I Call It Love) (1931) (Russ Columbo, Con Conrad, Gladys DuBois, Paul Gregory)
You Try Somebody Else (1931) (B. G. DeSylva, Lew Brown & Ray Henderson)
You're My Everything (1931) (Mort Dixon, Joe Young, Harry Warren)

FILMOGRAPHY

Gus Arnheim & His Cocoanut Grove Orchestra (1928–29) ("Vitaphone Varieties" musical short)
Appeared with Gus Arnheim vocal trio; also played violin solo.

Gus Arnheim & His Ambassadors (1929) ("Vitaphone Varieties" musical short)
Appeared with Gus Arnheim vocal trio; also played violin solo.

Wolf Song (1929) Paramount Pictures
Was originally slated for a part as Ambrosia Guiterrez and to sing the Leo Robin, Richard A. Whiting and Harvey Ferguson ballad entitled: "To Lola."

> Director/Producer: Victor Fleming
> Story: Harvey Ferguson
> Music: Richard A. Whiting, Arthur J. Lamb, A. Terres, Harry Warren

Wonder of Women (1929) M-G-M
In this heretofore lost film, Columbo supposedly ghost-voiced for Lewis Stone on the German tune "Ich Liebe Dich." The presence of a smooth, high-baritone sounding like Russ has yet to be determined.

> Director: Clarence Brown
> Original music: Sam Wineland, Arthur Lange, William Axt
> Adapted by: Bess Meredyth, from novel *The Wife of Stephen Tromholt* by Herrmann Suderman

Street Girl (1929) RKO Radio Pictures
Plays as part of Gus Arnheim and His Ambassadors, who provide the film's off-camera music. Through the years, various Columbo-watchers have spotted Russ in brief cameos that take place inside a café. WARNING: the more one looks, the more many of the men in the café scenes start to resemble Columbo. This book's authors believe they have spotted him in a very brief cameo in the first scene, which opens to a band (led by Jack Oakie) that is faking to the Ambassadors playing "Lovable And Sweet." As the scene moves out to establish the café setting, Columbo appears at a table, having dinner with friends and even tilting his head to look straight into the camera. In another scene, he appears to be among those standing to applaud as a royal Prince makes a grand entrance. Russ appears again, seated, sporting a black bow-tie and white carnation, while watching Compson serenade the café patrons with "My Dream Memory"—a version that he is likely playing on what would have had to be a pre-recorded track.

> Director: Wesley Ruggles
> Screenplay: Jane Murfin
> Musical Numbers: Oscar Levant & Sidney Clare
> Based on story "The Viennese Charmer" by W. Carey Wonderly

Dynamite (1929) M-G-M
Appears in a sumptuous but uncredited role as a "Mexican Boy" in a prison cell, singing "How Am I To Know?"

> Director: Cecil B. De Mille
> Story: Jeanie MacPherson
> "How Am I To Know?"
> Music: Jack King
> Lyrics: Dorothy Parker
> Musical score: Herbert Stothart

Hello, Sister (1930) Sono Art-World Wide Pictures (James Cruze, Inc.)
"Russell Colombo" is credited for the musical score. He also wrote the song "(What Good Am I) Without You?"

> Director: Walter Lang
> Script: Brian Marlow
> Music: Russell Colombo
> Lyrics: Jack Gordean
> Musical Director: Howard Jackson

The Texan (1930) Paramount Pictures
Another supposed ghost-voice for a singing Gary Cooper. He is also purported to have an uncredited cameo appearance as a "singing cowboy" at a campfire.
> Director: John Cromwell
> Story: Daniel Nathan Rubin
> Adapted from O. Henry's "The Double-Dyed Deceiver"

Hell Bound (1931) Tiffany Productions
Composed the melody for the song "Is It Love?"
> Director: Walter Lang
> Story: Edward Dean Sullivan & Adele Josephson
> Music: Russell Colombo
> Lyrics: Howard Coombs

That Goes Double (1933) Vitaphone
Plays dual role as himself and alter ego Clarence the Clerk
Sings "My Love," "Prisoner Of Love" and "You Call It Madness (But I Call It Love)"
> Director: Joseph Henaberry
> Script: Burnet Hershey, A. Dorian Otvos

Broadway Thru A Keyhole (1933) Twentieth Century Pictures—A United Artists Release
As the sensitive crooner Clark Brian
Sings "You're My Past, Present and Future" and "I Love You, Pizzicato"
> Director: Lowell Sherman
> Screenplay: Gene Towne & Graham Baker
> Original story: Walter Winchell
> Music: Harry Revel
> Lyrics: Mack Gordon
> Musical Director: Alfred Newman

Moulin Rouge (1934) Twentieth Century Pictures—A United Artists Release
Appears in staged duet with Constance Bennett (along with The Boswell Sisters) on "Coffee In The Morning And Kisses In The Night."

Director: Sidney Lanfield
Screenplay: Nunnally Johnson & Henry Lehrman
Original story: Nunnally Johnson
"Coffee In The Morning (And Kisses In The Night)"
Music: Harry Warren
Lyrics: Al Dubin
Musical Director: Alfred Newman

Wake Up and Dream (1934) Universal Pictures
As crooner Paul Scotti
Sings "Let's Pretend There's A Moon," "When You're In Love," "Too Beautiful For Words," and (in the film's opening) a few bars of the "Wake Up And Dream" title theme.
> Director: Kurt Neumann
> Original story and screenplay: John Meeham, Jr.
> Music & Lyrics: Russ Columbo, Bernie Grossman, Jack Stern, Grace Hamilton, Sid
>   Cuttner, Gordon Clifford
> Musical Director: Sam K. Wineland
> Additional music and orchestrations: Howard Jackson

DISCOGRAPHY

ON LPs, 78s AND 45s:

Songs Made Famous by the Golden Voice of Russ Columbo (Victor P-95)

This four-disc album of eight recordings on 78 rpm was issued originally in 1946.

Call Me Darling/Save The Last Dance For Me/Sweet And Lovely/Prisoner Of Love/Paradise/Good Night, Sweetheart/Auf Wiedersehn, My Dear/Where The Blue Of The Night (Meets The Gold Of The Day)

Love Songs by Russ Columbo (RCA Victor LPM-2072) 1959

Call Me Darling/Sweet And Lovely/Just Friends/Where The Blue Of The Night (Meets The Gold Of The Day)/You Try Somebody Else/You're My Everything/All Of Me/Time On My Hands/Save The Last Dance For Me/Living In Dreams/Auf Wiedersehn, My Dear/Paradise

Prisoner Of Love (Pelican Records 141) 1975

Among few releases containing most of the material he recorded with the studio incarnation of the Russ Columbo Orchestra.

Peach Of A Pair/Street Of Dreams/The Lady I Love/I Called To Say Goodnight/I Don't Know Why (I Just Do)/I See Two Lovers/You Call It Madness (But I Call It Love)/Lonesome Me/My Love/Lost In A Crowd/Make Love The King/Guilty/Prisoner Of Love/Good Night, Sweetheart

Russ Columbo: A Legendary Performer (RCA CPL1-1756(e) 1976

This collection includes a twelve-page illustrated booklet, with text by Mort Goode.

I Don't Know Why (I Just Do)/You Call It Madness (But I Call It Love)/Time On My Hands/Prisoner Of Love/Where The Blue Of The Night (Meets The Gold Of The Day)/Just Friends/Save The Last Dance For Me/All Of Me/Auf Wiedersehn, My Dear/Paradise/Just Another Dream Of You/My Love

The Films of Russ Columbo (Golden Legends 2000/2) circa 1970s

These recordings were taken directly from the films *Broadway Thru A Keyhole, Wake Up And Dream, Moulin Rouge,* and *That Goes Double.* The album also includes some of the dialogue. The selections from *Wake Up and Dream,* however, are not the screen versions that Howard Jackson conducted but the Jimmy Grier Brunswick Recordings.

Columbo tracks: *You're My Past, Present And Future/I Love You, Pizzicato/When You're In Love/Too Beautiful For Words/Let's Pretend There's A Moon/Coffee In The Morning And Kisses In The Night/My Love/Prisoner Of Love/You Call It Madness (But I Call It Love)*

Russ Columbo—"On The Air" (Totem Records 1031) 1978

This collection of some of the original NBC airchecks includes the entire broadcast from July 15, 1934.

More Than You Know/Time On My Hands/My Past, Present And Future/Kisses In The Dark/Lover/The House Is Haunted/Time On My Hands/Easy Come, Easy Go/With My Eyes Wide Open, I'm Dreaming/Star Dust/True/Rolling In Love/I've Had My Moments/I'm Dreaming

Russ Columbo On The Air: Rare Recordings by the "Romeo of Radio," 1933-1934 (Sandy Hook Records SH 2038) 1980

This contains the exact recordings on the Totem album only of somewhat less quality.

Return to the Legendary Past with Russ Columbo, Vol. 1 (Broncoli Gegend 32/34) circa 1970s

Produced in Palermo, Italy, this has essentially the same tracks as the other *On The Air* collections (with a couple of incorrect titles). It has the one advantage, however, of being among the few (if not only) albums to include "I've Got To Pass Your House (To Get To My House)." Side Two consists of Dick Powell performing "Live."

...GONE... But Not Forgotten: 51 Great Songs by the Romantic Voice of Russ Columbo (Russ Columbo Archives, Inc.) 1982

Every Columbo fan loves to poke fun at this misleading collection. Columbo sings only two of the tunes, but there are two Columbo compositions performed by others: "Until Eternity" (sung by Billy

Eckstine) and "I'm Yours To Command" (possibly sung by Gordon MacRae or Herb Jeffries). [Note: Eckstine recorded the single "Until Eternity" b/w "Everything Depends On You" on MGM 11396).] There is another track (with songwriting credits attributed to Columbo and Benee Russell) called "Love Is Like That (What Can You Do?)." The "archivist" DID include Columbo's hard-to-find hit "As You Desire Me," along with an alternate take of "Too Beautiful For Words" on which Columbo likely sings while accompanied by a lone accordion.

AMERICAN POPULAR SONG: Six Decades of Songwriters and Singers

(The Smithsonian Collection of Recording, in association with Columbia Special Products R-031 LP Edition, P7 17983) 1984

This boxed set of seven LPs or cassettes includes Columbo's version of "Street Of Dreams"

TREASURY OF IMMORTAL PERFORMANCES: COLUMBO, CROSBY, SINATRA (RCA) (issued both as 10" LP and 45 rpm boxed set) 1953

Includes Columbo's "Prisoner Of Love" and "Good Night, Sweetheart."

ON COMPACT DISC:

Save The Last Dance For Me (Take Two Records) 1994

20 songs, includes two tracks taken directly from the films *Broadway Thru A Keyhole* and *Moulin Rouge.*

Prisoner Of Love: 23 Crooning Hits, 1928-1934 (ASV Living Era Series) 1997

A fine collection of Columbo's best, even though it includes the likely erroneous listing of Columbo as vocalist for the track "Glad Rag Doll."

Art Deco: The Crooners (Columbia/Legacy) 1993

As far as crooner anthologies go, this two-disc tribute is often a bit too jazz-slanted in its song selections, but it does offer superbly remastered versions of Columbo's "Let's Pretend There's A Moon" and his final recording, "I See Two Lovers."

The First Crooners, Volume Two: 1930-1934 (Take Two Records) 1996

Take Two assembles twenty essential tracks from early crooner history, including Sam Coslow singing "Learn To Croon." Columbo appears with his hit recording of "Good Night, Sweetheart."

They Called It Crooning (ASV Living Era Series) 1984

Columbo performs "Living In Dreams" in this "smooth singers" salute to the crooner pioneers.

Hits Of '31 (ASV Living Era Series) 1997

This various artists collection contains Columbo on "Prisoner Of Love."

Great Crooners (Life Times & Music) 1996

This assortment, featuring crooner pioneers like Gene Austin and Nick Lucas, also includes Columbo on "When You're In Love."

PRISONERS OF LOVE

(A Selective Discography of "Prisoner Of Love" versions by other major recording artists)

When he sang "Prisoner Of Love," Columbo brought out the song's melodic approximation to the weeping sound of a violin. It was intended as a sweet ballad, but several jazz performers have adapted it to their idiom (perhaps because of its structural similarity to the much more bluesy "Body And Soul," which Johnny Green had published a year before "Prisoner" was released). Through the years, the song's uncompromising theme of romantic devotion and degradation has struck an inspiration chord in many performers. That is why it has found a home in the hearts of pop, country, blues, reggae, soul, and, last but certainly not least, the easy-listening instrumental. The following list is a sampling of various versions, identified by musical category and mood.

Listed by artist, album or disc title, record label, and catalog number (stereo numbers listed on appropriate titles):

ROMANTIC POP BALLAD

Pat Boone—I'll See You in my Dreams (Dot DLP-25399)

Perry Como—Perry Como: Yesterday & Today—A Celebration in Song (RCA 07863-66098-2) #1/1946 (Billboard's Pop Chart)

Bing Crosby—Legendary Singers (Heartland)

Connie Francis—White Sox, Pink Lipstick… & Stupid Cupid (five-Disc box set) (Bear Family—Germany)

Les Paul & Mary Ford—Hitmakers (Collectables Records)

Jimmy Roselli—Rock-A-Bye Your Baby (M&R)

Frank Sinatra—Sinatra & Strings (WEA/Warner Bros.)
LP: Reprise 1002 (1961) also on The Complete Reprise Studio Recordings

Tiny Tim—Resurrection / Tip Toe Thru The Tulips (Bear Family—Germany)

Tiny Tim (featuring Clang)—Prisoner of Love: A Tribute To Russ Columbo (Vinyl Retentive)—This version is amazingly identical to both the singing style and orchestration on Columbo's original Nat Shilkret session.

Jerry Vale—I Remember Russ (Columbia 8016) CD: Sony/Columbia CK 63549

The Vogues (single: 20th Century 2085) #37/1974 (*Billboard*'s Adult Contemporary Chart)

EASY LISTENING INSTRUMENTAL

Herbert Rehbein—Music to Soothe That Tiger/ Love After Midnight (Taragon)

Santo & Johnny—Encore (Canadian-Am. 1002)

Lawrence Welk—A Tribute to the All-Time Greats (Dot 25544)

Roger Williams—Ivory Impact (Bainbridge Records BT 8002)

COUNTRY

Troy Cory—Troy Sings Bing Crosby & Russ Columbo (BBC Radio Play)

Willie Nelson & Don Cherry—Augusta (Sundown—UK)

Ray Price—Prisoner of Love (BMG/Buddah Records)

BIG BAND / SWING-ERA POP

Billy Eckstine—Billy's Best! (Uni/Verve) #10/1946 (Billboard's Pop Chart)

Keely Smith—Because You're Mine (Jasmine)

Teddy Wilson & His Orchestra, featuring Lena Horne—Soundtrack For A Century–Pop Music: The Early Years 1890-1950 (Sony)

BLUES / JAZZ

Mildred Bailey—Mildred Bailey 1939 (Classics)

Etta James—The Essential Etta James (Uni/Chess)

Art Tatum—Complete Pablo Group Masterpieces (Fantasy/Pablo)

Lester Young—Complete Lester Young Studio Sessions (Uni/Verve)

FOUR-PART HARMONY

The Ink Spots—Anthology (Uni/MCA) #9/1946 (Billboard's Pop Chart)

The Platters—Four Platters & One Lovely Dish (Bear Family—Germany)

ROCK 'N' ROLL / R&B

James Brown—Ballads (Uni/Polydor) #18/1963 (Billboard's Pop Chart)

Conway Twitty—Rock 'N' Roll Years (Bear Family—Germany)

REGGAE / SKA

Flo & Eddie—Rock Steady With Flo & Eddie (Epiphany)

FOLK

Lonnie Johnson—Complete Folkways Recordings (Smithsonian Folkways)

RUSS COLUMBO TRIBUTE ALBUMS

I REMEMBER RUSS—Jerry Vale (1958)
CD: Sony/Columbia CK 63549
Original album: Columbia CS 8016

This album, among Vale's best efforts, is also important for including the lush, cushiony string arrangements of Glenn Osser.

PRISONER OF LOVE: A TRIBUTE TO RUSS COLUMBO—Tiny Tim (with Clang) (1995)
CD: Vinyl Retentive VRP-005

Tiny Tim makes a magnificent effort to recapture the exact sound of the Nat Shilkret Victor Sessions back in 1931 and 1932. He sings with such conviction that the listener can only wonder if Mr. Tim had channeled Russ at the time.

THE RUSS COLUMBO STORY —Paul Bruno (with Orchestra directed by Lon Norman) (1960)
LP: Coral: Mono: CRL-57327 / Stereo: 757327-S

Coral was essentially grooming Paul Anthony Bruno to be a Columbo reincarnation. The liner notes describe him as being 26 (Russ' age at death) and "the youngest of his Italian parents' nine children." The album closes with the Al Jacobs song "No More Rivers To Cross," Bruno's tribute to Russ.

A TRIBUTE TO RUSS COLUMBO—Gordon Lewis (1964) LP: Diplomat DS-2331

TROY CORY SINGS BING CROSBY AND RUSS COLUMBO LP: BBC Radio Play Music Records (1978)

DENNIS PENNA: TRIBUTE TO RUSS COLUMBO CD: Feather DRP-324
(www.dennispenna.com)

OTHER VERSIONS OF COLUMBO'S "I'M YOURS TO COMMAND"

On February 13th 1951, John Columbo and Carmela Tempest signed an agreement to transfer the copyright on several Russ Columbo compositions to Algonquin Music, Inc. The agreement also stipulated that 50% of the shares would go to the Columbo estate, while the other half would go to Russ' occasional co-writer Robert Milton, who now represented the publishing company. The songs included in the document were "So This Is Paradise" and "I'm Yours To Command" (on which Columbo and Milton collaborated), as well as the Columbo-Coombs title "Just For You."

The Smithsonian National Museum of American History has on file the sheet music to "I'm Yours To Command," with the 1951 Algonquin Music copyright renewal printed across the bottom. The sheet also lists "Words and Music by Russ Columbo" with no mention of Mr. Milton. A web search for versions of the song recorded that same year so far yields the following:

"I'm Yours To Command" / "What Will I Tell My Heart?" (1951)
Billy Eckstine (MGM 10944)

"I'm Yours To Command" / "Love Me" (1951)
Herb Jeffries (Coral 60425)

"I'm Yours To Command" / "I'll Buy You A Star" (1951)
Gordon MacRae (Capitol 1471)

ACKNOWLEDGMENTS

The authors would like to express heartfelt gratitude to Bill Nelson, for his emotional, intellectual and spiritual assistance throughout this project and to Adam Parfrey for helping to pull the forces together.

Particular thanks to:

The American Academy of Motion Picture Arts & Sciences
Frankie Avalon
John Beam
Jim Bedoian
Buddy Bregman
The Late Carmela Columbo
Hedi El Kholti
Robert Anthony Foster
Joe Franklin
Vince Giordano
Robert Heide
Ron Hutchinson at The Vitaphone Project
Paul M. Jensen
Janet Klein
Miles Kreuger
Tim Lanza
Al Martino
Lou Miano
Henry Nieves
Sam Penna
Howard Prouty
Susan Strange at The Smithsonian
National Museum of American History
Jerry Vale
Ian Whitcomb
"Woody" of Hollywood Attic Video
And to all of the others who helped in various capacities along the way.
A special appreciation to:
John "Russ" Columbo
And to
Max Pierce for his studious assistance and tireless dedication in creating the "Russ Columbo Remembered" website: www.russcolumbo.com

INDEX

BUBBLEGUM MUSIC IS THE NAKED TRUTH

THE DARK HISTORY OF PREPUBESCENT POP, FROM THE BANANA SPLITS TO BRITNEY SPEARS

Edited by Kim Cooper and David Smay

"Escapism is our birthright and the editors of *Bubblegum Music is the Naked Truth* have just the antidote for the current malaise. With over 50 contributors from all over the pop culture spectrum this book leaves no stick unwrapped in its search for the meaning and message of Bubblegum. It also seriously calls into question the accepted Rock Crit dogma of Bubblegum as vacuous music made by untalented charlatans while Artists like Dylan and Bruce Springsteen are celebrated as original performers of impeccable integrity. The naked truth seems to be the music business is, was and always shall be ruled by outside songwriters, session musicians and sharpy label owners, and Bubblegum music represents the apex of these hated figures' art."—**Blag Power.**

7x10 ✦ 344 pages ✦ Extensively Illustrated ✦ ISBN: 0-922915-69-5 ✦ $19.95

VOLUPTUOUS PANIC

THE EROTIC WORLD OF WEIMAR BERLIN

Mel Gordon

The perverse spectacle of Weimar Berlin prior to the Third Reich. "*Voluptuous Panic* is a phenomenal, guiltily absorbing and beautiful coffee-table sized masterpiece. A must for every perv who wishes they were living back in the good old days, when sex and porn still had the good taste to be as elegant as they were nasty."

—**Jerry Stahl**, *Shout Magazine*

"The sexiest—and strangest—volume of the season."
—*Talk magazine*

Deluxe full-color paperback original revised contents new cover

8 1/2 × 11 ✦ 278 pages ✦ full color illustrations ✦ ISBN: 0-922915-58-X ✦ $29.95

THE HOT GIRLS OF WEIMAR BERLIN

Edited by Barbara Ulrich
Introduction by Jerry Stahl

"Even as Death, smiling like a sadistic Domina, lowers her high-heeled boot on your face, you can smile, and grind, and know that, for one tragic and ecstatic moment, release is yours. And you can forget about the obliteration to come. The Hot Girls of Weimar Berlin could make anybody forget."
—**Jerry Stahl**

Feral House's second full-color investigation into the sexual culture of pre-Nazi Germany this time focuses on women, their fetishistic ascendance over men and legionary consumption of drugs. Fashion, Sapphic cults and psychiatric case studies fill the pages.

Over 140 paintings, illustrations and photos.

8 × 11 ✦ 120 pages ✦ in full color ✦ ISBN 0-922915-76-8 ✦ $19.95

To order from Feral House: domestic orders add $4.50 shipping for first item, $2.00 each additional item. Amex, MasterCard, Visa, checks and money orders are accepted. (CA state residents add 8.25% tax.) Canadian orders add $9 shipping for first item, $6 each additional item. Other countries add $11 shipping for first item, $9 each additional item. Non-U.S. originated orders must be international money order or check drawn on a U.S. Bank only. Send orders to: Feral House, P.O. Box 13067, Los Angeles, CA 90013.